D1562435

EMERSON AND HIS LEGACY

*Essays in Honor of
Quentin Anderson*

Edited by
STEPHEN DONADIO
STEPHEN RAILTON
and
ORMOND SEAVEY

SOUTHERN ILLINOIS UNIVERSITY PRESS
Carbondale and Edwardsville

Copyright © 1986 by the Board of Trustees,
Southern Illinois University
All rights reserved
Printed in the United States of America
Edited by Lynn de Gerenday
Designed by Quentin Fiore
Production supervised by Kathleen Giencke

"The Generation of Whitman," by Paul Zweig, is derived from
WALT WHITMAN: The Making of the Poet, by Paul Zweig.
© 1984 by Paul Zweig. Reprinted by permission of Basic Books,
Inc., Publishers.

Library of Congress Cataloging in Publication Data
Main entry under title:

Emerson and his legacy.

Bibliography: p.
1. Emerson, Ralph Waldo, 1803–1882—Criticism and
interpretation—Addresses, essays, lectures. 2. Emerson,
Ralph Waldo, 1803–1882—Influence—Addresses, essays,
lectures. 3. Anderson, Quentin, 1912–   . I. Anderson,
Quentin, 1912–   . II. Donadio, Stephen. III. Railton,
Stephen, 1948–   . IV. Seavey, Ormond.
PS1638.E4   1986   814'.3   85-1763
ISBN 0-8093-1218-2
89 88 87 86   4 3 2 1

Contents

CONTENTS

Preface

The essays in this volume continue a dialogue between two periods in the history of American culture. The first of them took place in New England in the quarter century before the Civil War, largely in response to the thought of Emerson. The Second centered in New York beginning in the 1930s, among a group of intellectuals simultaneously concerned with the political consequences of liberalism and of Marxism and with the imaginative implications of modernism. In both episodes the vexing relation between politics and literary expression has been the common concern of a distinctive group of thinkers aware of one another's work. It has been one of the achievements of Quentin Anderson to have maintained this dialogue at an appropriate level of seriousness and intellectual depth. For that reason among others these essays are dedicated to him.

American culture has not been rich in occasions in which a large view of the contemporary human situation has been collectively at issue. The first generation of American Puritans shared a synthesis of intellectual preoccupations, but the centrifugal tendencies inherent in their polity and in their geographic dispersion gradually dissolved that early community of concerns. With the marked exceptions of antebellum New England and mid-twentieth-century New York, American thought has turned to fragmented specialization and consequent mutual isolation. Many of the achievements of this attenuated culture have been impressive, but a lack of larger resonance can be felt in even the best of its work. (The rapid evolution of the Fugitives from their first agrarian gestures in *I'll Take My Stand* to the refuge in the New Criticism or the curious vestigial politics dabbled in by the current articulators of critical theory are only two of the ready examples of this cultural indisposition.)

Nor did either of these occasions acquire in their moments of flourishing the sort of acknowledged centrality enjoyed, for example, by an unbroken series of Parisian intellectual generations extending back to the seventeenth century or by the central figures of British intellectual life in the eighteenth and nineteenth centuries. Emerson's struggle to be heard during the period of his most important works has no parallel in the careers of Mill or Arnold. For all their range and brilliance, the American intellectuals whose writings regularly appeared in *Partisan Review* could not escape noticing that they wrote mostly for each other. The cant denunciation of these movements as peripheral "elite" phenomena arises not so much from an egalitarian affirmation as from a distaste for a world presented in such large and complicated terms. One of the lamentable aspects of Emerson's legacy, in fact, has been the cultural habit of trimming the world to the dimensions of the observer's capacities and interests. The centers of intellectual gravity in Europe do not customarily permit this sort of free-floating ignorance to establish much claim to attention.

Quentin Anderson has always been a difficult writer, addressing difficult and basic questions. He has also had a career of controversy, operating as he has in a milieu of intense polemics and corresponding investments of feeling. The authors whose work is included in this volume have not always agreed with him, or with one another. They have gathered here, however, in honor of a largeness of spirit they have all felt and in a common feeling that Anderson has rightly seen how the terms and origins of American expression, as they have come down to us from Emerson and Whitman, have subverted attempts to imagine the United States as a society. They share his bemusement at a literature which can excite us by the prospect of denying so many of our human needs. Anderson's own commitment—to his teaching as well as to the fate of American culture—has always led him, despite the formidable personal manner described in Jacques Barzun's essay, into keeping open an intercourse with the world. The contributors to this volume—colleagues, students, and intellectual associates—can all speak for the enduring success of that effort.

The editors wish to acknowledge gratefully the assistance and support of several people: Sacvan Bercovitch for his counsel, Kenney Withers of Southern Illinois University Press for his assistance and good will, Emmie Donadio, Ilene Railton, Thelma Anderson, Brom Anderson, and Max Anderson.

EMERSON
AND HIS LEGACY

1. Emerson as Itinerant

ORMOND SEAVEY

In September of 1832, after a career that had outwardly appeared to establish him in the vocation of his ancestors, Emerson resigned the ministry of the Second Church of Boston. In the years following, he did not cease to preach, however, and his career as a lecturer was in a sense a continuation of his past preaching. He had become an itinerant, one who travels from place to place addressing audiences who have gathered specially to hear him. The outwardly placid course of Emerson's life and his disposition to deny the reality of opposition and struggle make it difficult to appreciate how much Emerson was breaking from the cultural context that had engendered him. In becoming an itinerant, he was basically revising his notion of what an audience was, and ultimately of what society was.

Growing up in New England as a descendant of many ministers, Emerson understood the implications of leaving a congregation and setting up on his own as a self-designated spokesman for the truth. A long history of church controversies gave his decision a resonance he well understood, despite his own attempts to render it as the expression of an idiosyncratic preference. It was an act of muffled defiance, whose echoes could be heard most clearly on that occasion when he recommended his choice of vocation to the assembled company of future Unitarian ministers in "The Divinity School Address."

When he entered the ministry, Emerson followed a

procedure that had changed little since the seventeenth century. A young man who felt a calling to preach served a sort of apprenticeship while he acquired learning, experience, and an accumulation of favorable impressions. Approbation to preach here and there was given to him during this stage, but his full identity as a minister could only be granted by a congregation, which might, in turn, divest him of it. The first-generation American Puritans had drawn a distinction between kinds of ministry: there were extraordinary ministers, such as apostles, prophets, and evangelists, and ordinary ministers, such as pastors and teachers. The post Emerson would hold in Boston was, of course, part of the ordinary ministry; he was appointed to it not directly by God but by a particular congregation. With some private murmurings, Emerson had gone along with this pattern until 1832.[1]

American Puritans in particular had insisted on the powers of congregations to create their own ministers. Ordination was not permanent, as it was in most other churches, whether Catholic or Protestant. Nor was it done in the name of the Church as a whole; only the local congregation could ordain, and it was doubtful whether a minister's delegated powers could be exercised anywhere but in his own church. The minister, once called, had first to be a member of the congregation before he could be ordained, so he underwent the same tests for regeneracy that the congregation applied to other members.[2]

Ninety years before Emerson's decision, this established pattern was fractured and religious life revolutionized by the sudden appearance of itinerant preachers, creating what was soon called the Great Awakening. George Whitefield, Gilbert Tenant, and James Davenport toured New England, preaching to whatever congregations would receive them and even at times in public places, always to large crowds. The itinerants themselves made their own claims to being true to tradition, in their case to the exacting theology of Calvin and the first-generation Puritans. But they were also identified as the "New Lights" or the "New Side." The itinerants set about deliberately to disrupt the established network of social relations that held together towns and churches; instead of distinct congregations of independent believers, they assembled mass audiences of thousands who gathered for the sake of the large religious excitement and then dispersed. The itinerants directly attacked the old stability by posing repeatedly the question of whether ministers were converted, lifted out of their natural state by grace. Defending the transports of joy, the music and noise of the revival, Jonathan Edwards warned the disaffected clergy of their similarity to the older brother of the prodigal son in the parable, who "stood at a distance, sullen and much offended, and full of invectives against the young prodigal."[3] In the view of the itinerants, the minister was to be a continually disruptive element in the community, like a detachment of Red Guards during the Cultural Revolution, agitating for a renewal of the conditions of revolution in a postrevolutionary society.

Despite the claims of the New Lights to be the true heirs of Calvin and the Reformation, there was something about the itinerants that was fundamentally in keeping with the eighteenth century, with its sense of itself as an age in which traditional social bonds were increasingly discredited or reinterpreted. The eighteenth century offered considerable encouragements to those selves who wished to detach themselves emotionally from the community. The Great Awakening and the Methodist field preachers emerged at the same time as the first English novels, with their depiction of movement across the social landscape in search of some sort of self-fulfillment. The two phenomena were curiously complementary. Toward the end of his life, Emerson read *Pamela* and endorsed the genre as a stimulant to piety; the most prominent revival preacher of Emerson's own time was Charles Grandison Finney, named for the protagonist of Richardson's last novel.[4] Both in fiction and in life, eighteenth-century selves left home to discover philosophical truth or to become what they felt they might yet be: Benjamin Franklin leaves Boston for Philadelphia, Rasselas leaves the Happy Valley, Candide is exiled from the castle of Thunder-ten-tronckh, Tom Jones leaves the house of Squire Allworthy, Samuel Johnson leaves Litchfield, Rousseau leaves Geneva. Whitefield, the Great Itinerant, was continually on the move, and his audiences often had to travel unfamiliar distances to hear him. The access to wisdom was achieved in all of these cases by leaving home.

The power of the itinerants over their hearers came partly from the brief intensity of their presence and thereby from a mode of eloquence new to the colonies. In the first important anticipation of the Awakening in New England, the revivals centered around Northampton in 1734 and 1735, Edwards had discovered that a new minister appearing in the pulpit could sometimes command an attention which the usual minister could not. For instance, Sarah Edwards, his wife, was brought to her greatest transports of devotion by the sermons of Samuel Buell, a yount itinerant, while the sermon of Edwards that apparently provoked the greatest emotional response was delivered in Enfield, Connecticut. Whitefield's reputation preceded him as he made his way through the colonies, never staying for more than a few weeks in a single place. All the testimonies suggest that he was quite a new thing. In his youth, he had acted in plays, and his pulpit presence evidently employed an actor's sense of movement, timing, and vocal range. Fifty years after Whitefield's death, Emerson and his brother Edward visited John Adams in Quincy and heard the eighty-nine-year-old man reminisce about hearing Whitefield preach when he was a freshman at Harvard. "He had a voice such as I never heard before or since," Adams told the young Emersons. "He *cast* it out so that you might hear it at the meeting house (pointing toward Quincy Meeting h[ou]s[e]) and had the grace of a dancing master, of an actor of plays. His voice & his manner helped him more than his sermons."[5]

Eloquence, of the sort heralded by Whitefield and then displayed by the succeeding itinerants, was almost by nature a transient thing, encountered suddenly like the always-unexpected grace of God. The association between eloquence and divine power was not gratuitous; the power of the itinerants to move their audiences to crying and singing was perceived as evidence of the sanctified character of the Awakening. As one pious witness expressed it, referring to Whitefield's appearance in the pulpit at Middletown, Connecticut, "When I saw Mr. Whitefield come upon the scaffold, he looked almost angelical; a young, slim, slender youth, before some thousands of people with a bold undaunted countenance. And my hearing how God was with him everywhere as he came along, it solemnized my mind and put me into a trembling fear before he began to preach; for he looked as if he was clothed with authority from the Great God, and a sweet solemn solemnity sat upon his brow, and my hearing him preach gave me a heart wound."[6]

The transience of eloquence, like the transience of the Awakening itself, posed a problem for the New Lights—a problem which Emerson himself would inherit. Edwards had insisted from the first that the revival of religion was a permanent thing, altering the behavior of most of those affected and changing the whole character of their communities. Even after his dismissal from the Northampton pulpit, he denied that the Awakening had been a whimsical aberration, and he had always been a prudent but committed defender of the authenticity of the religious experience stirred up by the itinerants. No one expressly defended the transitory character of heightened religious feeling and its provocations, but in the aftermath of the Awakening the evangelical party was obliged to perceive the spirit as something which comes and goes, with inevitable, even desirable, alternating periods of intensity and slackness. The first generation of Puritans were more likely to describe authentic sanctification in terms of steadiness and persistence; Edwards, though, chose his own wife's capacity for ecstatic experience as an evidence of the continuing operation of the spirit. The possibility of renewed spiritual excitement becomes the distinguishing mark of grace. By the nineteenth century, the evanescence of religious feeling was seen almost as a virtue. Charles Grandison Finney, speaking on revivals of religion in 1834, asserts that collectively there is little authentic religious experience that does not emerge from these outbreaks of extraordinary belief. "Almost all the religion in the world has been produced by revivals. God has found it necessary to take advantage of the excitability there is in mankind, to produce powerful excitements among them, before he can lead them to obey. Men are so sluggish, there are so many things to lead their minds off from religion, and to oppose the influence of the gospel, that it is necessary to raise an excitement among them, till the tide rises so high as to sweep away the opposing obstacles."[7]

From the beginning of the Awakening, the Boston clerical establishment was hostile to the phenomenon of itinerancy and to the emotional responses aroused by the itinerants. Enlightened, sedate, and protective of the public order, they asked why these new preachers were on the move. Did they not have congregations of their own, their primary responsibilities? The issue was not merely a problem in church polity. Where did the authority to speak come from that the itinerants claimed? If they were ordinary ministers, it was their relationship to a specific congregation that licensed them to speak. If they were extraordinary ministers, then their authority had to come directly from God, a dangerous assertion to make. Itinerancy appeared to imply a condition of divinely ordained unsettledness, both in the itinerants and among their hearers.

Charles Chauncy, minister of the First Church in Boston, became the principal spokesman for the "Old Lights," the opponents of the itinerants and itinerancy. In his most extensive attack on the Great Awakening, *Seasonable Thoughts on the State of Religion in New England* (1743), he touches on what he refers to as "the *present settled State* of the *Church*," which requires a close tie between minister and congregation. The minister "is devoted to the Service of the LORD JESUS CHRIST, in a *particular* Place, and over a *particular* People. His Work, as a Minister, does not lie at large; but is restrain'd within certain Boundaries . . . his stated, constant Business is with his *own People*. These have been committed to his Care; these, he has solemnly engagd [*sic*], before GOD, and the LORD JESUS CHRIST, and *holy Angels*, to do the Duties of a Pastor to."[8] Chauncy's extended argument against the so-called field preachers is buttressed with quotations from the Cambridge Platform of 1648, the early consensus description of Congregational church polity, and from Increase Mather; the traditions of the New England Way are mustered in opposition to this disruptive innovation.

Twelve years after Chauncy's death, Emerson's father succeeded to the pulpit in the Boston First Church. William Emerson's only literary labor of any size was a history of the First Church, the sort of antiquarian effort which liberal New England clergymen felt called upon to do. In that plodding and generally lifeless work, one of the few moments of energetic and engaged narration appears in the senior Emerson's description of Chauncy's opposition to itinerancy and the Great Awakening. The population, he reports, was "no longer satisfied with the cool and moderate strain of preaching, practised by the generality of New England ministers"; it had developed a taste for "a loose incoherent kind of sermons, which contained strong appeals to their imagination and senses." Whitefield's eloquence itself had been a cause for repudiation by the Old Lights. According to a story told by William Emerson, Chauncy prayed that he might never be eloquent. Echoing Chauncy, William Emerson denounces the "rantings and censures and irregular preachings of the itinerants, and the swoonings and screams of their converts." William Emerson summarizes with approval the argument of Chauncy's *Seasonable Thoughts*; like Chauncy he recognized the danger that itinerancy presented to the settled traditions of respectable liberal congregations. His own attachment to the First Church extended beyond the history, which was left uncompleted at his death; he even named two of his sons after previous ministers of the church, including his youngest son, Charles Chauncy Emerson.[9]

Chauncy and William Emerson both attack the Awakening as a dangerous and disorderly innovation. Their greatest objections are not to the itinerants' theology but to their rhetoric; field preaching and the kind of emotional appeals to a mass audience they considered a dangerous novelty, not a revival of the plain and powerful preaching of the early seventeenth century. These forerunners of American liberal thought spent their careers in affirming their ties with tradition; their embrace of an undemanding latitudinarian benevolence was linked to a notion of communities and congregations that had changed little since the seventeenth century. Belief was to be centered in the stability of town and village life, a world where good taste rather than eloquence was to be the minister's goal. Joseph Stevens Buckminster's funeral sermon refers approvingly to William Emerson's "extraordinary correctness of manners, and disposition to method in the disposal of his time" and "the punctilious discharge of the duties of his profession." Both Buckminster and the departed senior Emerson would have understood correctness and punctiliousness as signs of spiritual merit. Buckminster describes William Emerson's own pulpit style as "a happy example of [the] correct and rational style of evangelical preaching." The compliment unintentionally betrays the limitation.[10]

When the successors of the Old Lights drifted into Unitarianism at the beginning of the nineteenth century, they preserved the old Puritan church polity. In fact, among the first Unitarian churches the connection between the minister and the civil body was a good deal tighter than it was among the Congregationalists, the descendants of the New Lights. Unitarianism had gained its foothold in eastern Massachusetts in the 1820s by means of the so-called Dedham decision, a Massachusetts Supreme Court ruling which determined that a minister was to be selected by the voters of a town, not only by the church members of the congregation. The Unitarian minister, then, owed his professional identity to a political body. For the generation of Emerson's teachers and senior colleagues, this political arrangement assured the security of an enlightened theology. It is an early instance of a recurrent phenomenon, a liberal practice securing itself against the popular will by judicial action.[11]

The Unitarian ministers saw themselves as part of what Coleridge, around the same time, was describing as the clerisy —a special class of educated people, domiciled in each parish in the country to serve as exemplars of civilization and good order. In Coleridge's view, the church and its ministers were charged with preserving and transmitting the national culture. The mature Romantics responded in much the same way as the Old Lights and Unitarians when confronted with the disturbances generated by the eighteenth century. Wordsworth and Coleridge, after their initial revolutionary enthusiasms, came to look for correctives to the unsettled lives and values that were the legacy of the previous age; the first Romantics were reacting as much to the emotional excesses of the eighteenth century as to its overblown diction and constrained prosody. It had been, among other things, an age of religious enthusiasm, of passionate and unexpressible emotion, and of political turmoil—the Methodists and the German Pietists, the sentimentality of Sterne and Goldsmith, the Sons of Liberty and the Jacobin Club. Against these modern developments, poetry and genteel religion were to lend their softening influences.

Charles Chauncy and the Old Lights had seen and abhorred these disruptive forces in the 1740s, and they appealed to the traditional New England social values as their standard. But the force of the Awakening had shown that the ideal of solidarity inherited from seventeenth-century American Puritanism was no longer emotionally sustaining. The crowds who listened to the itinerants had left home; they were finding themselves somewhere else. Most of the hearers had never been in so large a group before, crowds of thousands assembled out of the villages and farms. Out of that rural landscape, the itinerants created momentary cities of the saved. In leaving the ministry, Emerson was also leaving home. By 1832 he could no longer conceive of a particular human community that could provide an adequate response for him. Only by continually changing his audience could he hope for the necessary distance from the burden of felt human needs that his message requires.

When he decided on the ministry in 1824, Emerson had associated himself with his father, in manner and profession. "But in Divinity I hope to thrive," he writes in his journal, after casting a somewhat wistful eye at other professions that required gifts that he felt were not his. "I inherit from my sire a formality of manner & speech, but I derive from him or his patriotic parent a passionate love for the strains of elo-

quence."[12] The "but" in the last sentence suggests
how much his inheritance from his father was perceived as a limitation; the compensating love of eloquence is less definitely attributed to William Emerson. The full entry explores the responsibility of the
minister to display a certain kind of warm-hearted and
sustained connection to others, along with the responsibility to be eloquent. Young Emerson has no great
hopes that he can acquire a warmer heart; his reliance
is on eloquence. The association of his father with
what he was always prone to consider his greatest limitation of character may suggest how ambivalently he
was entering into the family vocation; to be a minister
would require him to present himself in some open
and genuine way to the people of his congregation in
their shared daily life.

Emerson read his father's respectful account of the
past ministers of the First Church, but he did not share
his father's reactions. He alludes to Charles Chauncy a
few times in his lectures, in particular in one called
"Eloquence." As an illustration of what was in his view a
glaring defect, he tells the story of how Chauncy had
once fumbled an opportunity to improve a sad occasion.
"The doctor was much distressed, and in his prayer he
hesitated, he tried to make soft approaches, he prayed for
Harvard College, he prayed for the schools, he implored
the Divine Being 'to—to—to bless to them all the boy
that was this morning drowned in Frog Pond.' Now this
is not want of talent or learning, but of manliness. The
doctor, no doubt, shut up in his closet and his theology,
had lost some natural relation to men, and quick application of his thought to the course of events."[13] Just the
tendencies in himself that Emerson found most an ancestral curse he attributes to his father's role model.
Elsewhere, in his journals, he records an anecdotal confrontation between Chauncy and Whitefield. " 'Where
are you going Mr. Whit[e]field?' said Dr. Chauncy. "I'm
going to Boston, sir.'—'I'm very sorry for it,' said Dr. C.

'So is the Devil' replied the eloquent preacher."[14] Manliness, boldness, a certain rude strength were always the hallmarks of eloquence for Emerson. It was not achieved by study or refinement; it came rather like grace, unforeseen and as a divine gift, imparting to the speaker the sort of power the apostles received at Pentecost.

Emerson left the ministry because of a disagreement with his congregation over the institution of the Lord's Supper. So he asserted in his negotiations with the church committee, who were disposed to make accomodations and were sorry to see him go. The formulation of Emerson's objections, as he stated them to the committee and elaborated them later to the congregation, is, to say the least, peculiar. He argued that the practice was not intended to be observed by Christ's followers, yet he did not urge its abolition. "I have no hostility to this institution," he said in his farewell sermon to the congregation; "I am only stating my want of sympathy with it. Neither should I ever have obtruded this opinion upon other people, had I not been called by my office to administer it. That is the end of my opposition, that I am not interested in it. I am content that it should stand to the end of the world, if it please men and please Heaven, and I shall rejoice in all the good it produces."[15] Emerson did not readily allude to the indefinite future; a note of impatience and distaste can be felt in this apparently broadminded statement.

He was hardly being consistent with his earlier views in taking his stand against the Lord's Supper, and despite his celebrated indifference to consistency, we are entitled to wonder why he reversed himself. In the ordination sermons he had preached three years earlier, he had described the ordinance as a "symbol of holy affection. And so it opens the doors of the heart. He therefore who adventures to break the bread and pour out the waters of life should be himself susceptible of emotion. The minister should be a man of feel-

ing, or I feel he will vainly endeavour to excite movements in other souls that have no archetypes in his
own."[16] The Lord's Supper was observed monthly in
the Second Church, so Emerson would have had frequent occasions to see his own capacity for feelings
tested. Later that same year, he preached a sermon on
the Lord's Supper in which he argued that the feast of
remembrance should be made open to all who seek it.
It has been pointed out that Emerson's digestive system failed him in the weeks of polite confrontation
with his congregation while the question of the ordinance was between them; a case of diarrhea caused
him considerable loss of weight. Naturally, in Emerson's developing thought, the notion of anything like a
sacrament, a means to special powers that derived
from the acknowledged connection with a past historical moment, would be unsustainable for the fully imperial self. But the Unitarian Lord's Supper had nothing
to do with ritual or mystery. I think the institution
became so unbearable for Emerson because it called
upon him to eat with his congregation. He knew what
the love feast was supposed to be, and he had no appetite for it.[17]

Emerson had earlier written in his journal that "in
order to be a good minister, it was necessary to leave
the ministry. The profession is antiquated. In an altered age, we worship in the dead forms of our forefathers. Were not a Socratic paganism better than an
effete supcrannuated Christianity?"[18] But in his farewell sermon, he could end only with the rather plain-
tive statement that he felt a "want of sympathy" with
the institution of the Lord's Supper.[19] That want of
sympathy was just the sort of inner inadequacy his
early journals refer to so frequently. The situation Emerson found himself in is a familiar one; he faced the
recognition of his own limitations in relation to the
largest realm of human possibilities. Yet somehow Emerson, in this same period and in the months following,

was able to assert that he was, in fact, a divine person and that his own distinctive characteristics were not limitations but rather evidences of his extraordinary status. His journal modulates gradually from a record of self-examination to a meditation on divine things. And what keeps this from being a wholly delusional state is his insistence that others might see the same divine qualities in themselves. Rather than proclaiming himself the new Messiah, he becomes John the Baptist for all the unwitting American Christs. It was to them that he felt called to preach, not to the irreducibly human congregation of the Second Church.

Henceforth, his ministry was extraordinary, rather than ordinary. During the weeks of his dispute with the congregation, he read through a life of George Fox, noting that the first Quaker "on almost all occasions preferred to preach out of doors. When the church was manifestly the only convenient place, he went in. He told the priests that he was no man-made priest."[20] Emerson was inclined to say that there was really no more place for an ordinary ministry, of the sort that his ancestors or the Unitarians engaged in. Times had changed, and historical Christianity was "antiquated" and "superannuated." As for the future, it was no mere extrapolation from the past and present. In the period around 1833 and 1834 Emerson was fond of noting in his journal that "the whole future is in the bottom of the heart."[21] For him the immediate present, the moment when modernity as he saw it had set in, opened the way to a future which could exist only in the mind. The escape from the constraints of place, time, and culture, then, came simply by leaving the past for the future.

So when the seniors at Harvard Divinity School invited him to deliver their graduation address a few years later, he was ready to proclaim that the kingdom of the new gods all around him was at hand. "The Divinity School Address" has a crucial place in his work because it states explicitly much that is only implicit elsewhere in his published work and because of the controversies that followed it. But it is also a very curious sort of manifesto, with an odd sort of rhetoric and an authorial personality that is particularly elusive. Emerson always counted on his *"aliquid immensum infinitumque,"* his capacity to appear sweetly removed from the human scene, to get him through various tight fixes, but here before the prospective Unitarian ministers he wished to be both places at once—in the timeless ether and also in Cambridge.

The argument is couched as an attack on "formalists" and on "historical Christianity," so he could disguise his ideas in the rhetoric the Unitarian themselves used to separate themselves from their Calvinist counterparts. But it is more or less clear that the "formalism" to which he objects is to be seen in the pulpits of Unitarians. What does "formalism" mean? It denotes the attachment to theological ideas or liturgical observances; the word is associated with a dry, spiritless condition that is supposed to come from too much preoccupation with forms of thought and worship. "Whenever the pulpit is usurped by a formalist, then is the worshipper defrauded and disconsolate."[22] But the adapted rhetoric fits the case poorly; the Unitarians were hardly steeped in dogma or ritual. The evidence of formalism to Emerson was the lack of excited response from congregations; not inadequate ideas but an inadequate spirit was to blame. William Ellery Channing, speaking fourteen years earlier, had noted the necessity in those times of an emotionally stirring message, yet even he had had to admit that Unitarians were accused of lacking fervor.[23] Emerson's denunciation of lifeless preaching is probably the most emphatic derogation he ever made publicly in his life. For him, the mark of inadequacy was the absence of an authentic acknowledged connection between the speaker's life and his thought. Speaking of such a preacher, he says, "The capital secret of his profession, namely, to convert life into truth, he had not yet learned. Not one fact in all his experience had he yet imported into his doctrine. This man had ploughed, and planted, and talked, and bought, and sold; he had read books; he had eaten and drunken; his head aches; his heart throbs; he smiles and suffers; yet was there not a surmise, a hint, in all the discourse, that he had ever lived at all" (DSA,86).

The alternative to formalism and the staleness of historical Christianity was for all ministers to be poets. "Yourself a newborn bard of the Holy Ghost—cast behind you all conformity, and acquaint men at first hand with Deity." Priest and poet are interchangeable terms; either is a man enamored of excellency. Emerson suggests that the young ministers before him be "[n]ot too anxious to visit periodically all families and each family in your parish connexion" (DSA, 90), responsibilities that Emerson found himself utterly unsuited for. Rather they should, "when you meet one of these men or women, be to them a divine man; be to them thought and virtue" (DSA, 90). It is significant that the word most commonly used both by Congregationalists and by Unitarians to refer to the office for which his audience had trained—the word *minister*—is used only once, in a derogatory connotation, while *priest* and its derivatives are used several times and always favorably. One needs only to think of the different associations for the two words: a minister has duties to persons and is subordinate to a master; a priest is the representative of a divine being. And a priest has no binding and necessary connection to any congregation, any more than a bard has to his immediate hearers.

It is not surprising that "The Divinity School Address" provoked severe criticism when it was delivered. What is surprising is that Emerson should be so generally praised for the address since his time, as if it were fully honest testimony or a coherent criticism of Unitarian practice. The Emerson who exhorts these prospective ministers is a slippery character who will not be located clearly either in or outside of the company which he is addressing. He calls the young men to their holy office; he calls them friends and brothers; he asks what they can all do to remedy the growing unbelief of the times. The characterization of desirable virtues that he draws for them is a disguised portrait of his own personal ideal, someone who rejects the commendation of society for the sake of communion with God. "There are sublime merits; persons who are not actors, not speakers, but influences; persons too great for fame, for display; who disdain eloquence; to whom all we call art and artist, seems too darkly allied to show and by-ends, to the exaggeration of the finite and selfish, and loss of the universal" (*DSA*, 91). Emerson's hortatory imperatives do not spring from his own experience; they are, rather, a summons to extrahuman modes of behavior. Even when he says, "Be to them a man," his "man" is a being whose like has never existed since the Fall. And as for the means of eloquence he cites, his hearers would have listened in vain for any indication that he had ever "ploughed, and planted, and talked, and bought, and sold." Emerson says that one could not know of a bad preacher "what age of the world he fell in; whether he had a father or a child; whether he was a freeholder or a pauper; whether he was a citizen or a countryman; or any other fact of his biography" (*DSA*, 86). Nor could one know any of those things about the Emerson of the address.

Emerson knew what he was up to in his efforts at disrupting theological training at Harvard. When ministers are expected to be poets, congregations can expect not coherence and a comprehensive accord between what is asserted and other things known, but rather a lyrical brilliance that disturbs all standing relations among the previously perceived facts of experience. "Truly speaking," he says in the address, "it is not instruction, but provocation, that I can receive

from another soul" (*DSA*, 80). Disruption and provocation should be characteristic of all serious discourse;
for Emerson, at least during this most radical period of
his life, they are very nearly to be seen as good in
themselves. " 'Overturn, Overturn, and overturn,' " he
writes in his journal, quoting his step-grandfather Ezra
Ripley on a blustery December day at the end of 1834,
" 'until he whose right it is to reign shall come into his
kingdom.' "[24] It was the world of settled social relations that was to be overturned, a world of persons and
their ensnaring interrelations. The very word "person"
had for him a disagreeable connotation, deriving in part
from its theological associations with the three persons
of the Trinity and the person of Christ. "The soul
knows no persons," he says in the address (*DSA*, 80).
He puts it most strikingly in his journal, on the same
December night of 1834. "When any one comes who
speaks with better insight into moral nature he will be
the new gospel; miracle or not, inspired or uninspired,
he will be the Christ. . . . Persons are nothing."[25] Emerson was given to sudden enthusiasms when some new
influence—Carlyle (whom he called on first reading an
unsigned piece "my Germanick new-light writer whoever he be"[26]), Alcott, Thoreau, Whitman—would set
up a pleasing disturbance; but the flash always sub-
sided when it proved to be of human origin.

"The Divinity School Address" in particular shows
how different Emerson was from the predominant values of the English Romantics. Those emotional states in
which the Romantics found the highest value were characterized by serenity, calm, and repose—even the emotional intensity they valued was conditioned by tran-
quility. Wordsworth, though he speaks continually of
freely ranging, asks characteristically, "What dwelling
will receive me? in what vale / Shall be my harbor?
underneath what grove / Shall I take up my home?" And
there is the continual presence of that silent audience
for both Wordsworth and Coleridge who is called

"Friend," someone who provides the surety of a known human response. Coleridge's Mariner reaches, after all his wanderings, the point where it is sweeter "To walk together to the kirk, / And all together pray, / While each to his great Father bends, / Old men, and babes, and loving friends / And youths and maidens gay!"[27] Whatever detached appreciation Emerson may have felt for such scenes of human fellowship, he calls in the address for a sort of piety that separates man from men. "In such high communion, let us study the grand strokes of rectitude: a bold benevolence, an independence of friends, so that not the unjust wishes of those who love us, shall impair our freedom, but we shall resist for truth's sake the freest flow of kindness, and appeal to sympathies far in advance" (*DSA*, 91). The apparent human warmth and sweetness of Emerson's appeal masks the bleakness of the human landscape he invites the young ministers into. Perhaps he had been forced to do without friends himself—his brothers, his first wife—and was obliged to embrace his privation as a virtue. In any case, he is calling his audience away from all settled relationships.

Andrews Norton, the Dexter Professor of Sacred Literature at Harvard, led the attack on Emerson following the address. His *Discourse on the Latest Form of Infidelity* is both heavy-handed and oddly revealing. Emerson is not mentioned in Norton's lecture; the apparent subject is the German Romantic theologians and students of religion—Schleiermacher, Strauss, and others—with whom Norton implicitly associates certain American developments. These represent the latest form of infidelity because, despite their apparent concurrence with organized religion, their thinking subverts it by denying the historicity of the miracles described in the gospels. Emerson had, to be sure, passed slightingly over the gospel miracles and no doubt was aware of the contemporary context of discussion. But these are hardly his issues, and Norton's attack may seem at first beside the point. The suggestive oddity of Norton's *Discourse,* however, comes from his determination to locate Emerson (and his Concord colleagues) in some sort of context. To imply that Emerson represented the latest form of infidelity suggested a determinable mode of thinking; to call it latest, suggested comparison with earlier forms. In the months following, Emerson was at pains to deny that he could be thus located in a context; to his old colleague Henry Ware, Jr., he objected that he was "from my very incapacity of methodical writing a chartered libertine, free to worship and free to rail, lucky when I was understood but never esteemed near enough to the institutions and mind of society to deserve the notice of the master of literature and religion."[28] Despite this pose as a sort of court fool for the Unitarian clerisy, Emerson could not fully escape the charge that he had arguments and ideas. He had in mind something more than just an exhortation for more lively preaching. And those ideas, as Norton's hammering discourse insisted, had historical associations. The latest form of infidelity was to be seen as another version of that earlier one, so often called by New England Federalists and their descendants "the French infidelity," or, in other words, the French Enlightenment.[29] Foreseeing such an association, Emerson had explicitly dissociated himself in the address from the religion of the French Revolution, because that mode of worship had been political and transitory. But it was clear enough to Norton that the individual resolutions of consciousness that Emerson was propagating would yield the same result that the *philosophes* had campaigned for, the downfall of institutional religion.

Yet Emerson was also right to object to his being treated as a thinker. He was a poet, as even his attackers knew; ideas appear in "The Divinity School

Address" only to be dismissed. As Emerson puts it, using the terms borrowed from Coleridge, "There is no doctrine of the Reason which will bear to be taught by the Understanding" (*DSA*, 81). In effect, the most important ideas could not be communicated except by an outpouring of the spirit, producing an intuitive acceptance. His audience was not listening to something directly addressed to their minds; instead, they overheard someone who appeared to be conducting a conversation with himself. The isolation of that figure has recurrently brought up the accusation of antinomianism: was he out of reach of the human community? The question has been answered variously with considerable subtlety.[30] It may be said, for one thing, that his relationship to experience is not merely reported but also propagated, and nowhere more than in "The Divinity School Address."

Itinerancy, enthusiasm as a good in its own right, and the disruption of settled life as a necessary condition of genuine feeling—these were the heritage of the Great Awakening and of evangelical Protestantism in the nineteenth century that Emerson turned to literary use. They are also the most disturbing aspects of his legacy. Emerson's audience—and to some considerable degree it is true of the American audience—will measure intellectual discourse by the excitement it can register more than by the coherence of its connection to what is already established. The discontinuous character of American critical discourse is symptomatic of the Emersonian appetite for overturning the known and bringing in the new. And the attitude of expectation that pose Emerson took on so readily, has established in the thin air of the future a city of promised impossibilities. "I look for the new Teacher, that shall follow so far those shining laws, that he shall see them come full circle" "A nation of men will for the first time exist" "I look in vain for the poet whom I describe"—the present is always pitiful in comparison to what must inevitably come. The act of casting aside a settled vocation for an unsettled condition of unlimited promise was the most significant single event of Emerson's life, and he promulgates the mentality behind it as a law by which we all should live.

2. Emerson at First: A Commentary on Nature

DENIS DONOGHUE

I have Emerson's license for beginning before the beginning, as his *Nature* (1836) started with two items
before coming to chapter 1. The first was an epigraph
from Plotinus, the second a body of two or three hundred words which might well enough have been called
chapter 1. My own preliminary matter goes into several paragraphs, and consists of observations which
have no other aim than to indicate my general sense of
Emerson: they haven't at all the merit of supplying the
qualifications they would need if they aspired to be
precise. I give them in a stark sequence, numbering
them to mark their limitations.

One: I assume that Emerson's essays propose to
assert "the sufficiency of the private man," a phrase
he uses in "New England Reformers" a page or two
before his more elaborate version of it, "the private,
self-supporting powers of the individual." It follows
that "an institution is the lengthened shadow of one
man," as Emerson maintained in "Self-Reliance," a
phrase T. S. Eliot recalled inaccurately in "Sweeney
Erect"—

> (The lengthened shadow of a man
>   Is history, said Emerson
> Who had not seen the silhouette
>   Of Sweeney straddled in the sun.)

—but accurately enough, since Emerson went on to say that "all history resolves itself very easily into the biography of a few stout and earnest persons."

Two: I interpret the sufficiency of the private man as Emerson's gloss on what in *Nature* he calls the soul. I assume, too, that the soul is not synonymous with the mind or the will, but with their conjoint power. I haven't found any passage in which Emerson refers to the mind as separable from the will.

Three: Emerson works on the conviction that the soul is adequate to whatever obstacles it encounters, and lifts every burden. He acknowledges necessity under the name of Ananke, but it is only a condition or circumstance; it doesn't defeat the soul or bring its activity to an end. The soul acts by giving its objects a certain form of attention. As Santayana says in "The Optimism of Ralph Waldo Emerson," "he passes easily from all points of view to that of the intellect."

Four: The adequacy of the mind isn't entirely dependent upon its power of abstraction. Nothing in Emerson contradicts the assumption, in Valéry and Stevens, that the mind fabricates by abstraction, unless they mean solely by abstraction. Emerson's sense of the mind's adequacy is closer to Coleridge's, especially in *On the Constitution of the Church and State*, where Coleridge describes an idea as "that conception of a thing, which is not abstracted from any particular state, form, or mode, in which the thing may happen to exist at this or at that time; nor yet generalized from any number or succession of such forms or modes; but which is given by the knowledge of *its ultimate aim.*" In Emerson, the particular form of attention the mind gives to an object is such as to respect not its immediate attributes but its ultimate aim. The act of the mind is concerned not with the object as it is or as it appears to be but with its destiny. Only the mind can say what destiny is.

Five: In the gap between the object and its destiny

we come upon a problem Robert Martin Adams has considered, without reference to Emerson, in his *Nil*, where he resorts to a vocabulary of void and nothingness. His theme is not the rift between experience and consciousness, so far as that might be considered a wretched predicament: it is the rift insisted on and gloried in, as if only a vulgar satisfaction could accompany the coincidence of mind and experience. "From Julien Sorel to des Esseintes, from Keats to Mallarmé, from Novalis to Ibsen, they all testify that anticipation, imagination, and memory (any relation as long as it is *distant*) are richer experiences than experience itself." In Emerson, the mind holds its power by keeping its distance, and by enforcing the distance between an object and its destiny. It is the mind's power to do this which ensures that no account of life is necessarily predicated upon a crisis or a rupture. Two forms of satisfaction are entailed. The mind is not intimidated by what it deals with, and a sense of history can proceed on the assumption not of ruptures and dissociations but of a continuous sufficiency of soul to the world it lives in.

Six: The characteristic defect of thought is prematurity: the mind settles upon familiar forms of itself, and loses the force of a contingent relation to its occasions. To counteract this tendency, Emerson trusts to the whim he praises in "Self-Reliance," and takes as his motto a sentence from "Circles": "our moods do not believe in each other." He repudiates consistency and repose. Again in "Self-Reliance" he says that "power ceases in the instant of repose; it resides in the moment of transition from a past to a new state, in the shooting of the gulf, in the darting to an aim." It is true that in "Art" he says that "the virtue of art lies in detachment, in sequestering one object from the embarrassing variety," and praises artists and orators for giving "an all-excluding fullness to the object, the thought, the word, they alight upon." Emerson's own affection for the character of an essay speaks to the same sentiment: a genre that takes contradictions lightly because it doesn't claim to be comprehensive. But what Emerson takes pleasure in is his assurance that the mind, having committed itself to "the tyrant of the hour," then passes to some other object, "which rounds itself into a whole, as did the first." The same rhetorical process could be applied to a few objects, seeing them from the vantage of different moods, thus introducing mobility where there seemed to be nothing but fixity. As Santayana wrote of Emerson in *Interpretations of Poetry and Religion:* "He differed from the plodding many, not in knowing things better, but in having more ways of knowing them."

Seven: Emerson's persuasiveness is based on the renewed claim that all men are equal—a charming claim, especially at a time when social and economic arrangements, notably industrialization and capitalism, were conspiring to make people unequal, and to emphasize their inequality by giving them unequal wages and conditions of employment. Emerson told his readers and audiences that people who are treated unequally in social and economic life can find their dignity in themselves, by seeing society in the light of nature and diminishing its force in that light. When people feel that they are dominated by systems and institutions, Emerson offers to disconnect these structures of power, on condition that each person will take up the slack upon his own responsibility.

Eight: The offer Emerson's essays make goes somewhat like this: "Wouldn't our lives be much as I describe them, if we took seriously the sufficiency of the private man, exerted mind and will together as power, and regarded the whole world as having been given to us for our instruction and use?" It is not surprising, then, that Emerson was just as readily available to Pragmatism as to Transcendentalism: the vocabulary of property, commodity, use, exchange, instrumental-ity, and value made him available to William James, Peirce, Dewey and any other sages who wanted to make the best of the given world.

So much for preliminaries and prejudices.

Emerson begins *Nature* by dissociating himself from belatedness and the acceptance of it: insisting on the new as providing "an original relation to the universe." Paul's First Epistle to the Corinthians (chapter 13) prophesied the supersession of prophecy and knowledge: the time will come when we shall see God face to face, without mediation. Emerson reverses Paul's vision. Our forefathers, he says, "beheld God and nature face to face": why must we see them only through their eyes?

So the oppositions begin: originality, against retrospection; insight, against tradition; revelation, not history; the living generation, against sundry masquerades; "floods of life" against the "dry bones of the past," this last being another reversal, since Ezekiel 37 has always been interpreted by Christian readers as a sign of resurrection. Emerson says that the universe is composed of Nature and the Soul; otherwise put, the Me and the Not-Me. Man is like and unlike Nature in the sense that action in him precedes knowledge and presumably can persist without knowledge. But man has the faculty of apprehending as truth what he has acted as life. Nature hasn't. Nature can only do, ignorantly and slavishly, what Wisdom ordains it to do, so the possibility of discovering what Wisdom is by divining its plan for Nature can only devolve upon man. This discovery would amount to a new relation to the universe: it would be indistinguishable from firstness. Hence the aim of Science is to propound a theory of Nature, sufficiently abstract to explain everything that needs to be explained. Man's destiny is in knowing; but since knowing and willing are never found apart, the terminology of action still applies.

Chapter 1: Nature

Appropriately, the "attitude" that prefigures the "act" of science is that of walking out into the fields and looking at the stars; astronomy being the privileged science to a sage who would set his thinking astir by reflecting upon the soul and nature. Not so appropriately, the stars are humanized by a flick of the sentence, the paragraph ending with reference to "their admonishing smile." The reason for the personification is clear enough, but hardly justifies grandiloquence.

The chapter begins with sensory events—the stars and their rays as a man sees them—but soon rises to concepts of understanding, invoking the faculty of recognizing unity among a multiplicity of sensory events: "the integrity of impression made by manifold natural objects." So the mind sees as a tree the bits of timber Nature supplies; distinguishes a landscape from the several farms which provoke this understanding; sees distant objects and calls the impression they make the horizon. What gratifies the mind is not the natural objects but the unity they unknowingly make. "There is a property in the horizon which no man has but he whose eye can integrate all the parts, that is, the poet." A few sentences later this property becomes "virtue"; in either case, a capacity of the mind is fulfilled. The allusions are mostly to Wordsworth, and to childhood as he praised it. But in the most famous passage, ideas of reason are transposed into modes of "the sublime" by way of Wordsworth and Schiller: "Crossing a bare common, in snow puddles, at twilight, under a clouded sky, without having in my thoughts any occurrence of special good fortune, I have enjoyed a perfect exhilaration. I am glad to the brink of fear . . . . Standing on the bare ground—my head bathed by the blithe air, and uplifted into infinite space—all mean egotism vanishes. I become a transparent eyeball; I am nothing; I see all; the currents of the Universal Being circulate through me; I am part or parcel of God." "Mean" shows that the egotism Emerson mentions is an attribute of the understanding when it refuses to allow a man to rise above it or otherwise disengage himself from its claims. In "New England Reformers," anticipating Stevens's "major man," Emerson says that "the man who shall be born, whose advent men and events prepare and foreshow, is one who shall enjoy his connection with a higher life, with the man within the man." Here, in *Nature*, Emerson is such a man, transparent rather than opaque—a juxtaposition that comes readily to Emerson when the despotism of sense and understanding is set against the higher fact of Reason.

"I am glad to the brink of fear." Emerson's version of "the sublime" involves, like many other versions, the presence of two contradictory perceptions. Schiller says, in his essay on the sublime, that such a combination irrefutably demonstrates our moral independence: "For since it is absolutely impossible for the very same object to be related to us in two different ways, it therefore follows that we ourselves are related to the object in two different ways; furthermore, two opposed natures must be united in us . . . By means of the feeling for the sublime, therefore, we discover that the state of our minds is not necessarily determined by the state of our sensations, that the laws of nature are not necessarily our own, and that we possess a principle proper to ourselves that is independent of all sensuous affects." Reason is Emerson's word, as it was Coleridge's, for the principle proper to ourselves: the exercise of it is further proof that, as Schiller goes on to say, "man's will is in his own hands."

Chapter 2: Commodity

Virtually a commentary on George Herbert's poem "Man," two lines of which Emerson quotes here, postponing till chapter 8 a more ample selection of stanzas.

But the two lines—"More servants wait on Man, / Than he'll take notice of."—are enough to establish the affiliation between "service" in Herbert and "commodity" in Emerson. "Under the general name of Commodity, I rank all those advantages which our senses owe to nature": the O.E.D. quotes this sentence to document "commodity" as "advantage, benefit, profit, interest: often in the sense of private or selfish interest." Not that it has that latter sense in Emerson: on the contrary, in him it means the availability of natural objects for entirely proper use, "Nature, in its ministry to man." Indeed, the chapter is a somewhat secularized version of Herbert's notion of "service" as the human form of mediation between Nature and God: "That, as the world serves us, we may serve thee, / And both thy servants be." If for "God" or "thee" we read Reason, we can still retain Herbert's domestic analogies and Emerson's vocabulary of use, profit, and service—with a fine equivocation on "ministry."

Chapter 3: Beauty

The love of beauty is a human attribute, but Emerson has to take care not to present Beauty as an intrinsic good: it must be seen as useful, of instrumental value. He concedes, in the first of his three numbered paragraphs, that "the simple perception of natural forms is a delight," but the delight is quickly made to consist of the exercise of certain human powers, notably the power of seeing a horizon, and of having eye and light cooperate to enforce a perspective upon natural forms. Perspective is an integrating act. There is also the admitted desire to find natural forms somehow significant: this paragraph asks "what was it that nature would say?" and "was there no meaning in the live repose of the valley behind the mill?" What are the wild waves saying was an incorrigible question, not only in *Dombey and Son*. But Emerson's version of it can't allow the natural forms to say or intend anything, since that would make Nature share some of Man's power of knowledge. So he must hold Nature at the point of trying to say something, but failing: he gives it an air of meaning, short of meaning. The word he uses for that condition is "expression," which is responsive to the human desire for communication but not committed to saying anything in particular. The word is especially convenient because it can lean toward meaning or be held in reserve, as in a later reference to "the face of the world."

At the end of this first numbered paragraph Emerson warns that the beauty of Nature should not be sought. Why not? Because it should be ancillary to the human acts it accompanies. But also because, if it is sought, enjoyed, or intrinsically cultivated, it prevents us from going further. So, in the second numbered paragraph, Emerson has these revealing sentences: "The presence of a higher, namely, of the spiritual element is essential to its perfection. The high and divine beauty which can be loved without effeminacy is that which is found in combination with the human will." Without effeminacy? There is no point in fudging the issue. Emerson thinks of the face of the world as a woman's face, and of that as expressive without expressing anything in particular. Nature is a woman. Mind is a man. Effeminacy is what a man falls into, or indulges himself in, when he is less than himself: Samson yielding to Delilah. Here, Emerson is warning us against cultivating the beauty of Nature, and the sentiment of being present to it: such a thing would mean luxuriating in matter, and suspending the will. In the fifth chapter of *Nature* he refers to "the analogy that marries Matter and Mind," and it is clear how the analogy goes. In the fourth chapter the assertion couldn't be clearer: "That which, intellectually considered, we call Reason, considered in relation to nature, we call Spirit. Spirit is the Creator. Spirit hath life in itself.

And man in all ages and countries embodies it in his language as the FATHER." If a doubt remains, consider this passage, again from the fourth chapter: "All the facts in natural history taken by themselves have no value, but are barren like a single sex. But marry it to human history, and it is full of life." It follows that the beauty that can be loved without effeminacy is that of the human will; a manly act, acknowledged for the heroic character it has by the feminine expressiveness that accompanies it. So this second numbered paragraph gives several instances of human virtue, all of them in a man's world.

In the third numbered paragraph the beauty of the world is linked to a still higher consideration; not delight or even virtue but thought: beauty "as it becomes an object of the intellect." This is work for scientist and artist. The scientist—Emerson refers to "the intellect," but it is clearly the work of science—"searches out the absolute order of things as they stand in the mind of God, and without the colors of affection"; without, that is, effeminacy. He seeks a theory of nature. Meanwhile the artist creates his work of art as "an abstract or epitome of the world": "it is the result or expression of nature, in miniature." As an aesthetic, Emerson's argument is unsatisfactory: it doesn't allow for an artist's creativity, his work is confined to an epitome of what is already there. In fact, the artist's faculty, according to Emerson's description here, is merely an extreme instance of the general human power of composing "the integrity of impression made by manifold objects." The artist's subject, like the orator's, is for the time being the sequestered object on which he lavishes attention: integrity of impression, provoked by the object but transcending it, is in turn an epitome of the integrity of the world.

At the end of the chapter, Emerson reverts to the vocabulary of use, Nature's ministry to man. "The world thus exists to the soul to satisfy the desire of beauty": truth, goodness and beauty "are but different faces of the same All." Goodness is clearly a moral virtue, truth a moral discovery: lest beauty appear to be an attribute of the natural object rather than of the mind that perceives it, Emerson makes it, in any event, entirely instrumental: "But beauty in nature is not ultimate. It is the herald of inward and internal beauty, and is not alone a solid and satisfactory good." The 1870 edition has "eternal," not "internal" beauty, presumably because inward and internal are nearly synonymous and the herald may be allowed to proclaim his master's message in the grandest terms. The relation between herald and master—between the message and its authoritative source—is a problem Emerson leaves for the next chapter.

Chapter 4: Language

Three numbered assertions set this chapter in motion. One: Words are signs of natural facts. Two: Particular natural facts are symbols of particular spiritual facts. Three: Nature is the symbol of Spirit. But Emerson doesn't distinguish between sign and symbol; we are free to think them synonymous. The scheme of things would work out somewhat like this. Start by positing Reason or Spirit or Universal Soul. Then allow that Spirit—choosing one of the synonyms for easy reference—necessarily manifests itself in material forms, the ensemble of which is called Nature. Finally, link words to Nature as "signs of natural facts." I concede that Emerson prefers to take the opposite direction: he likes to start with sensory events, and move with decent speed to a higher perspective, and thence to the perspective-beyond-other-perspectives which he calls Reason or Spirit or Universal Soul.

While the doctrine of this chapter is Swedenborgian, the details are organized in such a Wordsworthian manner as to make the chapter a devout allusion to the

Preface to the second edition of *Lyrical Ballads*. But the arguments, if put together in a more prosaic sequence than Emerson's, would culminate in yet another defense of Science.

Such a sequence would begin with the assertion that the Original Cause has ordained the world on the principle of "the centrality of man in nature, and the connection that subsists throughout all things"—phrases I have taken from the chapter on Swedenborg in *Representative Men*. The laws of Nature include relations and correspondences, and a privileged relation between mind and matter. Man's access to these mysteries is by way of analogy: nature is a text he tries to read in the light of radical consanguinities. The linguistic forms of kinship are figures, notably metaphor: the conceptual forms are types, emblems, and allegories.

Man's knowledge of the laws of nature is merely partial. Some people have no sense of the relation between mind and matter, but even those who are alive to it have only partial apprehension. "By degrees," Emerson says, "we may come to know the primitive sense of the permanent objects of nature, so that the world shall be to us an open book, and every form significant of its hidden life and final cause." There are far more symbols in nature than we can interpret; our dictionary is incomplete, and therefore so are we. "Did it need such noble races of creatures, this profusion of forms, this host of orbs in heaven, to furnish man with the dictionary and grammar of his municipal speech?" At this point Emerson glances at a question alien to him, whether the natural forms—mountains, waves and skies—are significant of themselves, or "have no significance but what we consciously give them, when we employ them as emblems of our thoughts?" Strictly speaking, Plotinus should have settled the question, but Emerson is struck by what seems to be the disproportion between the profusion of natural forms and the penury of our meanings. If "the whole of nature is a metaphor for the human mind," we don't seem to have learnt much. It is a difficult moment in the chapter. Emerson turns away from it and finds consolation again in Coleridge. "Every object rightly seen unlocks a new faculty of the soul," Coleridge said in a passage Emerson quotes now from *Aids to Reflection.*

Chapter 5: Discipline

The most scandalous chapter, this one is largely responsible for the assumption, audible as clearly in the elder Henry James as in W. B. Yeats, that Emerson was totally devoid of a sense of evil. I don't know whether or not it would improve Emerson's reputation in this respect to explain that when he appears a monster—as again in parts of "Self-Reliance"—it is because he has committed himself to the dominion of the act of consciousness over any conditions it meets. If those conditions include objective facts of evil, suffering, and pain, so much the more resolutely is the particular act of consciousness urged to transcend them. It could be argued, then, that the lack of a sense of evil and suffering in Emerson is a consequence of his logic rather than a defect of sympathy: but this doesn't help much, since it invites the retort that it is monstrous to take one's logic more strictly than the suffering of others. The mind can transcend the conditions it meets only by keeping them at a distance or by rising above the level on which they are met.

The second of these devices is favored by Schiller, who thought that the mind should exercise itself upon artificial or imagined misfortunes and assert its independence in that practise. "The more frequently the mind repeats this act of independence, the more skilled it becomes, the greater the advance won over the sensuous impulse, so that finally, should an imaginary and artificial misfortune turn into a real one, the mind is able to treat it as an artificial one and transform actual suffering into sublime emotion." For most people, Schiller's argument is nonsense: imagined pain is not the same as actual pain, and can't be mistaken for the real thing, unless the mind in the case is deranged. But I have to concede that Schiller's point has many ancient traditions behind it, and not merely Epicureanism: as a method of dealing with one's alienation, it has had its adherents.

Emerson's life had more than its share of sorrows; he saw those he loved in pain and misery. It is true that he brought his notion of compensation to bear upon these occasions: also that in his distinction between Understanding and Reason he insisted on regarding the inexplicable opacity of evil as a matter for the first, and every uplifting consideration as issuing from the second. Quentin Anderson has argued in *The Imperial Self* that Emerson "played with the idea that every evil was in the end compensated for, not because he deeply believed it, but because it offered a defense against the notion that the self could not embrace the world if the world was indeed fatally plural, intractable, and evil." This is well said, but I don't think it disposes of the question. We would then have to ask why Emerson so desperately needed what Anderson calls "his fantasy of the primacy of the self"—needed it so badly that he couldn't allow it to be threatened by appalling evidence.

The passage of most extreme scandal in this respect turns up in the present chapter, where Emerson argues that Nature is a discipline, and that every property of matter is a school for the Understanding. His general point is that the lessons the Understanding learns from the disposition of the natural world are the exercise of the will and the experience of power. Reason then "transfers all these lessons into its own world of thought," where they are translated into moral terms. Even the tedious details of daily life are valid, seen as instruction: "The same good office is performed by Property and its filial systems of debt and credit. Debt, grinding debt, whose iron face the widow, the orphan and the sons of genius fear and hate; debt, which consumes so much time, which so cripples and disheartens a great spirit with cares that seem so base, is a preceptor whose lessons cannot be foregone, and is needed most by those who suffer from it most." There is no point in saying that this is heartless: it is clear from its cadences ("Debt, grinding debt . . .") that the experience it generalizes are as familiar to Emerson as to anyone else. It is the lack of a dramatic context, sufficient to question the generalizations and bring them to the test of particular suffering, that distinguishes it from passages of fiction that might be produced from *Hard Times* or *The Mayor of Casterbridge.* What the sentences mostly evince is not hard-heartedness but pedantry, which pursues the logic beyond any reasonable degree of need. If the passage had stopped before its last phrase, the pedantry would not have to be insisted on; but that phrase ("and is needed most by those who suffer from it most") offers the poorest people an educational program when what they need at once is bread and money.

The first device I mentioned, by which the mind keeps its distance from whatever conditions it has to meet, is a technique of generalization and survey: in Emerson, it depends upon his privileging the sense of sight, and the light in which that sense acts. One of the consequences of this privilege is that when we see an object in the light of its idea, what we mostly see is the idea, not the object. But even if this is not necessarily the case, the privileging of sight has other consequences. Hans Jonas has pointed out, in *The Phenomenon of Life,* that "seeing requires no perceptible activity either on the part of the object or on that of the subject": "Neither invades the sphere of the other: they let each other be what they are and as they are, and thus emerge the self-contained object and the self-contained subject . . . . Thus vision secures that standing back from the aggressiveness of the world which frees for observation and opens a horizon for elective attention. But it does so at the price of offering a be-calmed abstract of reality denuded of its raw power." Denuded, too, of its power to hurt.

It is idle to ask which came first in Emerson, his privileging of the sense of sight rather than, say, the sense of touch and the conviction of reality which a sense of touch insists on; or his "fantasy of the pri-macy of the imperial self" in a world that threatened to undo it?

Chapter 6: Idealism

Emerson doesn't indicate, in this chapter, what form or degree of Idealism he favors, but it is clear enough that it is Critical or Transcendental Idealism: "a system of thought in which the object of external perception, to-gether with the whole contents of our experience, is held to consist, as known to us, but not necessarily in itself, of ideas." In "The Transcendentalist" he sufficiently de-scribes the position. The Idealist "affirms facts [which are] not affected by the illusions of sense, facts which are of the same nature as the faculty that reports them, and not liable to doubt." These are facts "which it only needs a retirement from the senses to discern." The Idealist manner of looking at things "transfers every object in nature from an independent and anomalous position without there, into the consciousness."

It is enough for Emerson to make these assumptions. One: Nature is a phenomenon, not a substance; but there is no need to deride it for that or any other reason. Two: "to the senses and the unrenewed understanding belongs a sort of instinctive belief in the absolute existence of nature." But the presence of Reason "mars this faith." "The first effort of thought tends to relax this despotism of the senses, which binds us to nature as if we were a part of it, and shows us nature aloof, and as it were, afloat." (Emerson's position here coincides with Coleridge's, especially when Coleridge attacks "the delusive notion that what is not *imageable* is likewise not *conceivable.*" The idea that the eye is "the most despotic of our senses" is also found in Wordsworth.) Three: Imagination, which Emerson describes as "the use which the Reason makes of the material world," perceives "real affinities between events (that is to say, ideal affinities, for only those are real)" and thus enables the poet— Shakespeare is Emerson's example—"to make free with the most imposing forms and phenomena of the world, and so assert the predominance of the soul." Four: Idealism has this advantage over the popular faith, "that it presents the world in precisely that view which is the most desirable to the mind."

I assume that this phrasing alludes to Bacon's description of poetry, that "it doth raise and erect the mind, by submitting the shows of things to the desires of the mind; whereas reason doth buckle and bow the mind unto the nature of things." Bacon's vocabulary in the latter part of the sentence wouldn't suit Emerson, who has a quite different idea of Reason and wouldn't attach such weight to "the nature of things." No wonder he misquoted Bacon, as René Wellek has noted, and turned him into an out-and-out Platonist. Poetry, Emerson has Bacon saying, "seeks to accommodate the shows of things to the desires of the mind, and to create an ideal world better than the world of experience." Not that it much matters: the only point is that what Bacon attributes to poetry, Emerson attributes to Reason as such. It is then from Emerson that Stevens begins, brooding upon poetry, fictiveness, and the desires appeased by the fictive capacity of mind.

Chapter 7: Spirit

The title is misleading, so it is not a surprise that the chapter has little to say about Spirit and much about more tangible things. Emerson's concern with Spirit was nearly exhausted by the act of positing it. He was far more interested in the consequences of the act than in the act itself or its meaning. He remarks in his journal for 22 April 1837: "I say to Lidian that in composition the *What* is of no importance compared with the *How*. The most tedious of all discourses are on the subject of the Supreme Being." If someone were to ask him what he meant by Spirit, Emerson would have to answer: by Spirit I mean the Supreme Being or the Creator or the Universal Soul. But he wouldn't have wished the interrogation to go much further. Whereof one may not speak, thereof one might as well be silent.

So here we have him referring to "Spirit, that is the Supreme Being," and to God, the Creator, and "the divine mind." The elder Henry James once complained that Emerson "found certain transcendentalist and platonic phrases named beautifully that side of the universe which for his soul . . . was all-important." The problem was and is: can the reader do anything more with these phrases than take them as lyric cries, sites of desire?

Emerson posits Spirit, and then derives from it two further terms, Man and Nature. "The world proceeds from the same spirit as the body of man. It is a remoter and inferior incarnation of God, a projection of God in the unconscious." The world differs from the human body in one respect: it exhibits a serene order, independent of the human will. For that reason, the world is to us "the present expositor of the divine mind." There is another difference, which Emerson doesn't specify here. The world is ignorant of itself, but Man—as a projection of God in consciousness—"has access to the entire mind of the Creator, is himself the creator in the finite."

But Emerson is moody with these terms. Sometimes he represents Nature as an unconscious drudge, a donkey; sometimes as the Christ who sat on one.

These discrepancies wouldn't matter, indeed, if they were merely signs of compensatory moods within a genial acknowledgement of man and nature. If a Wordsworthian sense of man and nature were to obtain, as "a wooing both ways"—Blackmur's phrase in another connection—one's mood of the moment could safely tip the balance now in favor of one, now of another. But in this chapter Emerson deduces from the inviolable order of nature and the supposed disorder of man that "we are as much strangers in nature, as we are aliens from God." But the only proof he offers is that we're not on easy terms with bears and tigers; we don't know much about bird-song. The chapter ends with a very strange notion: "Is not the landscape, every glimpse of which hath a grandeur, a face of him? Yet this may show us what discord is between man and nature, for you cannot freely admire a noble landscape, if laborers are digging in the field hard by. The poet finds something ridiculous in his delight, until he is out of the sight of men." Why so? A Marxist would say that a middle-class poet should indeed be embarrassed, indulging himself in intimations of the grandeur of a landscape at a time when laborers are digging in the next field. But the embarrassment wouldn't have anything to do with discord between man and nature; it would testify to discord between man and man, and invite a strictly historical explanation. If Emerson finds something ridiculous in his delight, it can only be because he is in a position to turn fields into a landscape by raising his mind above the stubble, while the laborers aren't.

Chapter 8: Prospects

The crucial word in this chapter is Idea. Each fact is to be seen "under the light of an idea." The question is not: what is an idea? But rather: how is the correlation established between a particular fact and a particular idea? If we look again at Coleridge's definition of an idea, it now appears more questionable—that conception of a thing "which is given by the knowledge of its ultimate aim." On the next page Coleridge associates it with Law, his reiterated point being that an idea in mind is to a law in nature as the power of seeing is to light. Specifically: "That which, contemplated objectively (i.e., as existing externally to the mind), we call a LAW; the same contemplated subjectively (i.e., as existing in a subject or mind) is an idea." But it's not clear whether an idea, or a law, in Coleridge's sense, is deemed to be already known, or still to be known. Is "its ultimate aim" already known to the mind, so that at most it only needs to be fulfilled; or is it already fulfilled?

The question is crucial for our sense of Emerson, because he is hostile to fixity: an idea would have to be sufficiently mobile to have a further life. Mobility could be gained if we said that while the laws of Nature are in force, we don't yet know them. Science knows some of them, but not all. A total theory of Nature is Emerson's project for Science, so the activities of Understanding and Reason should continue indefinitely. The power of an idea would consist in the power of the mind lavished upon achieving a more and more complete knowledge of it; it would not be already in place, fixed and retrospective.

This distinction is well established: it is possible to distinguish between two meanings of the word "idea." Erwin Panofsky's book *Idea* recalls Michaelangelo's use of the words *concetto* and *immagine*. "Both of these words might reasonably be translated as 'idea,' " Panofsky says, "but with a crucial difference." In its proper and literal sense, already formulated by Augustine and Thomas Aquinas, "*immagine* means that notion which *ex alio procedit*, that is, which reproduces an already existing object." *Concetto*, on the other hand, "when it does not simply stand for 'thought,' 'concept,' or 'plan,' means the free creative notion that constitutes its own object, so that it in turn can become the model for external shaping: as the Scholastics put it, the *forma agens*, not the *forma acta.*" The distinction turns on a matter of grammatical tense. *Immagine* is the code of past feelings, invoked even at the risk of replacing them with a code. *Concetto* is a project, a gesture—Newman's idea of a university, Eliot's idea of a Christian society—toward a future in which the project may or may not be fulfilled. If we brought this meaning—*concetto*—to bear upon "idea," then a fact seen in the light of an idea would mean "in the light of the further possibilities of the fact, its possible development by correlation with the further phases of the mind that attends to it." Awkwardly phrased, I know, but the important point is that the fact would have a future commensurate with the most developed activities of the mind.

Coleridge's way of gaining mobility for his Idea was by compromising its ultimacy and "perfection": not that that was his intention. In "Constancy to an Ideal Object," Coleridge invokes the ideal object as an absolute, "the only constant in a world of change"; then thinks of another absolute, his love for Sara, a passion just as constant. Emerson's writings—his essays and poems—are not as immediately personal as Coleridge's poem; so in theory he could be content to regard an idea as an archetype, which doesn't depend upon its embodiment in a substance. But he, too, like Coleridge, disturbs the archetype to the point at which it becomes a *concetto* rather than an *immagine;* but for a different reason. He hasn't any particular need to concentrate his mind on the merging of an absolute with a human embodiment; or on the hyperbole to which Coleridge's feeling drives him. But he has an interest, just as keen, in giving his mind the latitude of experience and the indefinitely extensive scope which I have been describing as mobility. Mobility is the quality of Emerson's desire, too, though the object of the desire is the "supreme fiction" of his mind: the "ultimate aim" which characterizes an idea must be such as to give the mind that aspires to it—or yearns for it—an historical development as large as Emerson's ambition.

Postscript

Granted that Emerson is not a philosopher; it is enough that he is a poet and a sage. He is not in competition with Hegel or Schelling. But the site of his poetry and his sageness is the history of voluntarism. The more we read *Nature,* the more clearly it appears that the whole essay is predicated upon the capacity of Will. Not knowledge but power is its aim; not truth but command. Human will is deemed to participate in the vitality of natural forms. Mind is a chosen direction of Will. In "The Poet" Emerson writes: "This insight, which expresses itself by what is called Imagination, is a very high order of seeing, which does not come by study, but by the intellect being where and what it sees, by sharing the path or circuit of things through forms, and so making them translucent to others. The path of things is silent. Will they suffer a speaker to go with them?" The vitality of natural forms is the circuit of things through forms; the aim of the poet and sage is to present the circuit as if it were subject to his command. Mind, as a chosen direction the will takes, is charted in *Nature* through the phases of sensibility, understanding and reason. An extreme "moment" in that progress is self-command, which corresponds to Heidegger's notion, in *Being and Time,* of choosing to "let be." So if we go back to the transparent eyeball passage and read it as a voluntarist act rather than an instance of the Sublime, we find that the eyeball becomes transparent because a light higher than its own sensory light is made to shine through it. "The currents of the Universal Being circulate through me"; that is, I will that no sensory obstacle—and therefore no opacity—shall impede the progress of the power that is in me.

Voluntarism is an accurate name for this commitment, provided we do not think of it as issuing in an ego psychology. Harold Bloom well distinguishes, in his *Agon,* between *psyche* and the Emersonian spark or *pneuma*—"this Gnostic true or antithetical self, as opposed to *psyche* or soul." The difference can only be that *psyche,* as asserted by ego psychology, is known by the particular structure of the attributes which embody it: *pneuma* has only this sole attribute, that it is one's willful possession of the energy at large in a living world. *Pneuma* is a spark of life, of the force of life as such, before any further attributes are located or recognized. Not a psychology but a pneumatology explicates Emerson's work: we have access to it only by recourse to the vocabulary of Will and to its social form, a pragmatics of the future.

Reference to such a pragmatics is enough to remind us that Emerson is not merely a poet and a sage: he is the founding father of nearly everything we think of as American in the modern world. To the extent to which the sentiments of power, self-reliance, subjectivity, and independence attract to themselves a distinctly American nuance, its source is Emerson. Harold Bloom has named as Emersonian the only form of religion he is willing to recognize as American. So it is clear that American scholars and artists have invested much of their energy in the values we associate with Emerson.

That there are "answers" to Emerson is well understood, but we hear little of them nowadays. Twenty or thirty years ago a critic writing on Emerson would have felt obliged to face Yvor Winters's argument, in *Maule's Curse,* that Emerson presented the commonplaces of the Romantic movement in the language of a Calvinistic pulpit: "He could speak of matter as if it were God; of the flesh as if it were spirit; of emotion as

if it were Divine Grace; of impulse as if it were conscience; and of automatism as if it were the mystical
experience." It follows, according to Winters's argument, that Emerson and those who listened to his lectures and read his essays "were moral parasites upon a
Christian doctrine they were endeavoring to destroy."
At this point the argument merges with another,
which we find in the Southern critics and especially in
Allen Tate and Robert Penn Warren, that Emerson
made available a genteel form of secularism which was
particularly attractive to people who wanted to escape
from the responsibilities of crime and punishment, sin
and expiation.

Eliot's poem "Cousin Nancy" extends these arguments: its implication is that Emerson and Arnold, by
encouraging Nancy to think of herself as the privileged
center of culture and experience, merely released her to
fall for every fashion that came along, mistaking futile
rebelliousness for self-determination:

> Upon the glazen shelves kept watch
> Matthew and Waldo, guardians of the faith,
> The army of unalterable law.

The irony of "guardians" reaches conclusion in the
mockery of "law." The total effect of Arnold's philosophy, Eliot maintained in his essay on Arnold and Pater,
"is to set up Culture in the place of Religion, and to
leave Religion to be laid waste by the anarchy of feeling." So Arnold was responsible for the easiest forms of
Humanism, and for Pater and Wilde. What Emerson
was responsible for, Eliot doesn't explicitly say. But the
strongest indication of Eliot's condescending estimate
of Emerson is the fact that he excluded him from the
American tradition he took most seriously. In "The
Hawthorne Aspect" he said of Emerson, Thoreau and
Lowell that "none of these men . . . is individually very
important; they can all, and perhaps ought to be made
to look very foolish; but there is a 'something' there, a

dignity, about Emerson for example, which persists after we have perceived the taint of commonness about some English contemporary, as for instance the more intelligent, better educated, more alert Matthew Arnold." But in describing the kinship of Hawthorne and James, which he presented without wishing to diminish James's relation to Balzac and Turgenev, Eliot pointed to what he regarded as the best the New England mind had to give, a best by comparison with which nothing in Emerson, Lowell, Thoreau, Longfellow, or Margaret Fuller was quite good enough. What Hawthorne and James had, a possession requiring full consideration in any account of their genius, was "a very acute historical sense," a sense even more acute in Hawthorne than in James. By the criteria this sense enforced, Emerson didn't come into the reckoning.

It is not my intention to document "the case against Emerson." Indeed, I wouldn't have mentioned it but for the fact that such a case appears to have been quite forgotten. In the past several years, Emerson has been called upon to sponsor many different programs: he can be quoted to nearly any purpose. There is no question of adjudicating between Emerson's adherents and his opponents: one would have to start with a consideration of Original Sin. The critical question might be met, far more briefly and delicately, by yet again reading *Nature:* if our first reading concentrated upon the privilege accorded to Mind, and the second upon the primacy of Will, a third would register not chiefly Will, but the misgivings that should attend the claims Emerson makes for it as nothing less than a moral principle.

3. Seeing and Saying: The Dialectic of Emerson's Eloquence

STEPHEN RAILTON

> It was the happiest turn to my old thrum which Charles
> H Warren gave as a toast at the ΦBK Dinner. "Mr Presi-
> dent," he said, "I suppose all know where the orator
> comes from; and I suppose all know what he has said. I
> give you *The Spirit of Concord. It makes us all of One
> Mind.*"[1]

"Imperial" is a much more accurate word than "dialectical" to describe the vision Emerson announced and
the self he celebrated at the beginning of his career as a
prophet. Why, then, do so many recent commentators
on *Nature* emphasize the dialectical quality of its
thought? Emerson's first book, which seemed to him
as scrupulously structured as "the multiplication ta-
ble,"[2] is organized dialectically, but a distinction has
to be made between Emerson's ideas and the exposi-
tory strategy by which he seeks to express them. Even
Kenneth Burke, the first critic to analyze the dialectical order of *Nature*, implies this distinction, though he
does not develop it, when he refers to the essay's "dialectical maneuvers."[3] The organization of *Nature* is
like its titular subject: just as Nature is real, manifold,
and objective only to the fallen man, but dissolves into
the One Soul as soon as he regains his sovereignty, so
is *Nature*'s structure Emerson's concession to the Understanding—it exists to be seen through; it too must

float and soar. Nowhere in the essay does Emerson suggest that Reason has anything to learn from dialectical experience. Indeed, he begins by transcending all dialectical divisions: he has just barely made the most fundamental of these—the separation of existence into Me and Not-Me—when he reveals how, walking across a bare common or in the woods, he has felt that dichotomy break down. Every di-vision, all theses and antitheses, give way to the one vision. No dialectical thinker would recognize that "transparent eyeball" moment as a synthesis, for in it oppositions are not reconciled. They are simply dismissed.

This announcement of an imminent apocalypse, and not the arrangement of its chapters, is what is most characteristically Emersonian about *Nature,* and what clearly distinguishes his program from the one defined by his romantic counterparts in Europe. How similar the "transparent eyeball" moment is to—yet how different from—the comparable moments in *The Prelude* or *Sartor Resartus.* By the time Wordsworth's "I" is vouchsafed its vision on Mount Snowdon, or Carlyle's Teufelsdrockh arrives at his "Everlasting Yea," the realms of history, society, otherness have been fully engaged. As M. H. Abrams points out in his brilliant discussion of the Romantics' program, "the familiar Romantic model of a self-formative educational journey" is rooted in a sense of experience as dialectical: the Romantic Self "moves through division, exile, and solitariness toward the goal of a recovered home and restored familial relationship."[4] Emerson, on the other hand, chose not to recount the growth of his prophetic Soul, although as readers of his journals know, his own experience during the 1830s with doubt and alienation could certainly have been worked up into an autobiography as powerful as either Wordsworth's or Carlyle's. Emerson's unwillingness to acknowledge that experience reveals not only his temperamental diffidence, but also his epistemological refusal to root the truth he attained in dialectical ground. The society of Boston, the creeds of Unitarianism, the deaths of a wife and a brother: his Self does not move through these antitheses toward its climactic reunion with the Over-Soul. What Wordsworth and Carlyle must encounter, Emerson can seem to ignore.

The a-dialectical supremacy Emerson bestowed upon the Self can be understood, as Quentin Anderson has demonstrated, as a quintessentially American aspect of his thought. Unlike the English Romantics, Emerson could persuasively assert the Soul's exemption from all constrictions of time and place and other people. Not even a "common" seemed inextricably set in the middle of a society, and the primordial woods just beyond his door made all man's social or historical "operations" seem so insignificant that, in the introductory section of *Nature*, "the mixture of [the human] will" with the "essences unchanged by man" seemed irrelevant from the start. In a sense, this preliminary disposition of Me and Not-Me, by including society and history with Nature, contains its own abrogation: saying that it does not matter whether we use "Nature" "in its common or in its philosophical import" moves us right to the verge of Emerson's final redefinition, where we make the leap into the kingdom of power, where it does not matter whether we say Nature or Soul. Yet as soon as we start talking about Emerson's lexical maneuverings, we approach the problem of his style—which, since style for Emerson was a function of rhetoric, is another way of referring to the problem of his relationship to his contemporary American audience. And this, I believe, is one aspect of his program to which the adjective "dialectical" can legitimately be applied.

Emerson himself indicates the terms of the rhetorical dialectic I want to discuss in one of the few passages in his early prose which refer to moving between two specific poles. "How hard it is to write the truth," he noted in his journal in 1836; "so soon as I have seen the truth I clap my hands & rejoice & go back to see it & forward to tell men" (*JMN*, 5: 181). Here Emerson locates the most stubborn of the antitheses he was forced to try to reconcile: the conflict between seeing and saying, between the radical truth he was privately convinced of and his desire to share that truth with a public whose values were hedged in by Victorian decorums—for Emerson did not want to rejoice alone, and in fact needed to hear others clap their hands.[5] If, as a seer, he was "an endless seeker with no Past at [his] back," as a sayer he was always acutely conscious of the audience in front of him. The reader of his essays looks in vain through their assertions for any acknowledgment that life is dramatic; when we look at how those assertions are made, however, we become aware of the drama that is being enacted between Emerson and his contemporary audience, a drama in which the texts of his lectures and essays play a mediatory role. The strategies of his style were shaped by the exigencies of his relationship to his public.

Several times in his journal Emerson exhorts himself to "deal plainly with society," even to shock his listeners (*JMN*, 7: 105), and throughout the 1830s identified strongly with the model of George Fox, who was as prepared oratorically to shout down the enemies of truth as he was physically to suffer their abuse. Yet in 1862, when he wrote his eulogy to Thoreau, he displayed in a dozen ways his own discomfort with what he called his friend's stylistic "habit of antagonism." Only one of Emerson's performances—"The Divinity School Address"—verges on confronting his audience, and even there the surface of his text seeks to deny the existence of any friction; rhetorically, his stance on that occasion was explicitly defined by such blithe assertions of agreement as "All who hear me, feel that the language that describes Christ to Europe and America . . . is appropriated and formal." Emerson was the rarest of prophets: the one who declined to attack his listeners. He had done a brave thing by resigning from his church in 1832. Exchanging a Unitarian pulpit for the lyceum platform meant that henceforth he would meet his audience as Ralph Waldo Emerson, not as a minister. Without a commissioned role, with no institutional authority from which to speak, he took it upon himself—and his language—to work out the terms of a public identity. Emerson celebrated the lyceum lecture as the literary genre least encumbered with tradition (cf. *JMN*, 7: 224–25), but the ad hoc nature of a lecture also made it a truly existential encounter. The people who filled the hall met on no common ground besides that which Emerson could supply in his text for the evening. As a speaker, he finally had no other sanction for his words than his audience's consent to them. In that most democratic of forums, he had "to put on eloquence as a robe" (*JMN*, 2: 242)— he had no other costume of office.

A comparison of Emerson's early lectures with his journal entries for the same years reveals his many and varied concessions to the sensibilities of his audience and to his own ambition to speak as "the mere tongue of us all" (*JMN*, 5: 102). There is, for example, a pronounced pattern of suppression, so that many of the thoughts we now associate most intimately with Emerson were not given public utterance for many years.[6] There are unequivocal instances of self-censorship.[7] There is also his habit of evading responsibility for his most radical ideas, best known in his creation of that fictive Bard at the end of *Nature* (*JMN*, 5: 179–83 leaves no doubt that the Bard's words were really Emerson's), but also present in the lectures in the systematic way he relies on explicating someone else's ideas—Luther's or Fox's or even (of course out of context) Jesus'[8]—to express principles that he is not yet willing to assert in his own person. In fact, Emerson's own person is impossible to pin down in his lectures. He uses the first person singular most regularly to refer to himself in his role as the lecturer, to announce a new subject or apologize for a digression, but is much more likely to use the plural whenever he advances a principle of thought: "in all our reasonings respecting society this is assumed," "on the whole, then, we think." The most conspicuous example of this mode of commonality must be his lecture on "The Transcendentalist" (1841), in which Emerson uses "we" to indicate those people—himself and his listeners—who want to understand "the transcendentalist," and speaks about the transcendentalist himself (whom most of his contemporaries would obviously have assumed was Emerson) exclusively in the third person. There is no public lecture, not even "The Protest" (1839), in which Emerson does not presume to be taking sides with his audience—going so far, for instance, as to quote his own deeply personal words from the journal as those of "a youth," "our young Hamlet," and then disingenuously to suggest to his listeners that such a "fantastic young person might find a friend in each one of us"![9]

Probably the most characteristic of Emerson's rhetorical strategies, though, involves the kind of lexical sleight of hand that Anderson has already noted: "To appropriate the language of politics or poetry or conventional morality was to set up a tension between the expectations that language gave rise to in Emerson's audience and the voice of the self, which devoted all these terms to the use of the inward empire."[10] Emerson especially needed to manipulate the vocabulary of contemporary theology, for he knew that he and his audience were nowhere further apart than on the issue of religion: "In all my lectures, I have taught one doctrine, namely, the infinitude of the private man. This, the people accept readily enough, & even with loud commendation, as long as I call the lecture, Art; or Politics; or Literature; or the Household; but the moment I call it Religion,—they are shocked."(*JMN*, 7:

342) To note only one among the innumerable instances of Emerson's willful appropriation of language, we can recall the fifth sentence of *Nature*, which syntactically turns a pair of antonyms into synonyms: "Why should not we have a poetry and philosophy of insight and not of tradition, and a religion by revelation to us, and not the history of theirs?" A thesaurus would endorse the way Emerson matches tradition and history, but to pause over his marriage of insight with revelation is to be amazed at how much he attempted to get away with linguistically. Emerson knew, and later, after "The Divinity School Address" had publicly put him at odds with the religious establishment, could acknowledge that he knew, what "revelation" meant—"the idea of a revelation which obtains in modern Christendom ... see how degraded it is."[11] His own prophetic project can be summed up by saying that he sought to convince his contemporaries that their allegiance to revelation (what God had enjoined from without) had to be replaced by an absolute faith in their insights (what the godhead within reveals). But Emerson would not have been Emerson had he been this explicit. Instead, he attempts in this sentence, and again and again in his prose, to stretch the meaning of words far enough to include both his truth and his audience under their spell.

This lexical tension is there for the critic to note, but the rhetorical purpose it serves is rather to preclude any tension between Emerson and his audience: "never compare your generalization with your neighbor's. Speak now, & let him hear you & go his way. Tomorrow, or next year, let him speak, & answer thou not. So shall you both speak truth & *be of one mind*; but insist on comparing your two thoughts ... & instantly you are struck with blindness, & will grope & stagger like a drunken man." (*JMN*, 7, 40; my italics) Emerson could admit that he and his audience might think different thoughts, but was compelled to try to subvert the difference. "The length of the discourse indicates the distance of thought between the speaker & the hearer" (*JMN*, 7: 50). His operative mode of discourse—the Emersonian style—was to use words themselves as the means of bridging that distance. When we consider how "revelation" functions in the sentence I quoted, we can see the dialectical struggle between seeing and saying being (implicitly) carried forward at the most local level. We might even consider Emerson's public diction as his idiosyncratic version of the Romantic journey that Abrams describes.[12] For in Emerson's ab-use of words we can see his tacit acknowledgment of societal dividedness and individual alienation. As a rhetorical persona, Emerson always claimed to be at home with his audience in the same truths; "O my brothers" is among his favorite oratorical interjections. His Self cannot be displayed in any conflict with their world. But in his diction he was forced to send his truths out to engage their words.

While his prose had an obligation to those truths, it was still more severely constrained by Emerson's need to share his vision with others. His audience, conceived as an entity, had an authority over him that he granted to nothing else: "The audience is a constant meter of the orator."[13] In their presence his omnipotence could not be taken for granted, and although he was a convincing advocate of solitude, although all forms of human relatedness could be denied in his essays, Emerson himself, as his journals reveal, never found a solitude retired enough to wholly exclude his consciousness of that audience. To himself he could confess that "the infinitude of the private man" had limits. The writer, at least, is never alone—much less the writer who takes as his genre the lyceum lecture: "The child is sincere, and the man when he is alone, *if he be not a writer*, but on the entrance of the second person hypocrisy begins" (*JMN*, 4: 314; my italics). That second person, the public before whom he performs, was by Emerson's own implication always present. Going forward to tell men meant being forced to anticipate their response, as Emerson also confessed in a startling aphorism (for which we now have the cancelled phrases): "Let the painter unroll ⟨again⟩ his canvas; ⟨& spread it with hope before his solitary eyes.⟩ millions of eyes look through ⟨them⟩ his" (*JMN*, 6: 321). "Hypocrisy" was Emerson's Victorian judgment on the strategies he felt forced to used to close the gap that separated his convictions from his public's pieties. We need not be so harsh. But we should bear in mind that, despite our respect for them as literary artifacts, the texts of Emerson's work he himself considered primarily as a means.

What was the end? In the fall of 1834, when he moved to Concord, Emerson confided in his journal a hope that would be reiterated there: "The high prize of eloquence may be mine, the joy of uttering what no other can utter & what all must receive" (*JMN*, 4: 324; also 5: 219, 449). This was the most fundamental of his aspirations. And if the first of his conditions suggests that he suffered some anxiety about influence and priority, it is nonetheless the second—"what all must receive"—that declares the deeper of his concerns. How much deeper is revealed in a journal entry from 1839, when he was still trying to digest the official reaction to his "Divinity School Address" the summer before; in an extraordinary passage, he appeals to what others have already uttered to reassure himself about what his audience will eventually receive from him, forsaking any claim to an original relation to the universe for the sake of a more reciprocal one with his public:

To him who said it before. I see my thought standing, growing, walking, working, out there in nature. Look where I will, I see it. Yet when I seek to say it, all men say "NO: It is not. These are whimsies & dreams!" Then I think they look at one thing & I at others. My thoughts, though not false, are far, as yet, from simple truth, & I am rebuked by their disapprobation nor think of questioning it. Society is yet too great for me. But I go back to my library & open my books & lo I read this word spoken out of immemorial time, "God is the unity of men." Behold, I say, my very thought! This is what I am rebuked for saying; & here it is & has been for centuries in this book which circulates among men without reproof, nay, with honor. But behold, again here in another book "Man is good, but men are bad." Why, I have said no more. And here again, read these words, "Ne te quae-siveris extra." What, then! I have not been talking nonsense. These lines of Greek & Latin which pass now current in all literatures as proverbs of old wise men are expressions of the very facts which the sky, the sea, the plant, the ox, the man, the picture, said daily unto me, & which I repeated to you. I see that I was right; that not only I was right, which I could not doubt, but my language was right; that the soul has always said these things; & that you ought to hear it & say the same. (*JMN*, 7: 180–81)

"You" here, of course, refers to Emerson's contemporary listeners, who are granted an independent existence and volition by the very form of the pronoun. This dramatic entrance of the second person, intruding into the seclusion of the journal, shatters the solipsistic self-sufficiency of the first two sentences, and indicates as plainly as the sense of the passage as a whole how real Emerson's audience was to him, and how much depended on their response.

The true theory may be its own evidence, but true eloquence, as Emerson defined it to himself, depends upon the evidence of the listeners' reception: "In the pulpit at Waltham, I felt that the composition of his audience was not of importance to him who possessed true eloquence. Smooth or rugged, good natured or ill natured, religious or scoffers, he takes them all as they come, he proceeds in the faith that all differences are superficial, that they all have one fundamental nature which he knows how to address. This is to be eloquent. And having this skill to speak to their pervading soul he can make them smooth or rugged, good-natured or ill natured, saints or scoffers at his will." (*JMN*, 5: 219) Similarly, though, any failure to convert that audience into "one mind" was a failure of the will: the end of rhetoric, "that which eloquence ought to reach," can be nothing less than "a taking sovereign possession of the audience."[14] There is no more obsessive topic throughout the journals for the 1830s than Emerson's concern with eloquence and oratory, with making every listener's heart vibrate at one pitch, and all men say Yes. Even the great man's greatness is apparently mortgaged to his ability to bring the huge world round to him, rhetorically: "I said to Alcott that I though the great Man should occupy the whole space between God and the mob. He must draw from the infinite source on the one side & *he must penetrate into the heart & mind of the rabble* on the other. From one he must draw his strength; to the other he must owe his Aim." (*JMN*, 5: 249; my italics)

Backwards and forwards, seeing and saying, the one and the other: Emerson consistently locates himself and his prose between the poles of the dialectic we have identified. This passage seems to claim a vast amount for the Self, but also lays down a program that does subject it, fatally, to the verdicts of time and place. To himself Emerson admitted that he was bound to this "Aim" by a necessity he could not resist, though he might complain: "What a mischief is this art of Writing. An unlettered man considers a fact to learn what it means; the lettered man does not sooner see it than it occurs to him how it can be told" (*JMN*, 4: 314). How to tell the truth meant solving the problem of getting all men to embrace it: "In perfect eloquence, the hearer would lose the sense of dualism; of hearing from another" (*JMN*, 7: 52). The new man whom Emerson announced from the platform was illimitable; the announcer himself, however, can be measured by the dimensions of his need to court his audience's assent.

Emerson's ambition, I had better say explicitly, was not mere popularity, that false republican idol against which he warned himself often enough in his journal—though there he could also wonder "Were it not a heroic adventure in me to insist on being a popular speaker?" (*JMN*, 4: 315), and he did keep careful track of how well he was doing with the public at the box office and bookstore (cf. *JMN*, 5: 411, 451, etc.). Neither, however, do we need to be satisfied with his own philosophical justification of his desire to avoid alienating anyone in his audience: that as there is one truth, so the best way to restore men to it is to talk past their disparate identities to their common soul: "Do not put yourself in a false position in regard to your cotemporaries. If your views are in straight antagonism to theirs, nevertheless assume an identity of sentiment,—that you are saying precisely that they all think, & in the flow of wit & love roll out your ultra paradoxes in solid column with not the infirmity of a doubt, knowing that really & underneath all their external denials & diversities, they are of one heart & mind." (*JMN*, 5: 504–5) What Emerson hoped consciously to accomplish through his oratory was to fulfill the prophet's public office: generalizing from lyceum audience to mankind, he believed that under the inspired idiom of a truly eloquent speaker, all men might meet on a higher platform: "an example of a perfect society is in the effect of Eloquence."[15] This, we may decide, this is why Emerson mounted again and again to the podium. But that is to focus on the effect he sought at the cost of ignoring the cause, the personal need that compelled him to seek it.

It is the fallen narcissist who looks at his own work through millions of other eyes. We certainly do not need to be reminded of Emerson's narcissism, although his published pronouncements about self-reliance have effectively disguised his private desire to see his sovereignty reflected in his contemporaries' assent.[16] "Stay at home in God," he wrote, but that too turns out to be as much a means as an end: "& the whole population will do homage with cap & knee" (*JMN*, 7: 173). On the other hand, how far he had fallen is revealed in the numerous journal comments about his crippling diffidence in the presence of others. Conscious of the public even in solitude, he was still more painfully conscious of himself in public: "The old experiences still return. Society when I rarely enter the company of my well dressed & well bred fellow creatures, seems for the time to bereave me of organs or perhaps only to acquaint me with my want of them. The soul swells with new life and seeks expression with painful desire, but finds no outlets. Its life is all incommunicable." (*JMN*, 7: 516) Even Emerson suggests that this fact of his personality has a legitimate relevance to the emphases of his thought: "We love to paint those qualities which we do not possess. . . . I who suffer from excess of sympathy, proclaim always the merits of selfreliance" (*JMN*, 7: 371–72). And Emerson himself, drawing the connection I would draw between the personality he could not escape and the role he could perform on the platform, saw his eloquence as a kind of compensation—in the Freudian, not the Emersonian, sense: "[Margaret Fuller] writes me that she waits for the Lectures seeing well after much intercourse that the best of me is there. She says very truly; & I thought it a good remark which somebody repeated here from S.S. that I 'always seemed to be on stilts.' " It is even so. Most of the persons whom I see in my own house I see across a gulf. I cannot go to them nor they come to me. Nothing can exceed the frigidity & labor of my speech with such." (*JMN*, 7: 301)

On the platform, in using eloquence to fill up that gulf, in seeking to unite himself and his audience through his words, in wanting always to be able to claim that *"All who hear me feel that,"* Emerson sought not only to communicate his life, but to live it: "If I could persuade men to listen to their interior convictions, if I could express, embody their interior convictions, that were indeed life" (*JMN*, 4: 346). Abrams' formulation for the goal of the Romantic's quest—"a recovered home and restored familial relationship"— can serve as well to define the end to which Emerson's rhetoric was the means. For behind the figure of Emerson addressing an audience we may recognize the anxieties of the infant who has begun to need to see the smile on his mother's face to affirm his own identity and eminence. Primary narcissism abandons its title to the world reluctantly. It is followed by a transitional stage in which other people are both perceived as subjective phenomena (part of the Me) and recognized as objective objects (part of the Not-Me). There is a striking illustration of this ambiguity in the passage, quoted earlier, "To him who said it before": there Emerson can lump "the man" in with "the sea, the sky" and so on, as mere manifestations of his thought—but at the very end of that same sentence "the man" reappears as "you," as a wholly separate entity whose resistance to Emerson's volition must be overcome. I suspect that many performers who need to confirm their identities in the live presence of an audience have had a major portion of their character arrested at just this point in their development, when the Self first becomes aware of the fatal fact of its limits and its dependency. By putting themselves at the center of an audience's attention, and then willing its unanimous approval of them, they keep seeking to triumph over their knowledge of the dividedness of the human condition. Whenever Emerson could feel that his eloquence had made him and his listeners "of one mind," he had managed to expand the circumference of his Self at least to the edges of the lyceum hall. Yet his need was finally as unbounded as the unfallen infant's sense of his potency; his aspiration, after all, was that all men would receive his thoughts as their own.

Thus we cannot easily exaggerate Emerson's dependency upon the responses of his audience. Restoring himself to a sense of his own omnipotence meant that he had, despite his impatience with the tendency in himself, to keep "gazing into the looking-glass of men's opinion" (*JMN*, 7: 400). His words, unlike Thoreau's or Whitman's, could be reabsorbed so easily by his culture because of his rhetorical exertions, even while declaiming against society as an abstraction, to avoid offending anyone among his listeners. Confronting an audience would have meant drawing a line between himself and them, reestablishing the boundary that his valuation of style as eloquence, his transformation of truth into rhetoric, was intended to transcend: "Very disagreeable rencontres are there all the way," he wrote after a "variously instructive" visit in 1836 to Groton, where he preached from a Unitarian pulpit; "To meet those who expect light from you & to be provoked to thwart & discountenance & unsettle them by all you say is pathetical" (*JMN*, 5: 214). For the rest of his career, on whatever platform he spoke from (including the pages of his essays), Emerson remained committed to the search for a rhetoric that would bring his audience round to him.

It is only after recognizing this that we are in a position to understand Emerson's style. While we are used to thinking of influence as something referred to with the past tense—how, say, what Coleridge had written influenced Emerson's ideas—we need to consider more seriously the kind of influence that can only be pointed to with the future tense. Emerson's expression was shaped by his anticipations of how his contemporaries would respond. Indeed, it seems to me that most analyses of his style leave out the crucial term. Style, for Emerson, was a performance. "In composition the *What* is of no importance compared with the *How*" (*JMN*, 5: 304–5); "Gladly I would solve if I could this problem of a Vocabulary" (*JMN*, 7: 149); "It is rhetoric that takes up so much room: the result of the book is very small & could be written down in a very few lines" (*JMN*, 7: 522)—in his anxieties about saying, Emerson also expresses the urgencies of his personality. Perhaps the most illuminating way to examine an Emersonian text, its strategies of organization, of diction, of syntax, rhythm, and tone, would be to relocate that text in the space between Emerson and his audience, and see how pervasively his pages are dominated by the implicit presence of that audience, how his rhetorical choices are governed by his desire to close that gap. In this aim he did not, of course, always succeed, as he himself learned when confronted by the adverse reaction to "The Divinity School Address."[17] That controversy, which he describes in "Uriel" as a fall, was unquestionably the most unsettling of all the events recorded in the journals. Yet in retrospect it may even have seemed to him, as it must to us, a *felix culpa*, because in the crack that that reaction opened between Emerson and the formal guardians of his culture, he found the room and courage to be more explicit, to publish many of the ideas he had previously suppressed, to insist upon his truths more emphatically. At the same time, however, he never yielded his desires, no more than he could change the definition of eloquence that was as rooted as the needs of his psyche.

Indeed, his journal reveals that he had even hoped to avoid discountenancing anyone in "the discourse now growing under my eye [and his audience's] to the Divinity School": "We shun to say that which schocks the religious ear of the people & to take away titles even of false honor from Jesus. But this fear is an impotency to commend the moral sentiment. For if I can so imbibe that wisdom as to utter it well, instantly love & awe take place. The reverence for Jesus is only reverence for this, & if you can carry this home to any

man's heart, instantly he feels that all is made good &
that God sits once more on the throne." (*JMN*, 7: 41)
Obviously Emerson knew that much of what he had to
say on this occasion would attack the values of the
faculty at Cambridge. But his hope was to convert, not
to confront them. His repetition of "instantly" betrays
the extremity of his hope: that even as he spoke, if he
could utter them well, his words would accomplish a
miracle that would have been worthy of Jesus, and Andrews Norton would find himself paying reverence to
the truth that Emerson, at the podium, had set upon
the throne. Eloquence's failure on this occasion led to a
prolonged period of self-doubt, cadenced by manic intervals of self-assertion, but in nearly all the journal
entries dealing with the controversy, Emerson cannot
stop until he has arrived at a redeclaration of his faith
in eloquence's promise:

> Society has no bribe for me, neither in politics, nor church,
> nor college, nor city. My resources are far from exhausted. If
> they will not hear me lecture, I shall have leisure for my
> book which wants me. Beside, it is an universal maxim
> worthy of all acceptation that a man may have that allow-
> ance which he takes. Take the place & attitude to which
> you see your unquestionable right, & all men acquiesce.
> Who are these mourners, these haters, these revilers? Men of
> no knowledge, & therefore no stability. The scholar on the
> contrary is sure of his point, is fast-rooted, & can securely
> predict the hour when all this roaring multitude shall roar
> *for* him. (*JMN*, 7: 60–61)

One passage in the essay "Eloquence" catches up
both these entries and provides a final testimony to the
role that the public played in Emerson's life and work:
"the highest bribes of society are at the feet of the
successful orator. He has his audience at his devotion. . . . He is the true potentate; for they are not kings
who sit on thrones, but they who know how to gov-
ern."[18] Eloquence, according to Emerson, was "pure
power." Yet his need to express the truth, to tell men,

points always to his fallen condition. He could not rest at the pole of seeing, because mere seeing, even if what he saw was Nature's pledge of his sovereignty as an imperial Self, could not sufficiently confirm his right to the throne. For that he was dependent on his audience. "Always the seer is the sayer": this turns out to be the burden of Emerson's career.

4. English and American Traits

CARL F. HOVDE

English Traits[1] is perhaps the most ingratiating of Emerson's major works. One suspects this is particularly true for the modern reader; admire Emerson as we do, we are less accustomed than our forebears to the heightened tone of his more typical performance, the urging toward his ideal and noninstitutional vision. *English Traits* charms with its freshness of detail, its air of being the result of particular attention. Its relaxed and occasionally casual tone seems to assure us that no ideological axe is being ground.

But Emerson rarely loses sight of his large purposes, and while his least examined long work is of course focused on the characteristics of our old home, the book is in some of its implications a work about America as well. This reference to America appears more often than one might suspect. Sometimes the allusions are direct comments, though more often they are matters of implication: together they come to suggest an "under-text" to the examination of England itself, an account evoked by a combination of Emerson's overt concerns, his enthusiasms, and his registered surprise. As he thinks about our old home, our new one is not long absent from his thoughts.

What strikes Emerson most about England is the sense it gives him of fully achieved form—the potentialities of the nation seem fully realized, for better and for worse. The glory of this is that England becomes for him a demonstration of mature identity—through a long history potentialities have been completely worked out, and the things admired are seen as the epitome of their types. Shortcomings also exist in final form, but even these provide the pleasures of certain knowledge. The melancholy note in all this clarity is Emerson's certainty that the country's future is one of decline. He looks on mid-nineteenth-century England as a kind of splendid game preserve: the fine animals run free in their native habitat, but they are living in a territory whose borders are no longer determined by their own energies and character. England is summed-up and memorialized in *English Traits*—it is not a work about what may come to pass.[2]

Above all else, England has for Emerson produced admirable men and women. Nothing is more powerfully celebrated here than the virtues of finished human presence, the spectacle of a person who cannot be imagined in any other way. This concern is the substance of Emerson's first chapter, about the 1833 trip: the main purpose, he tells us, was to visit those few figures who had been so valuable in his own reading—Coleridge, Wordsworth, Landor, De Quincey, and Carlyle. Besides these names, "there was not in Britain the man living whom I cared to behold, unless it were the Duke of Wellington." Given Emerson's usual concerns, his desire to see Wellington is notable—the ripe man of action who brought down the representative man Napoleon. The thought of Wellington precedes a sad reflection, looking forward to the visits about to be described, that the life of letters can hamper personality: "The conditions of literary success are almost destructive of the best social power, as they do not leave that frolic liberty which only can encounter a companion on the best terms." He recovers hope, however, by clinging "to my first belief that a strong head will dispose fast enough of these impediments and give one the satisfaction of reality, the sense of having been met, and a larger horizon."

That Emerson is vaguely troubled by the possible
effect of his own enterprise is made all the more intriguing by the strength of character he encounters all
about him in England, both in and out of the literary
life. He seems in this comment to equate social freedom with a spontaneity unmarred by professionalism
in intellectual affairs, but the Iron Duke is far from an
example of that "frolic liberty" which encourages companionship in those not smelling of the lamp. Emerson
seems to be generalizing a personal discomfort, the
concern he expressed in a letter home on his second
trip, that he had been getting on well in English society
because he had not yet been discovered to be the bore
he really was.

Emerson's sketches of these literary visits are
amusing, for he has a Charles Lamb-like appreciation
of vagary and the odd. Landor, visited in Italy, is made
to represent the "love of freak which the English delight to indulge." Coleridge, "old and preoccupied," is
a nonstop monologuist who puts forth strong views on
diverse matters. Less comedy is made with Carlyle, for
this is at once a serious relationship. Wordsworth im-
presses for his "great simplicity," but is "of a narrow
and very English mind; of one who paid for his rare
elevation by general tameness and conformity." Towards the end of *English Traits*[3] Emerson, on his second trip to England, visits Wordsworth again and continues to find him both conventional and eccentric:
the poet complains that " 'No Scotchman can write
English. . . . Incidentally,' he added, 'Gibbon cannot
write English.' " But Emerson gives him his due: " . . .
let us say of him that, alone in his time, he treated the
human mind well, and with an absolute trust . . . The
Ode on Immortality is the high-water-mark which the
intellect has reached in this age." In light of some of
Emerson's concerns about his own country, it is interesting that he records on his first visit that Wordsworth "has even said, what seemed a paradox, that

they needed a civil war in America, to teach the necessity of knitting the social ties stronger." Wordsworth
doubtless had a bitter lesson in mind, and the remark
was not the paradox it appeared.

Emerson's great tribute is to say that "the right
measures of England are the men it bred: that it has
yielded more able men in five hundred years than any
other nation."[4] The country's strength is that "the
power of performance has not been exceeded—the creation of value. The English have given importance to
individuals, a principal end and fruit of every society."
Emerson finds much to admire and to condemn, as he
does in any actual presence in the world, but it is not
for nothing that at the beginning of chapter 18 he calls
England "the best of actual nations." He was drawn to
it because in certain directions it had to his taste produced the largest gallery of defined and interesting
temperaments. That England had in his view developed as far as it would go did not lead him to underes-
timate its achievement, nor did his view that America
was the country of the future move him to unqualified
approval of his own land.

If England is the country of the achieved past, the
fact that America is the child of time is both its promise and its problem. America's advantage is that it can
presumably move on to a higher stage of human awareness and of development in social and political forms,
but the difficulty is that one does not know what these
are going to be. Along with the buoyancy of the view
that the future is open to American energies, there is
the necessary uncertainty in thinking about possibilities rather than about fact—it is imaginable that things
will go wrong as well as right, however bravely one
fronts the world. "Alas for America as I must so often
say," he notes in the journal. "America is formless . . .
Genius always anthropomorphist."[5]

Though Emerson does not write much directly
about American character in *English Traits*, his journal

and letters indicate that the matter was on his mind
when he was in England on the second visit, and in the
years leading up to the publication of the work. "The
facile American," he writes in one journal entry, "sheds
his Puritanism when he leaves Cape Cod, runs into all
English & French vices with great zest & is neither Unitarian, nor Calvinist, nor Catholic nor stands for any
known thought or thing; which is very distasteful to
English honour. It is a bad sign that I have met with
many Americans who flattered themselves that they
pass for English."[6] This is an observation about the ordinary run of Americans abroad, but this is just the point:
Emerson is stressing the uncertainty of personality and
commitment on the part of many countrymen. Unsure
of their own definition, they imitate another style, and
do not bring it off. Two years later, in notes on a conversation about America with Thoreau, he remarks that
"My own quarrel with America, of course, was, that the
geography is sublime, but the men are not; that the
inventions are excellent, but the inventors, one is
ashamed of."[7] Three years earlier he had written to Margaret Fuller, who was in Europe, that "The famine in
Europe only affects potatoes, the sterility in America
continues in the men . . . We cannot see where we are
going, preternaturally sharp as our eyes are at short distances, nor can we discern a single plant, animal, man,
house, temple, or god, and say confidently, It is this or
that; Here is a native reality.—Strange malady, is it
not?"[8] Reflections of this sort are a partial explanation
of why Emerson exults in firm identities, people whose
culture helps to let them know who they are.

   "England has produced more great men than any
other actual nation," he says in various ways in *English
Traits,* and while he periodically rises to declare America the land of the future, he does not do so without a
sense of what this old, hierarchical, and only partially
democratic society has produced: "though we must not

play Providence and balance the chances of producing ten great men against the comfort of ten thousand mean men, yet retrospectively, we may strike the balance and prefer one Alfred, one Shakspeare, one Milton, one Sidney, one Raleigh, one Wellington, to a million foolish democrats. [¶] The American system is more democratic, more humane; yet the American people do not yield better or more able men, or more inventions or books or benefits than the English. Congress is not wiser or better than Parliament."[9]

As the second voyage begins in chapter 2, Emerson uses the ocean crossing itself as a means of contrast between American potentiality and English achievement, though he is here dealing not with human character, but with the world's primal energies. The last physical sign of the North American continent is a "floating drift of boards, logs, and chips, which the rivers of Maine and New Brunswick pour into the sea after a freshet." These are the raw stuffs and by-products of people who are still dealing with basic forces directly, turning the forests into materials by which human forms are imposed, if only here and there, upon the energies which seem often enough to threaten human existence as well as to give it birth.

The natural threat is made vivid by the account of the voyage; Emerson evokes the ocean's danger as he gives account of the *Washington Irving* under tightly stretched sail—an American ship leaving America behind, and sailing into a nature which can never be tamed. "Watchfulness is the law of the ship,—watch on watch, for advantage and for life. Since the ship was built, it seems, the master never slept but in his day-clothes whilst on board." One becomes accustomed to the inconveniences of a pitching ship, "but the dread of the sea remains longer. The sea is masculine, the type of active strength. Look, what egg-shells are drifting all over it, each one, like ours, filled with men in ecstasies of terror, alternating with cockney conceit, as the sea is rough or smooth. Is this sad-colored circle an eternal cemetery?"

This oceanic violence, potential and actual, is the analogue of the forces which shape the American land as well; Emerson moves from the vast continent to the still-more-threatening sea, and in neither place is man really in charge. One can and must cooperate with these energies to create comprehensible, proximate order, but it would be a foolish and short-lived man who fancied himself master for very long. American nature, like the ocean, is seen as beyond our means of control; we interact with it not as equals, but as mere apprentices to the powers that be, and the long task implied in *English Traits* is the creation of a coherent relationship between the large natural energies found on the new continent, on the one hand, and the need for forms on the other. The ship *Washington Irving* was appropriately named for the transition from American to England: the first American author of fiction to write with the ease and sophistication of the English, the American who had put himself to school with English masters, to learn his craft.

Even as the ship skirts the land, England is presented as a triumph of realized order—there is fully achieved interaction between the human and the non-human. There is no raw nature to be found; everything speaks of the harmony achieved between the men who live there and the forces which lend themselves to man's purposes. As he arrives, "England is a garden. Under an ash-colored sky, the fields have been combed and rolled till they appear to have been finished with a pencil instead of a plough. The solidity of the structures that compose the towns speaks the industry of ages. Nothing is left as it was made. Rivers, hills, valleys, the sea itself, feel the hand of a master. The long habitation of a powerful and ingenious race has turned every rood of land to its best use."[10]

As he lands, he poses the curious traveler's question of why England is England. Near the end of the book, on the other hand, when his companions at Bishops Waltham ask him about his own country, the query is framed as to "whether there were any Americans?" It is not a country which one can take for granted; Englishmen ask the question, to be sure, but Emerson, in answer, speaks of ideas which no one actual creature fully embodies—not even the unnamed Thoreau, whose ideas he puts forward. He is talking about the country of his dreams, so to say, and the ironic horseplay before dinner about who is "most evil" points to common awareness of the fact.

At this point in chapter 16 Carlyle has for several days been Emerson's companion; this attractive if not unvexed friendship has often been noted. Unlike Coleridge or Wordsworth, Carlyle had been sympathetic to Emerson's early sense of his own mission; Emerson was much impressed at their first encounter, in 1833, and we know that the Carlyles were too. The amused tone with which Emerson describes the other lions is much softened in this other account; from the start Emerson deals with an equal rather than pays honor to a sage. In *English Traits* Carlyle provides companionship and occasional comments and questions, though Emerson does not let him or anyone speak for long in his own voice.

Carlyle looms large in the journal, however, from the time Emerson first read him, and during the second visit and the years just after it, Emerson is almost obsessively interested in the man's personal strength. In entry after entry he comes back to Carlyle's powerful presence—so formidable as to dismay many of those who come to meet the man who has meant so much to them. "It takes more than interest and reading German to talk with this man." Even when Emerson thinks Carlyle wrong, as he increasingly does, he respects the sheer force and consistency of temperament. Carlyle, that is, becomes for a time Emerson's example of developed character: a strong identity, no rounded edges, often enough no social geniality—just a hard, driving man who is unyielding and sometimes cantankerous. During the early 1850s the correlate in the journal to this view of Carlyle is Emerson's bitter disappointment in an American, Daniel Webster, who of course supported the Fugitive Slave Law. Before that action, going back many years, Emerson had written in the journal passages of high praise for Webster's rare combination of strengths—intellectual, personal, and even physical: he quite looked the part of the splendid public man. In 1844 Webster spoke at the Bunker Hill celebration, and in Emerson's account of it he generalized Webster's virtues into national traits: "Webster is very good America himself."[11] All this matters the more when for Emerson he shirks his moral duty, and it accounts for the betrayal expressed in the later entries. "The word *liberty* in the mouth of Mr. Webster sounds like the word *love* in the mouth of a courtezan."[12] And again, "Webster truly represents the American people just as they are, with their vast material interests, materialized intellect, & low morals . . . Webster's absence of moral faculty is degrading to the country."[13]

If Emerson sometimes views American character as morally inconsistent, he more often judges it, as one would expect, to be insufficiently interested in things of the spirit. In an 1853 letter to Carlyle, he writes of a lecture trip to Saint Louis, and describes the development of his western countrymen as arrested in material things:

The powers of the river, the insatiate craving for nations of men to reap & cure its harvests, the conditions it imposes, for it yields to no engineering,—are interesting enough. The Prairie exists to yield the greatest possible quantity of adipocere. For corn makes pig, pig is the export of all the land, & you shall see the distant dependence of aristocracy & civility on the fat fourlegs. Workingmen, ability to do the work of the River, abounded, nothing higher was to be thought of. America is incomplete. Room for us all, since it has not ended, nor given sign of ending, in bard or hero. Tis a wild democracy, the riot of mediocrities, & none of your selfish Italies and Englands, where an age sublimates into a genius, and the whole population is made into paddies to feed his porcelain veins, by transfusion from their brick arteries. Our few fine persons are apt to die.[14]

One has here both a physical nature so vast as to be resistant to human will, and a human nature not yet risen out of physical concerns. These attitudes bear on *English Traits*, which appeared only a few years later. Individual development and personal force were matters he had been thinking much about, and the results of English culture provided him with sharply defined examples of people who had made nature into a comfortable home, and who seemed not to wonder about their own identities.

But England is not given all the advantages. For all that Emerson praises the products of tradition, the primary fact for him about modern England is the industrialization which had already largely transformed the economy. In a letter to Lidian of 1 December 1847 he registers shock at the level of urban poverty: "you should see the tragic spectacles which these streets show, these Manchester & those Liverpool streets, by day & by night to know how much of happiest circumstance how much of safety of dignity & of opportunity belongs to us so easily that is ravished from this population. Woman is cheap & vile in England—it is tragical to see—Childhood, too, I see oftenest in the state of absolute beggary."[15]

He makes a comparison favorable to America here, though the difference is in part because the English industrial and urbanizing process is farther along than the American. It is interesting that this measure of surprise does not carry over into *English Traits;* there are several reasons for this. First, English conditions had significantly improved by the early 1850s when Emerson was seriously preparing the book. Further, since he wished in the work to generalize about the country's character, he seldom makes reference to particular and temporary conditions as he does at the very end of the last chapter. Too, he never looked on social disorder in England as a problem which the people could not work out in a peaceful way. Perhaps the best evidence in the book for Emerson's faith in England's capacity for peaceful change is what he does in chapter 14 with the famous description of England as made up of "two nations"; he says that the two nations are not the rich and the poor, but the small yet influential band of concerned intellectuals on the one hand, forming the mind and conscience of the country, and the great mass of practical materialists on the other, genius and animal force. This play of wit could not have been made by someone who feared for the life of the nation.

He gives frequent attention, however, to the social effects of industrialization. Emerson's openness to historical process made him more accurate than some of his English friends about what was under way in English society, at least about the possibility of major violence. On his second trip, Emerson arrived late in the "hungry forties," and he attended a Chartist meeting in London not long before the "great march" of 10 April 1848. Despite the agitation, he thought that in the long run accommodations would be made by those who had the wealth and power, to those who wished not to overturn the establishment but only to share its benefits. He was, of course, correct. "People here expect a revolution. There will be no revolution, none that deserves to be called so. There may be a scramble for money. But as all the people we see want the things we now have, & not better things, it is very certain that they will, under whatever change of forms, keep the old system."[16]

Emerson came to this view from two assumptions. First, coming from a more radically democratic country then England, he had less fear of an extended franchise than did inflexible defenders of the old order. While Carlyle was certainly not that, and had in 1840 in *Chartism* made a fine indictment of social irresponsibility and "self-interest" economics, as time went on his proposed remedies for social problems became less useful than his analysis of them. While Carlyle was certainly critical of the traditional sources of power in England, his view of human nature led him to want reformed leadership rather than a diffusion of authority among even greater numbers of fallible men. Emerson was clear-eyed about the mixed qualities of his friend; in an 1848 journal entry, he noted of Carlyle that "He draws his weapons from the skies, to fight for some wretched English property, or monopoly, or prejudice."[17]

Second, as Emerson argues in chapter 11 of *English Traits*, he felt that the relationship of the aristocracy to the land had long trained those in power to melioration in the face of injustice rather than to absentee indifference, and he thought this would prove true for the new industrial and commercial powers as well. Because industrial development has a leveling effect in a democratic culture, Emerson is sure that, as a result of industrial change, England, given time, will move in the direction of America. It is this certainty which gives the summational tone to the work; he describes a country which will not be the same much longer. All about him he sees irresistible pressures towards a diminished social hierarchy, an increasingly democratic political system, and a more equitable distribution of wealth. "The English dislike the American style of civilization," he notes in the journal, "yet are doing all they can to bring it in."[18]

Near the end of *English Traits*, Emerson and Carlyle visit Stonehenge, which even Carlyle had not seen before. On the second visit they make to the monument, they have a knowledgeable guide who explains aspects of the design, but the mystery of the place remains. Heretofore in England, all seemed yielding to analysis as bearing the mark of an identifiable hand, but, coming out of an ancient time, Stonehenge defies explanation. To Emerson, the visit "seemed a bringing together of extreme points, to visit the oldest religious monument in Britain in company with her latest thinker, and one whose influence may be traced in every contemporary book." An extreme point not mentioned is of course Emerson himself—the most visible American thinker of his moment and the prophet of a new ordinance of worship.

Emerson ruminates about America during this visit, and remarks to Carlyle that when he returns to his country, "I shall lapse at once into the feeling, which the geography of America inevitably inspires, that we play the game with immense advantage; that there and not here is the seat and centre of the British race; . . . and that England, an old and exhausted island, must one day be contented, like other parents, to be strong only in her children."

Because of its simplicity and good preservation, Stonehenge "is as if new and recent," and in thinking about the methods of construction, Emerson recalls that he "chanced to see, a year ago, men at work on the substructure of a house in Bowdoin Square, in Boston, swinging a block of granite of the size of the largest of the Stonehenge columns, with an ordinary derrick."

The "newness" of the stones and the varied theories of origin and meaning are the corollary in the past of the speculations about America which occur three paragraphs after their departure from this monument of an ancient religion. Just as there was heroic endeavor in the long-forgotten past, here associated with a primeval temple which seems timeless and fresh, so there are thoughts of great enterprise on the newly settled continent across the sea. Immediately on leaving Stonehenge, the two men reenter history—that which is past—returning to the England of forms both aristocratic and religious, at Wilton and at Salisbury.

Wilton Hall, the venerable seat of the earls of Pembroke, evokes a world of secular authority and beauty. For Emerson, it is a palace of art, "a house known to Shakspeare and Massinger, the frequent home of Sir Philip Sidney" and Fulke Greville. Carlyle lingers among the statuary and paintings, and in the grounds they cross a bridge designed by Inigo Jones; Emerson wonders if they are not indeed at Coleridge's pleasuredome. From Wilton, they go to Salisbury Cathedral, the triumph of English Gothic, with the highest spire in the country. The elaborate formality of this architecture, like that of Winchester Cathedral two pages later, is a strong contrast with the open suggestiveness of Stonehenge. Wilton and the churches are the loveliest expression of a culture which has taken on developed form; surrounded by the elegant shapes of a religion which is now for him a stage of history only, Emerson expresses his admiration in purely aesthetic terms.

Leaving Salisbury, they go to the home of "Mr. H" (Arthur Help) at Bishops Waltham, and the openness of Stonehenge has its parallel in the question asked by Emerson's companions about America: "whether there were any Americans?—any with an American idea,—any theory of the right future of that country?" Asked about a true "American" in this sense, Emerson thinks not of our public figures but "only of the simplest and purest minds," and having said that, he mentions particular people not at all, but speaks of "no-government and non-resistance," not even mentioning Thoreau's name in the process. "I said, it is true that I have never seen in any country a man of sufficient valor to stand for this truth, and yet it is plain to me that no less valor than this can command my respect." Emerson anticipates and partially records the fun his listeners make of this, but he is serious nonetheless. It is characteristic that he moves swiftly from an unnamed but real man to an ideal beyond possibility; the extremity of his expectations has not left him when he thinks of the future of his own country, no matter what detailed observations he has been making abroad.

The following day his friends question him not about American men, but about American conditions—"landscapes, forests, houses,—my house, for example." Emerson does not feel up to answering these questions because he thinks, in a remarkable passage, of American nature:

There, I thought, in America, lies nature sleeping, overgrowing, almost conscious, too much by half for man in the picture, and so giving a certain *tristesse*, like the rank vegetation of swamps and forests seen at night, steeped in dews and rains, which it loves; and on it man seems not able to make much impression. There, in that great sloven continent, in high Alleghany pastures, in the sea-wide sky-skirted prairie, still sleeps and murmurs and hides the great mother, long since driven away from the trim hedge-rows and over-cultivated garden of England. And, in England, I am quite too sensible of this. Every one is on his good behavior and must be dressed for dinner at six. So I put off my friends with very inadequate details, as best I could.

The passage on the one hand evokes a nature which is overwhelming in its force, and on the other describes an "untranscendental" discomfort born of man's contemplation of this power. The nature commonly conceived by Emerson and Thoreau, despite their differences, is one in which the energies of nature and the consciousness of man interact harmoniously when the imagination is poised to its proper tasks. The conception in this passage from *English Traits*, however, reminds one of those few moments in Thoreau when nature is suddenly seen as either alien or characterized by powerful sexuality: the Mount Katahdin episode or the skinning of the moose in *The Maine Woods*, and the sense of oceanic force in *Cape Cod*.

The center of emotion here is *tristesse,* born of the realization that nature is "too much by half for man in the picture." The sadness points to the incommensurability between man and nature in the American landscape, a new world where the ancient and primal energy, the wild, lives in ways irrelevant to man's need for order—in "rank vegetation of swamps and forests seen at night, steeped in dews and rain, which it loves." This swamp is the same one where Frost's protagonist in "The Wood-Pile" finds himself "far from home," and which Nick Adams in "The Big Two-Hearted River" does not want to enter because the fishing would be "tragic." In *English Traits,* man is sad in the face of this nature because "on it men seem not able to make much impression," and there is sexual anxiety in the proximity of disorderly generative force and appetite—the "great mother" still "sleeps and murmurs and hides" in the "great sloven continent."

This force (*the* force) has been driven away from the "trim hedge-rows and over-cultivated garden of England," but despite the negative ring of this comment, it would be a mistake to think that Emerson's approval is all for American circumstance. As is usual in Emerson, there is a polarity of interests, but here without the possibility of practical resolution. In England, man's dominion has become so strong that he is too far from the original energies of life; in America, the forces inhabit the landscape so strongly that man's need for order, for form, can lie only in high hopes for the future. If English civilization is characterized by undue deliberation and constraint, America has a long road to travel before fulfilling its promise, and while Emerson's usual tone makes a virtue of our possibilities, the occasional accompaniment of hope is an awareness that we are not yet as we should be.

When the book ends with the close of his "Speech at Manchester," Emerson comes back to an image he used in this paragraph from "Stonehenge": should England lose its courage in the current commercial crisis, Emerson will "go back to the capes of Massachusetts and my own Indian stream," and report to his countrymen that "the elasticity and hope of mankind must henceforth remain on the Alleghany ranges, or nowhere." In "Stonehenge," it is in the "high Alleghany pastures" that the "great mother" lives, and while one is optimistic when one hopes, there is the knowledge that expectation is not fulfillment.

That Emerson ended his speech by saying that the future lies in "Alleghany ranges, or nowhere" should not easily be taken to mean his automatic assurance that his hopes for America will come true; "nowhere" is also a possibility. I of course do not mean to question Emerson's affirmative stance about American prospects—only to point out that his optimism about the country's prospects is informed by his awareness of the distance between what is and what ought to be. He had not been a minister for nothing, and even after his celebrated 1832 resignation from the pulpit he continued the minister's task of awakening people to their potentialities not only by pointing to what they could become, but by making them aware that they had not gotten there as yet.

English Traits is not only a book about a foreign country; it is also admonitory about American characteristics. Emerson was not simple-minded about either nation; the work is not an unqualified celebration of English genius, but neither is it a work which exults America by putting England down. Emerson is much drawn to the English people because he admires, even when amused by, the assured identities which he so often encountered there. Emerson does not of course confuse his attractive English men and women with his truly ideal figure, with what he might have called "The English Scholar" (who would in any case be the same as "The American Scholar"), but he is attracted to what he sees around him as the self-assurance, sense of place, and personal strength in cultivated English society. This is for him a contrast with the encouragingly open but unfinished American character, a judgment which exists largely by implication in *English Traits*. The very steadiness of his concentration on the wonder of developed English forms and figures is a commentary *in absentia* on the promise of America, a promise in many ways still unfulfilled.

Emerson's reservations are of course more frequent in the journals and letters than in the public works; the very ideality of his public tone created a more private discordance with fact. If it is true that there are no meaningful standards except in relation to the highest ones, then Emerson's flag is surely at the top of the pole; for all his assurances about our ideal prospects, he is in actual judgments critical enough. One thinks of how he closes the essays in *Representative Men* by pointing to the shortcomings of Shakespeare and company, and one does not read far in "The American Scholar" before realizing that no human being can become what he has in mind. And when Emerson, like Thoreau, writes about the essence of friendship, relationships between those actually alive tend to rarify and disappear.

The corollary of these high standards is that no personal development is ever complete—not only because life is a process, but because no one can be all things. This is the underside of Emerson's buoyant hopes; the two views are reverse images of one another. It can be a great encouragement to argue that man is ideally without limit, and disheartening to see that he is bounded in fact. Much of *English Traits* is born of complex admiration for the roots of Emerson's America, and a not-untroubled view of the distance to go before America can come into its own country, let alone into the mountains of the mind.

5. Emerson, Poe, and the Ruins of Convention

STEPHEN DONADIO

> It is not every man who can build a house who can
> execute a ruin.
>
> William Gilpin

My purpose in these pages is to suggest how the dreamy contemplation of ruins frequently associated with the gothic sensibility may provide a means of grasping an aesthetic principle central to the development of modernist form in literature and the visual arts. More specifically, I mean to indicate how the veiled assault on literary convention which characterizes the commanding works of Emerson reflects an idea of organization which persists in dominating American imaginative expression well into the twentieth century. In order to evoke the range of concerns involved in this inquiry, I shall begin by focusing on certain formal ambitions which Emerson appears to share with another of our most audacious nineteenth-century writers—one with whom he is not commonly linked: Edgar Allan Poe.

For all their visionary power, in our everyday understanding, and in the organization of literary anthologies which reveal and reinforce that understanding, Poe and Emerson tend to be categorized rather narrowly, in ways that fail to take account of the impact of their imaginations beyond the limited range of

nineteenth-century American culture. And yet, beginning long before the turn of the century, the recognition by advanced European authors of the prophetic
force of these Americans appears to take the form of an
encounter with a second deeper and more innovative
self. "The first time I opened one of his books," Baudelaire observed of Poe, "I saw, to my amazement and
delight, not simply certain subjects that I had dreamed
about, but SENTENCES that I had thought of and that
he had written down twenty years before." Similarly,
Nietzsche, regarded by many as the most extreme and
daring thinker of his age, identified Emerson as "the
author who has been richest in ideas in this century so
far"; and so intense was his feeling of kinship with the
errant American divine that he asserted: "Never have I
felt so much at home, as—I may not praise it, it is too
close to me."[1]

More often than not, though, these Americans remain juxtaposed in our thinking in ways that suggest a
cartoon-like contrast between the canny, upright, vigor-
ous New England Mind (with its exacting but surprisingly versatile Puritan inheritance) on the one hand, and
the more defensive, languorous, and self-consuming
Mind of the South on the other. While Emerson's intentions seem to declare themselves in the bright glare of
moral assurance which pervades his public utterances,
those of Poe are often lost in a shadier, more dubious
element; his apparent lack of recognizable moral purpose, combined with a degree of cultivated eccentricity
and flamboyance—indeed, at times a downright junki-
ness and unreliability—finally led Henry James to remark that taking Poe too seriously signified a want of
seriousness in oneself, and that "an enthusiasm" for
that author was "the mark of a decidedly primitive
stage of reflection."[2] To James's estimate of Poe we
shall presently return; but at this point in our inquiry
let me make it plain that by arguing that these writers,
so different in their social and intellectual origins, liter-

ary character, and moral appearance, often shared a common aesthetic intention, I mean to be suggesting how far-reaching and radical the formal consequences wrought by romantic consciousness were in nineteenth-century America, and how, long before the development of cubism and surrealism, the possibility of abstract composition which incorporated familiar elements in unexpected settings—thus unsettling our perspective on the commonplace—began to emerge. As we shall see, it is as a consequence of the willful (although at first almost surreptitious) destruction of conventional forms and generic boundaries that such possibilities came about.

For the moment, let me suggest that one compelling characteristic that Emerson shares with Poe is a kind of studied tastelessness—tastelessness sometimes carried to the point of preciosity. In one way or another, this element has always figured in our evaluations of Poe (as it has in our estimates of writers like Melville and Stephen Crane, whose works reveal a similar disruptiveness, and a similarly refined scorn for conventional expectations). But Emerson's mild, remote, clerical demeanor has served to distract us from his evident rhetorical incoherence, as it served to distract many of his auditors. Yet in Emerson's own time, it was still possible to be upset by the unsettling shifts of level in the prose, as the Harvard Unitarian Francis Bowen made plain in his antagonistic assessment of *Nature*. Addressing the issue of "taste in composition" in Emerson's first book, Bowen noted that "some defects proceed from over anxiety to avoid common errors." Detecting in Emerson's prose a fastidiousness disguised as a frank insistence on simplicity and directness, he was moved to conclude that Emerson "is in love with the Old Saxon idiom, yet there is a spice of affectation in his mode of using it. He is sometimes coarse and blunt, that he may avoid the imputation of sickly refinement, and writes bathos with malice prepense, because he abhors forced dignity and unnatural elevation."[3]

In the works of Emerson as well as Poe, moreover, what may be judged deficient taste is often associated with an appearance of incoherence. Indeed, Bowen's account of the experience of *Nature* could serve as a perfectly plausible recapitulation of the effect of one of Poe's more ambitious fictions. "The reader feels as in a disturbed dream," Bowen observes, "in which shows of surpassing beauty are around him, and he is conversant with disembodied spirits, yet all the time he is harassed by an uneasy sort of consciousness, that the whole combination of phenomena is fantastic and unreal."[4] To a considerable degree, the sense of disorientation and pervasive disorder produced by such writings is related to their failure to distinguish conclusively among alternative modes of discourse. More precisely, there is a refusal in these works to separate the popular from the serious, the commonplace from the exalted, the ordinary from the improbable. In the end, this refusal signifies an underlying assault on institutional authority and its literary embodiment: an accepted hierarchical arrangement of discrete genres, forms, and modes of discourse. What remains striking about these writings of Poe and Emerson is the way in which they regularly represent themselves as conforming to established and familiar models which they proceed systematically to reduce to ruins; and what are ruins, finally, but structures rendered useless in their original function by the effects of time or damaging circumstances?

Necessarily, then, the focus of our inquiry is the experience of ruins, of fragmentary structures which have paradoxically come to be apprehended as aesthetic wholes. At the outset, let me state that for our purposes at present a ruin may be defined as a structure substantial parts of which are missing—which means that under certain circumstances it may be indistinguishable from a structure left uncompleted, abandoned before all the relationships among its formal elements have been fully articulated and developed. On the whole, however, the kind of experience we are concerned with here is less likely to be produced by the view of a building under construction than by the prospect of a building in the process of decomposition or demolition, since the process of disintegration, whether attributable to natural causes or accelerated by the wrecker's ball, usually appears more arbitrary and random, and as a consequence tends to produce more unpredictable effects, more dramatic and arresting juxtapositions. The important point is that whether we find ourselves wondering what the building actually looked like when it was intact, or how it would appear in its completed form, we are confronting essentially the same challenge to our powers of vision: that of a structure which is incomplete in the present and which can only be completed in imagination, a structure which is inconclusive in itself but which evokes a shifting range of possible aesthetic implications. In order for the aesthetic experience of such a structure to be rendered whole, the perceiver is required to contemplate the presence in the structure of elements which are evoked but absent.

"We ought to look into old established ruins for ourselves," one recent writer on the subject has advised, "and we ought to hang around buildings that are being torn down to catch what might be a splendid aesthetic experience coming out of some shabby elements."[5] One could hardly wish for a more appropriate introduction to the works of Poe—especially works like "The Fall of the House of Usher" (in which that provoking author brings the literal and symbolic house down) or the rather more perplexing *Narrative of Arthur Gordon Pym*. It is this latter work, Poe's longest and most ambitious prose fiction, that concerns us most in the present context, for I wish to argue that, despite its disorderly appearance, that work exemplifies the formal consequences of a precise aesthetic intention. *Pym* has of course generally been regarded by all but a few critics (some of whom, in recent decades, have seized on its bizarre black/white contrasts in order to address certain extraliterary issues) as one of Poe's most egregious and definitive failures. And indeed, it is extremely difficult to talk about the work in a way that does not seem to be merely an ingenious apology for shoddy workmanship and haphazard construction, an elaborate theoretical excuse for the work's evident defects. For what demanding reader could fail to be persuaded by Henry James's case against Poe? Reflecting on the breathtaking conclusion of the *Narrative* proper, the nation's preeminent expositor of the art of fiction observes that in this "would-be portentous climax . . . the indispensable history is absent . . . the phenomena evoked . . . are immediate and flat, and the attempt is all at the horrific in itself." "The result," James asserts, "is that, to my sense, the climax fails—fails because it stops short, and stops short for want of connexions. There *are* no connexions; not only, I mean, in the sense of further statement, but of our own further relation to the elements, which hang in the void." As a consequence, the novelist concludes, "we see the effect lost, the imaginative effect wasted."[6]

And yet in order to understand this judgment in perspective, it is important to remember that when, in an earlier essay, James compared Baudelaire and Poe, he noted that although "Poe was much the greater charlatan of the two," he was also "the greater genius." The power of that genius is attested to by the fact that despite his critical lament for the unachieved aspect of *Pym,* the extraordinary ending of the narrative clearly lingered in James's mind; his persistent admiration for it is reflected in that famous passage in the opening chapter of *The Golden Bowl* in which Prince Amerigo recalls having "read as a boy a wonderful tale by Allan

Poe . . . which was a thing to show, by the way, what imagination Americans *could* have; the story of the shipwrecked Gordon Pym, who, drifting in a small boat . . . found at a given moment before him a thickness of white air that was like a dazzling curtain of light, concealing as darkness conceals, yet the colour of milk or of snow."

James is referring here, of course, to the closing pages of Poe's work, and a few brief passages may help us to call to mind that ultimate phase of the adventure:

March 1. Many unusual phenomena now indicated that we were entering upon a region of novelty and wonder. A high range of light gray vapor appeared constantly in the southern horizon, flaring up occasionally in lofty streaks, now darting from east to west, and again presenting a level and uniform summit—in short, having all the wild variations of the Aurora Borealis. . . . The temperature of the sea seemed to be increasing momentarily, and there was a very perceptible alteration in its color.

. . . *March 3.* The heat of the water was now truly remarkable, and its color was undergoing a rapid change, being no longer transparent, but of a milky consistency and hue. . . . we were frequently surprised at perceiving, to our right and left, at different distances, sudden and extensive agitations of the surface—these, we at length noticed, were always preceded by wild flickerings in the region of vapor to the southward. . . .

March 5. The wind had entirely ceased, but it was evident that we were still hurrying on to the southward, under the influence of a powerful current. And now, indeed, it would seem reasonable that we should experience some alarm at the turn events were taking—but we felt none. . . .

March 6. The gray vapor had now arisen many more degrees above the horizon, and was gradually losing its grayness of tint. The heat of the water was extreme, even unpleasant to the touch. . . . A fine white powder, resembling ashes—but certainly not such—fell over the canoe and over a large surface of the water. . . .

March 9. The whole ashy material fell now continually around us, and in vast quantities. The range of vapor to the southward had risen prodigiously in the horizon, and began to assume more directness of form. I can liken it to nothing but a limitless cataract, rolling silently into the sea from some immense and far-distant rampart in the heaven. The gigantic curtain ranged along the whole extent of the southern horizon. It emitted no sound.

March 21. A sullen darkness now hovered above us but from out the milky depths of the ocean a luminous glare arose, and stole up along the bulwarks of the boat. We were nearly overwhelmed by the white ashy shower which settled upon us and upon the canoe, but melted into the water as it fell. The summit of the cataract was utterly lost in the dimness and the distance. Yet we were evidently approaching it with a hideous velocity. At intervals there were visible in it wide, yawning, but momentary rents, and from out these rents, within which was a chaos of flitting and indistinct images, there came rushing and mighty, but soundless winds, tearing up the enkindled ocean in their course.

March 22. The darkness had materially increased, relieved only by the glare of the water thrown back from the white curtain before us. Many gigantic and pallidly white birds flew continuously now from beyond the veil. . . . And now we rushed into the embraces of the cataract, where a chasm threw itself open to receive us. But there arose in our pathway a shrouded human figure, very far larger in its proportions than any dweller among men. And the hue of the skin of the figure was of the perfect whiteness of the snow.

James's refusal to accept this last movement of *Pym* as an artistic achievement (even though he apparently persisted in regarding it as a triumph of vision) derives in general from his characteristic and profound concern with fully realized literary forms, and in particular from his insistence on literary closure. In his view, the effect of the conclusion of *Pym*, no matter how impressive, was wasted because the narrative itself was not the vehicle which that momentous culmination implied; accordingly, it had to be judged as an effect which exceeded the form in which it figured, and for James such a disjunction invariably indicated the failure of the artist to construct a form adequate to his intentions. Indeed, in the preface to "The Altar of the Dead" in which his impatient judgment of *Pym* is presented, James makes his critical assumptions plain by emphasizing "the preference I have noted for the 'neat' evocation—the image, of any sort, with fewest attendant vaguenesses and cheapnesses, fewest loose ends dangling and fewest features missing."[7] Such a declaration makes it evident that James's aesthetic predilections (which are essentially—though hardly simply—those of literary realism) are in most important respects antithetical to those of the author of the shifty, inconsistent *Narrative*.

Still, some clue to Poe's suggestive intention in that work is provided by an early episode in which the main character, entombed in the lightless, suffocating hold of a ship, endeavors to read a message, previously torn into shreds, conveyed to him by his friend Augustus; after several unsuccessful attempts, Pym is at last able to see, in a momentary glimmer of phosphorous, three sentences, though in his anxious state he manages to read only "the seven concluding words"—the most significant of which is "blood":

having rubbed in the phosphorous, a brilliancy ensued as before—but this time several lines of MS. in a large hand, and apparently in red ink, became distinctly visible. The glimmer, although sufficiently bright, was but momentary. Still, had I not been too greatly excited, there would have been ample time enough for me to peruse the whole three sentences before me. . . . In my anxiety, however, to read all at once, I succeeded only in reading the seven concluding words, which thus appeared—"*blood—your life depends upon lying close.*"

Had I been able to ascertain the entire contents of the note—the full meaning of which my friend had thus attempted to convey, that admonition, even although it should have revealed a story of disaster the most unspeakable, could not, I am firmly convinced, have imbued my mind with one tithe of the harrowing and yet indefinable horror with which I was inspired by the fragmentary warning thus received. And "blood," too, that word of all words—so rife at times with mystery, and suffering, and terror—how trebly full of import did it now appear—how chillily and heavily (disjointed, as it thus was, from any foregoing words to qualify or render it distinct) did its vague syllables fall, amid the deep gloom of my prison, into the innermost recesses of my soul!

If we regard this passage as an indication of Poe's method of composition in *Pym*, it may help us to understand his use of fragments and incomplete utterances in that work as a means of evoking nameless possibilities, the precise details of which are to be supplied by the feverish imagination of the reader. It might be argued that the use of obsessive physical details in many of Poe's best-known shorter fictions serves as a similar function, compelling the reader to imagine for himself the harrowing, unspeakable implications of the detail, to complete the hallucinatory image in the dark theater of his own mind: consider, for example, the heart in "The Tell-Tale Heart," the teeth in "Berenice," the eyes in "Ligeia." In all such tales, moreover, the extraordinary vividness of the detail emerges in sharp contrast to the vagueness which surrounds it, and its evocative power is such that it almost immediately exceeds the plot which is supposed to contain it: the precise circumstances of its appearance may be easily forgotten, but the disconnected image, like that of the head of the Medusa, continues to haunt the imagination.

For James, the suggestion of an unearthly whiteness at the close of *Pym* is wasted because that suggestion is presented in a kind of narrative isolation—it "hangs in the void," in James's phrase (a phrase intended as sum-

mary judgment, but one which might impress us somewhat differently if it were applied to such characteristically indeterminate twentieth-century works as the
writings of Kafka or Duchamp's *Large Glass*). Nothing
in the earlier episodes prepares the reader for this extraordinary phenomenon, and so it can hardly be said to
unify, as conclusions commonly do, the earlier and later
portions of the work. But as the passage I have quoted
from *Pym* indicates, it was precisely this sort of mysterious disjunction that Poe found intriguing, and that he
was concerned with maintaining. Thus, when we compare the opening and closing sections of the work, what
we perceive is a radical contrast between what promises
to be a rather tedious and uninspired juvenile adventure
and an unstoppable imaginative journey leading us
quite literally out of this world. The commonplace earlier sections of the book do not prepare us for what is to
follow any more than everyday reality prepares us for
dreams. And since Poe's general concern is with rendering concrete experience as if it were dream, with showing how the elements of everyday reality (like Pym's
dog Tiger, who actually seems to become a tiger) may be
transformed without warning into the ambiguous elements of dream or the insistently menacing elements of
nightmare, the blurred discrepancy between precise
realistic notation and hallucinatory suggestion serves
his purposes very well. Although the original, mundane
outlines of the fiction remain vaguely recognizable, the
content of the work is altered radically, and at last we
become aware that the tale has been changing its aspect
before our eyes.

Accordingly, in reading *Pym* we gradually come to
discover that familiar narrative devices have been torn
free of an anticipated narrative logic—just as in our
perusal of a ruin we may unexpectedly come upon
structural elements which no longer serve a necessary
structural purpose, such as broken columns which support an absent roof, or stairways which lead us into

empty space. In other words, in this work the narrative structure as a whole has assumed an abstract rather than a mimetic function, and its elements are no longer subservient to a comprehensive architectural idea.

If the presence of certain realistic details leads us to expect a continuous realistic narrative in which events follow one another in some clearly definable sequence and abide by the laws of probability, then like James we will be displeased and frustrated by the apparent inconsistencies of *Arthur Gordon Pym;* but if, on the other hand, we consider the possibility that the inconsistencies are in some sense intentional, and that they provide the mechanism by which the reader, like Pym himself, may be reborn again and again out of realism into pure adventure and unfathomable mystery, then we may permit ourselves, as our writer on ruins suggested, "to catch what might be a splendid aesthetic experience coming out of some shabby elements." In this way, we may be delivered out of the everyday world in which a dog is a housepet and we use matches to light our cigars into a realm (like Poe's "Dreamland," "out of *Space*—out of *Time*") in which such items, isolated from the context of ordinary relations, assume a baffling and even magical aspect.

From the point of view of technique, what Poe discovered when he was writing *Pym* was that the effect of suggestiveness and awakened expectation which he wished to achieve could be prolonged and sustained at maximum intensity only if he eliminated virtually all the discursive or connective elements of plot. This procedure owes a great deal to his conviction (expressed in 1850 in the essay entitled "The Poetic Principle") that there is no such thing as a long poem, and that in all compositions which present themselves as such, "after a passage of what we feel to be true poetry". . ."there follows, inevitably, a passage of platitude which no critical pre-judgment can force us to admire." What Poe has done in *Pym* is to excise all the so-called "passage[s] of platitude"—the "prose" passages—the function of which would have been to link the moments of poetic intensity in a developmental sequence; he has simply not provided the tissue of connections which would keep the various episodes of the narrative clearly balanced and related to one another in a closed composition. (This tendency to subordinate form to effect is undoubtedly the source of the histrionic or decadent element in Poe, but merely to identify that quality as such is not to arrive at an adequate assessment of Poe's technical ambition, or of the momentous shift in artistic sensibility which that ambition reflects.)

The elimination of developmental sequence is intimately bound up with the conception of the curiously blank and undramatic central character of *Pym*. As W. H. Auden has pointed out, this hero "has no history . . . because he cannot change, he can only experience."[8] (This observation might also provide us, incidentally, with a way of understanding the curiously static, uncompleted personalities at the center of Mark Twain's *Huckleberry Finn* and Stephen Crane's *Red Badge of Courage*.) In order to keep alive the sense of unending wonder he wished to convey, Poe came to understand that he would have to create a central character whose actions had no lasting perceptible effect on the world in which he moved: the protagonist would have to exist in a state of detachment from his own experience, would have to be a powerless witness to the mysterious unfolding of his own life. Because his experience tells him nothing conclusive about who he is, he never experiences his personality as coherent. Moreover, if his adventures were related to the operation of his will, then those adventures would follow from and lead to purposeful action, would resolve themselves into a causal sequence which would ultimately be comprehended by the logic of personality, the laws of probability, and the dictates of literary realism. In sum, the adventures would cease to be entirely unpredictable and amazing. It is to this dimension of *Pym* that Auden is referring when he observes that in this story "of pure adventure the hero is as purely passive as the I in dreams." The aura of dreams is, as most of Poe's work indicates, very much to the point here. The vividly realized details of his fiction, like the details in dreams, regularly exceed the context in which they appear. It is for that very reason—because they break the frame of specific circumstances which ostensibly contains them—that those free-floating, isolated elements take on a larger evocative function.

This brings us at last to the characteristic form of Emerson's most memorable essays. For just as the individual elements in *Pym* (whether details or entire episodes) are conceived distinctly, even though the relationship among them remains inconclusive or ambiguous, so too in an Emerson essay the individual assertions appear sharply defined and intelligible in themselves, though taken together they seem to imply a larger and more comprehensive structure of relationships which remains undisclosed or absent. In sum, if Poe has created a work in which clearly articulated individual narrative elements persist but no longer serve to support a fully realized narrative structure, Emerson has employed the elements of the essay in a similar way in order to fashion an essay without a visible argument. The overall appearance and effect of argument are maintained, but the controlling logic of the sequence can no longer be specified or traced from point to point.

To put the matter somewhat differently: Emerson's most commanding work provides an intense spiritual experience which exceeds the conventional rhetorical form in which it appears. Comprehended in these terms, "The American Scholar" address of 1837, for example, may be seen as offering a prospect which dwarfs the broken facade of the traditional commencement address which is presumed to contain it. Similarly, "The Divinity School Address" of 1838 may be likened to a sermon in ruins; it presents us with an inherited form in which significant doctrinal gaps have appeared, and through these open spaces we may glimpse a widening range of spiritual possibilities. The effect of such literary performances resembles what we might experience if we were to find ourselves in a majestic, ruined cathedral and, looking up, discover that we could indeed see the celestial realm—the sky itself—where the massive vaulted ceiling used to be.

In place of concrete articulation, then, Emerson offers a distant liberating prospect: a deepening silence where we would expect the elements of a religious program. And yet the very absence of specific doctrine—even, it might be said, of definable subject—awakened in his audience the desire for ultimate, unbounded revelation. As one of his most devoted auditors, Elizabeth Peabody, once observed, "the 'golden silence' which heightened the effect of Mr. Emerson's 'silvern speech' when he preached those truths that he felt were hidden from his times by the prevalent technics of the pulpit" derived from "the unforgotten instinct of the child, who often cannot utter the name of God, precisely because he sees Him with the spiritual eye of pre-existence." According to Miss Peabody, "In Mr. Emerson, the Infinite of Being was an intuition 'beyond the reach of thought,' which is the act of the growing understanding, likened by himself to a man going out in a dark night with a farthing candle to find something":

What he discovered with his farthing candle he declared, in words that shine and words that burn, putting his readers at a stand-point open on all sides to the sky of the Universal Truth, which comprehends the seer and the seen too; and then, with the delicate reserve of a spiritual modesty which never says "I," he pauses, to let his hearer or reader supply the ellipses, not attempting to utter the unutterable, which we nevertheless know as we know the fixed stars, wondering what they are.[9]

Indeed, as Miss Peabody's language makes plain, and as their very titles ("Experience," "Circles," "Art," and so on) would indicate, it is as futile to attempt an inventory of the specific contents of an Emerson essay as it would be to catalogue the contents of a Beethoven symphony, and one can only reflect with a kind of grim amusement on those generations of unsuspecting students condemned to reduce those essays to "Harvard Outline" form—an ordeal the full hilarity of which only an Yvor Winters or an Evelyn Waugh could comprehend. The experience of such works simply does not lend itself to common-sense summary, to a rendering into what Poe would regard as "passage[s] of platitude." The unsettled language of the most compelling utterances characteristically evokes and distances itself from other, more familiar modes of expression. The resulting alternation of ordinary and extraordinary language, of expected and unexpected discourse, may mystify the reader, but it also encourages him to continue the difficult ascent to something more than everyday illumination. No matter how vague he may be about the precise nature of the process, the reader of an Emerson essay is aware that the sense of heightened possibility which he experiences at its conclusion is not simply a function of his assenting to the various propositions and injunctions of which the essay appears at first to consist. Instead, that sense of personal confidence and mysterious exhilaration which the work regularly produces would seem to be a function of its ability to detach our attention from the present moment, and from the specific context in which the words are being uttered, in order to lead us, through disconnected private reveries, toward complete deliverance from our worldly confinement, from our limited, oppressive historical condition, which our spiritual ambition demands. As Emerson observed of actual performances of Shakespeare (and his observation tells us much about the intended effect of his own performances): "The recitation begins; one golden word leaps out immortal from all this painted pedantry, and sweetness torments us with invitations to its own inaccessible homes."[10]

In his discussion of *The Poetic Principle*, Poe asserts that the true poet is not "he who shall simply sing, with however glowing enthusiasm or with however vivid a truth of description, of the sights, and sounds, and odours, and sentiments which greet *him* in common with all mankind." There is still "a something in the distance," Poe insists, that such a writer has been unable to attain, and toward which all deeply affecting poetry aspires. For beyond all power of expression, we have still "a thirst unquenchable," and that "thirst belongs to the immortality of Man. . . . Inspired by an ecstatic prescience of the glories beyond the grave, we struggle, by multiform combinations among the things and thoughts of Time, to attain a portion of that Loveliness whose very elements, perhaps, appertain to eternity alone. And thus when by Poetry—or when by Music, the most entrancing of the Poetic moods—we find ourselves melted into tears—we weep then—not . . . through excess of pleasure, but through a certain petulant, impatient sorrow at our inability to grasp *now* wholly, here on earth, at once and for ever, those divine and rapturous joys, of which *through* the poem, or *through* the music, we attain to but brief and indeterminate glimpses."

Such observations make it clear why Georges Poulet was led to conclude that Poe ultimately aspires to a condition that can only be described as "posthumous consciousness,"[11] but what is more significant about Poe's assertions in the present context is that they might serve very well as an account of the experience and pervasive intention of Emerson's most visionary writing. "I am born a poet," the Concord author confided to Lydia Jackson before they were married, "of a low class without doubt, yet a poet. That is my vocation. My singing, to be sure, is very 'husky,' and is for the most part in prose. Still I am a poet in the sense of a perceiver and dear lover of the harmonies that are in the soul and in matter, and specially of the correspondence between these and those."[12] One finds a similar emphasis on the apprehension of spiritual correspondences at the conclusion of *Eureka,* and it seems reasonably clear that what Emerson provided for his audience was an experience of discontinuous revelation analogous to that described by Poe: it is toward just such an effect that every element of his style strives. The utterance seems strangely disconnected: it brightens and darkens abruptly, and the general theme of the discourse is illuminated momentarily by flashes of intuition. Statements are not arranged in the form of an orderly progression through time, but according to some other logic only intermittently revealed, in sequences of short duration. Continuous passages are suddenly disrupted; conventional utterance suddenly gives way to breathtaking vision, and then once again the rhetorical prospect closes. The reader is consequently left with the sense of a world of meaning communicated only in fragments: he is haunted by a vision of wholeness which seems to be withdrawn almost as soon as it is offered, which seems to recede into another dimension at the very moment it appears to be within his grasp. In this way, again and again, the Emersonian audience is allowed a tantalizing glimpse of immortality—of a secure and rapturous order which exists beyond the limits of our mortal lives.

Thus, in their separate ways, the works of Emerson and Poe imply a principle of order which is always at the edge of consciousness but which can never finally be attained. All the discrete elements of the aesthetic experience may be grasped in isolation, but the whole that they appear to promise is never disclosed. Virtually all the continuities, all the logical, discursive links connecting one assertion (or incident) with another in an unbroken sequential chain have been eliminated to create the maximum poetic intensity—which for both Emerson and Poe involves the widest range of suggestiveness. And because the shape of the overall structure remains ambiguous, it becomes virtually impossible to render a comprehensive—let alone systematic—account of the experience, just as it is virtually impossible to achieve a comprehensive view of a ruin, a structure on whose general form one is allowed only discontinuous and incomplete perspectives. Moreover, just as in a ruin the perceiver may be permitted views of the inside and the outside of the structure simultaneously, so too in works of the kind we are discussing, inside and outside have become exceedingly difficult to distinguish: the structure itself has become open, fragmentary, and evocative rather than enclosed and self-contained. The detached structural elements come to serve as references to limiting modes of organization which the overall experience of the irregular configuration now exceeds. Indeed, in literary terms, it might be said that the very genre of the work, the kind of work it appears to be, has become an object of detached aesthetic contemplation, defining by implication a range of possible experiences which the author is endeavoring to transcend.

By refusing to limit the potential range of suggestiveness of a work by defining its form as the precise embodiment of a particular experience begun and brought to completion, writers like Emerson and Poe succeed in creating works which appear to remain in the process of being realized. For them, the fragmentary form of the work seems to embrace a whole range of still unrealized possibilities—possibilities which the perceiver has been freed to realize in consciousness for himself. In effect, then, the work has been left to the perceiver's imagination. It no longer presents itself to his consciousness as a completed artifact but as an occasion for an alteration in his state of mind, or in his relation to his everyday experience. (It is clear enough, I think, how this emphasis on the work of art as process or evocation might lead eventually to the devaluation of the artistic product—the material product which can be acquired and displayed—as it has in our own time in minimal, conceptual, or environmental art, for example.) In these advanced nineteenth-century writers, the unfinished, inconsistent aspect of the work suggests a range of terms in which it might potentially be unified and brought to completion; but because it never is completed in a single set of terms, the divergent possibilities are maintained through an internal tension, keeping the perceiver more or less disoriented but imaginatively engaged.

The considerations which I have been attempting to raise here may help to explain something of the aesthetic impulse connecting such apparently dissimilar literary compositions as the poems of Emily Dickinson, which almost routinely break through their own frames, and a work like Melville's "Bartleby the Scrivener," the main character of which is described at one point as resembling "the last column of some ruined temple . . . standing mute and solitary in the middle of the otherwise deserted room." It is an impulse which links the mode of composition of the early Eliot not only with that of Pound's *Cantos*—fragments of an enormous, ultimately inconceivable monument—but with that of Faulkner's *Absalom, Absalom!*, that triumph of the gothic imagination in which the reader, like the characters striving to comprehend it, must assemble the shattered history for himself. What I have been arguing, in sum, is that what finally asserts itself through the technique of Emerson and Poe is a romantic ambition which leads inevitably to that fragmentation which we have come to identify with modernism.

And I would like now to conclude my necessarily abbreviated discussion by considering one aspect of the work of the sculptor Rodin, an artist whose work vividly reflects the formal consequences of the transition from romanticism to modernism.

Rodin is especially significant for our purposes because he is the first artist to exhibit fragments (torsos, hands, feet, and so on) as completed works: the first artist to conceive deliberately of isolated elements of the human figure fully realized in their particulars but torn out of the context of relations in which they normally appear. The effect of this practice struck a number of Rodin's contemporaries as bizarre, not to say more than vaguely inhumane, but it is not to that issue that I wish to draw our attention here. Our own concern at this point is simply with determining what sorts of feelings might have moved Rodin to construct such works, and a clue to his frame of mind is provided by an observation he made about Michelangelo: speaking of the intensely brooding figures of that artist and of "the pressure of despair which fills them," Rodin observed that "when Michelangelo was old, he actually broke them. Art did not content him. He wanted infinity."[13]

It is a powerful and extraordinarily suggestive observation, and whether or not it tells us anything significant about the sensibility of Michelangelo, it certainly tells us a great deal about the profound impatience with form which is generated by romantic ambition. For Rodin, no completed form could satisfy or keep alive the sense of heightened expectation produced by a distinct fragment; in his view, any form, fully realized, would inevitably fall short of the vague, unrealized possibilities evoked in the perceiver's imagination, and would release the energizing tension between what has been given concrete existence and what is apparently still struggling to be born. Romantic form defines itself through just such tensions:

through the contrast between the vastness of artistic vision and the little that can actually be realized, between the possibility of perfection and the inevitability of human limitation, between articulated elements and the threat of formlessness—of emptiness—which surrounds them and which they attempt to overcome.

A fragmentary structure comes to dominate the space surrounding it by incorporating that space, transforming it into a charged field of implications. As the artist Hans Hofmann has suggested, "when a sculptured figure has lost its meaning as an architectural block . . . . Such a work must function independently. It represents an entity in itself. Its spiritual sphere does not end with its physical periphery. It has the power to enliven its environment. Its message is all embracing since it is of a metaphysical nature."[14] One might arrive at similar conclusions about the spiritual effect of Emerson's assertions when they ceased to be subordinated to a specific institutional religious program. Accordingly, if we imagine a perfectly ordinary doorway placed in an open field, a doorway through which, let us say, a sky with clouds is visible, we are imagining not only a possible work by the surrealist Magritte, or a contemporary work of so-called "environmental" art: we are imagining a concrete metaphor for an essay by Emerson. It is an invitation to enter the infinite world, a formal gesture which, for all its appearance of modesty and plainness, makes the world itself a work of art which we can enter and inhabit in imagination, secure from the threat of all that is without form and therefore without meaning. It offers us a vantage point from which the universe appears to be domesticated space, a space which reflects our will and which surrenders to our control. In this way, it serves as a threshold which permits us passage from our ordinary vague sense of the bewildering character of our common experience to a sudden awareness of that experience as the available ground of spiritual triumph. In the end, it invites us to apprehend, in that familiar "bare common," certain possibilities of exaltation which had not revealed themselves before.

6. The Generation of Whitman

PAUL ZWEIG

When Bronson Alcott first rode the ferry over to Brooklyn to visit Whitman in the fall of 1856, he noticed an unmade bed with a full chamberpot under it and three engravings—"a Hercules, a bacchus, and a satyr"—pinned to the walls of Whitman's bedroom. Half-jokingly, Alcott asked which of these pictures stood for the new poet; Whitman replied with an evasive shrug which seemed to indicate all three. Years later, this sort of memory irked him; for in time, he came to think of himself no longer as a natural man, one of the "roughs," but as a reassuring, prematurely old father, the good gray poet he thought America needed. Something Alcott did not mention seeing in the room is a large nondescript trunk, maybe the one Whitman took with him on his trip to New Orleans seven years before. But it was somewhere around, probably serving already as a repository for Whitman's past, a kind of substitute memory. In it, he deposited his odds and ends of manuscript, bundles of receipts, the articles he tore out of magazines, a file of his old editorials, pocket-sized notebooks made of folder paper, in which names and addresses mingled with book titles, scraps of poems, and anything else that drifted into his Sargasso of written bits.

This was the trunk Whitman had his mother send on to him in Washington, when he set up there during the Civil War. It was his one solid belonging in his drift from one roominghouse to another, during the

Washington years. It migrated with him to Camden, New Jersey, where, during the last decades of his life, its contents spilled over onto tables and chairs, so that to the visitors to his room on Mickle Street, Whitman seemed to be drowning in paper.

Not only did he hold on tenaciously to these fugitive scraps; he seems, from early on, to have lived with his pen in his hand. For years, this was his secret: the one thing he did not want to be, or look like, was a man of letters. He wanted his poems to sound as if they had come on their own, in the spare time left to him from merely living. An air of slowly moving flesh; a kind of garrulous ease in public, sitting next to the drivers on streetcars, or in Pfaff's, a bar and resturant on lower Broadway: this was how he wanted to be known. Writing was his secret because the poems were not supposed to be literature. Yet Whitman wrote all the time. Not only poems; but notes for lectures he never gave; stray opinions on various subjects; the names of young men, usually workingmen or soldiers, with, rarely, a personal note, "slept with me," raising the obvious question but not really answering it, the phrase not having yet become the euphemism for sex that it is today.

By the early 1850s, Whitman began to accumulate books of a few pinned-together pages, or in thicker bond notebooks, usually pocket-sized and therefore probably carried around with him on his frequent excursions around the city. With the doggedness of a self-taught man, he accumulated notes on the great writers of world tradition, collected articles on the history of the English language, and compiled a personal handbook of vernacular expressions, often with a note reminding him where he'd heard them spoken. Very rarely are these reams of notes personally revealing; they are never intimate, their connection to Whitman's published work is spotty. Yet he wrote them tirelessly, as if he needed this daily buckshot of words, this flotsam of language, however trivial.

For a while during the Civil War, the role of the notebooks changed, as Whitman poured into them his impressions of the hospitals, often while he sat in the long whitewashed rooms beside dying or suffering boys whom he thought of as his sons. During these years, when he served as a volunteer nurse in the Army hospitals around Washington, Whitman felt that his private life and the life of the nation had become one. The hospitals were the secret of the war; they were its inner life, so to speak; and Whitman moved through them, soothing, helping, writing. Later, he published his jottings in *Memoranda during the War* and then, in 1883, in his miscellany of autobiographical notes, *Specimen Days.* Having tried for years to form the notes into a real book, at last he gave up, deciding that their spontaneous, disorganized aspect was a good thing: a way of rendering into language the elusive shape of events, without any overlay of artifice:

If I do it at all I must delay no longer. Incongruous and full of skips and jumps as is that huddle of diary-jottings . . . all bundled up and tied by a big string, the resolution and indeed mandate comes to me this day, this hour . . . to go home, untie the bundle, reel out diary-scraps and memoranda, just as they are, large or small, one after another, into print-pages, and let the melange's lacking and wants of connection take care of themselves. It will illustrate one phase of humanity anyhow; how few of life's days and hours (and they not by relative value or proportion, but by chance) are ever noted. Probably another point too, how we give long preparations for some object, planning and delving and fashioning, and then, when the actual hour for doing arrives, find ourselves still quite unprepared, and tumble the thing together, letting hurry and crudeness tell the story better than fine work.

With these words prefacing *Specimen Days,* Whitman turned his wayward jottings into literature; and we think of Melville exulting midway through *Moby Dick:* "God keep me from ever completing anything. This whole book is but a draught—nay but a draught of a draught."

Since Whitman and Melville's day, modern readers have developed a love for the fragment, the sketch, the spontaneous jottings, as being, in some way, truer than the crafted final work. This love has expressed a distrust of culture, a sense that an artist is closer to the muse when—as Kierkegaard said of his own notebook experiments—the "umbilical cord of [the] first mood" still clings to his inspiration. With Picasso, the sketch became a major form. With Eliot, Pound, and Joyce, the fragment—in a wayward pastiche of other fragments, a quilt of moments accidentally yet somehow harmoniously thrown together—became an element of style— the basic molecule, so to speak, in a new idea of form. Those radical modernists, the Surrealists, believed that a man carried around in his mind and blood something like a living notebook—called the unconscious—that threw off telegraphic jottings, to be snatched as they flew past. Renaissance philosophers considered nature to be God's other book. In our day, the unconscious, taken as nature's most concentrated essence, has become God's other book; its language a form of anti-art, dissonant, elliptical, reveling in non-sense, grounded often in ugliness.

When Whitman revised "Song of Myself" for his 1882 edition, he added a sort of gloss to the first lines of the poem:

I harbor for good or bad, I permit to speak at every hazard, Nature without check with original energy.

The added lines tell the reader how to approach this puzzling text which spills erratically down the page in long flaglike lines, shifting elliptically from theme to theme, image to image, over fifty undivided, apparently indigestible pages. Whitman is saying: In this poem, you will hear nature speaking; that is why it is so unliterary, so uncrafted. For nature's language is spontaneous utterance. Nature knows only the present, never the past or the future. My poem therefore is like the crest of a wave, billowing into the present with no echo of its beginning, no forshadowing of its conclusion, that is to say, no form, as life itself has no form.

By the time Whitman added this couplet of lines to "Song of Myself," he had backed away from the extreme provocation of his first edition. The punctuation has been conventionalized. A scattering of thematic hints, such as the one I have quoted, have been added. Above all, the fifty pages of packed language have been skillfully divided into fifty-two stanzas. By 1882, "Song of Myself" has moved part way back into literature. But Whitman might have described the original 1855 version as "Incongruous and full of skips and jumps"; its passages reeled out of his notebooks, "just as they are, large or small, one after another, into print-pages . . . letting hurry and crudeness tell the story better than fine work," which made it maybe "the most wayward, spontaneous, fragmentary [poem] ever printed."

While this description is literally true of the text of *Specimen Days*, it tells another sort of truth about "Song of Myself." And yet, as I have suggested, it soon becomes apparent how thematically controlled and artful Whitman's greatest poem is, its apparent lack of form becoming a new kind of form. Yet the poem, and most of Whitman's writing, has effectively resisted the sort of critical intelligence lavished on other poets of Whitman's stature. It does not comfortably divide into a sequence of related parts; it themes, even its rhythms, seem too casual to support interpretation. As the poem slips through the hands of readers who have not such trouble with Wordsworth's *Prelude*, say, or even Blake's prophetic books, it seems to insist that nothing can or should be said about it; that it is simply itself; nature's unparaphrasable outpouring—God's other book—and therefore fundamentally different from a "mere" poem. To its first readers, on the other hand, and to many of its later critics, "Song of Myself" seemed literally to have tumbled pell-mell out of Whitman's trunk. To a conventionally literary eye, clutter and nature can resemble each other. Yet it is this fragmentary, elliptical aspect of Whitman's poetry that has made it seem modern: its unprepared shifts in tone; its maw of a long uniambic line that digests the unpoetic without a missed breath: all those qualities Whitman meant when he called his method "indirect" and contrasted it with the narrative method of the poets he saw himself replacing—Shakespeare, Milton, Walter Scott. Only by "indirection" could the entire man, and not merely his tellable actions, be expressed in language. "Indirection"—"elliptical and idiomatic," as he put it—was the democratic, truly American method, for it addressed itself to an obscure well of sentiments and impulses which everyman, no matter how ordinary, carried within him: his own complete "nature."

Is it too much to say that all of modernism sprang out of Whitman's trunk, as it did out of those other pell-mell masses of privacy—those trunks—that the nineteenth century turned into famous anti-books: Emerson's *Journals* and their decanted essences, his essays: the *journaux intimes* of Maine de Biron, Delacroix, or Amiel, those monuments to a lifetime's probing of the intimate rhythms of thought and feeling. Out of these grossly shaped boxes of words came the idea of a form that would be no form: words that would perform the ultimate mimetic act by pretending to be, and trying to be, life itself in all its unravelings. Proust, Joyce: epic trunks of language, devoted to the miraculous ordinariness of a man's inner being.

The idea that his life could be represented as a miscellaneous bag of bits may have come to Whitman from one of the century's underestimated books, Thomas Carlyle's *Sartor Resartus,* which Whitman read avidly during these years. Carlyle's philosopher-hero, Diogenes Teufelsdrökh, turns out to have left, in guise of an autobiography: "Six considerable Paper-Bags [containing] miscellaneous masses of Sheets, and oftener Shreds and Snips ... Anecdotes, oftenest without date or place or time, fly loosely on separate strips, like Sibylline leaves. Interspersed also are long purely Autobiographical delineations; yet without connection, without recognisable coherence ... Selection, order, appears to be unknown to the Professor ... Close by a rather eloquent Oration ... lie washbills marked *bezahlt* (settled). His Travels are indicated by the Street-Advertisements of the various cities he has visited."

By the early 1850s, the sheets, shreds, and snips had begun to accumulate in Whitman's trunk. When, three decades later, he came across a scrapbook of these clippings among the odds and ends scattered across his floor on Mickle Street, he mused to his young friend Horace Traubel: "It is a strange miscellany—a hodge-podge, some of it only pulp, some of it very vital: curious, rejected reviews, critiques, odds and ends of newspaper gossip—all of it in the past, the far past—gathered together fifty years ago and on from that time for many years. I have always had it about me as a book for personal reference...." "What has that particular book to do with *Leaves of Grass?*" "Oh! everything! is full of its beginnings—is the a b c of the book—contains the first lisps of the song.... Here was my first tally of life—here were my first tries with the lute—in that book I am just like a man tuning up his instrument before the play begins."

Sometime during 1854, Whitman had sufficiently tuned up his instrument, and began to write out the poems that make up his first book. His trunk full of notebooks and scraps give us some idea of how he went about this. Many of the poems were in fact worked up from prose notes Whitman had made during the preceding years, some of them arranged experimentally into a cascade of more or less rhythmic verse. Then, as if the conception of the poems and their long rhythmic line had suddenly become clear to him, Whitman recast all this material into the form we know, with its Biblical parallelisms, its anchoring nouns, and floating, indefinite verbs.

The poet's loosely reeled-out line could accommodate a startling variety of tones; its range of subject matter was vast. He picked through his poetic notebooks and his old editorials, the scrapbook of newspaper items he had begun to keep half a dozen years before. He bracketed passages in books on geology and astronomy. These were his sources, and he worked them into the new line, inventing, pastiching, paraphrasing.

There is another, less appreciated side to Whitman's remarkable breakthrough at this time. As he wrote and rewrote the material accumulating on his desk, he began to shape it into a vast central poem—this would eventually be "Song of Myself"—and the shaping was unprecedented. Unlike virtually every other long poem of the century, this one did not tell a story or unfold an argument. The material in it included sensational erotic passages, fantasias of geology and astronomy, a series of impressionistic travelogues, a sketch of a sea battle, another of a wartime massacre, remarkable tableaux of a horse, a butcher, a fleeing slave, a sad lonely woman, the prayerful invocation of natural "miracles" reverberating with echoes from Carlyle's Sartor Resartus. All of this contributes to the changeable portrait of a man, named on line 499 as "Walt Whitman," who, we are told, is creating this uninterrupted flow as a form for himself, as a celebration of himself.

Whitman was remarkably adroit. Without any narrative or clear subordination of themes, he arranged his armfuls of poetry into a single text. It is fascinating to see how he grouped together lines taken from all over his notebooks, and juggled passages, until they complemented each other and completed each other. The fragments and portraits and "catalogues," the sexual deliriums, and the reflections on poetry contribute to a whole effect (as the sounds of the instruments contribute to an orchestral piece). Among modern poems, perhaps T. S. Eliot's *The Waste Land* comes closest to "Song of Myself," in its deliberately various styles, its indirect unity consisting in repeated images and themes, its undercutting of narrative.

For half a century, *The Waste Land* has haunted readers, because its intricate balancing of themes seems to call out for interpretation: surely the poem "means" something; yet it slides out of reach, hovers amid a plurality of meanings, until, giving up, the reader understands that the poem is simply itself—a musical whole, spoken by a disembodied voice, in turn playful, mournful, satirical, mystical. "Song of Myself" has puzzled its readers in many of the same ways. Eschewing narrative, Whitman, too, balanced themes and images; he created a voice in turn playful, mournful, satirical, mystical. The idea of a musical structure was promoted by Whitman, who claimed that his method was that of the Italian opera: an interplay of arias and recitatives. The triumph of the poem lies, finally, in its architecture.

The task of organizing an extremely long poem without any overarching narrative is formidable. Some of Whitman's finest middle-length poems are framed by a single setting: the night ("The Sleepers"), or the East River just before sunset ("Crossing Brooklyn Ferry"), or a beach on Long Island ("Out of the Cradle Endlessly Rocking"). But "Song of Myself" takes the universe and all of time as its setting. Within the poem, there are occasional smaller unities: the sun rising unobtrusively through several stanzas, two staggeringly busy journeys taking up almost half the poem, an ecstatic awakening of the sense through half a dozen stanzas. Nonetheless, the poem flows from surprise to surprise; nothing seems too peculiar to find a place in it. The catalogues are bristling and random, and their randomness is important. For they are extended symbols of a mind that excludes nothing. A random list is, by definition, merely a sample of an unspoken list containing everything; and "Song of Myself," similarly, contains everything.

The great epic poems have been masterpieces of inclusion. To the classical Greeks, the *Iliad* was a kind of Bible, not only because of its solemn heroic code, but because the poem moved in expanding circles of knowledge. While telling about Troy and Helen, Hector and Achilles, it scrupulously caught up quantities of knowledge about rituals, techniques of warfare, a medically exact description of serious wounds, weapons making, and, in the extended similes, countless tableaux of ordinary living. In this sense, "Song of Myself," too, is an epic. It, too, is a masterpiece of inclusion, although it deliberately inverts the familiar epic ambition: it does not tell a story; its hero has not accomplished any grand actions; or, rather, his grand action is the poem itself. The hero of "Song of Myself" is an ordinary man (Hollyer's frontispiece engraving makes sure the reader knows this) who had led a remarkably commonplace life, as Whitman insists when he invokes the

People I meet . . . the effect upon me of my early life . . . of
    the ward and city I live in . . . of the nation,
The latest news . . . discoveries, inventions, societies . . .
    authors old and new,
My dinner, dress, associates, looks, business, compliments,
    dues,
The real or fancied indifference of some man or woman I
    love,
The sickness of one of my folks—or of myself . . . or
    ill-doing . . . or loss or lack of money . . . or depressions
    or exaltations.

Whitman's "singer" glories in his anonymity. We don't know his name or how he earns his living. His actions of any sort are few, but everything—the "everything" that is the poem—happens to him. The "singer" bestrides the poem and is the poem, reciting, celebrating, ironizing. Whitman's unified setting for "Song of Myself" is not a place but a voice various and broad enough to say "everything." The poem is an extravagant monologue; or, rather—to use Whitman's model for the genius of pure voice—it is an opera; an opera, moreover, in which all the voices are one. Whitman's "singer" resembles no one more than that extraordinary celebrator of his own irruptive nature: Diderot's character of Rameau's Nephew, who also bursts the confines of his social self, in a hilarious, moving, endlessly surprising performance that deliberately evokes an operatic aria.

Remember the lines Whitman added to the final version of "Song of Myself": "I harbor for good or bad, I permit to speak at every hazard, / Nature without check with original energy." Whitman is trying to help the reader here, by seeding his poem with parenthetical comments, like stage directions inserted between the lines of a play or, more exactly, like the unspoken plea of a novelist whose naïvely truthful tone tells us his reader: what you are reading here really happened, I didn't make it up; this is not literature, but fact.

As our first important anti-literary genre, the novel took its reader by ruse, developing a remarkable bag of tricks by which it claimed to tell only the truth. The novelist openly renounced his claim to be an artist: he was an amanuensis, a mere scribe of history; facts spoke through him. The reader suspended disbelief, agreeing to be beguiled by a new kind of artistry which consisted in "lying like the truth," as was said of Daniel Defoe, the first modern novelist.

"Nature without check with original energy." Whitman, too, is saying, there is not art here, and no poem; there is only "nature," only spontaneous utterance. Don't look here for second thoughts or cunning echoes, for foreshadowings and formal development. Here is a voice speaking before it thinks, "for good or bad." Now everything is explained: the overabundant images, the vagaries of subject matter, the sudden shifts and leaps, the sense of a voice reeling out of control. There is a kind of brinkmanship, as the poem veers from surprise to surprise. It is the brinkmanship of life itself, which takes place at the very edge of an unwritten future. To be sure, it is all art no less than a novel is art. Whitman's bag of tricks is deep. His claim, too, is the novelist's: this is merely truth, not literature.

"Song of Myself" is not only a voice, then. It is a voice that cannot stop "singing," delighted with its own fullness, plunging into its unuttered future. The poem's present tense is so reckless and hurried ("I speak at every hazard . . . without check") that it seems to have no past, no memory: that is to say, the poem is not about anything, any more than life is about something. It is simply happening: it is about itself. How much like Whitman, to have written a provokingly unliterary poem (a frank outpouring, pure "nature") which yet plays humorously, even erotically, with the theme of its own creation:

I believe in you my soul. . . . the other I am must not abase itself to you.
And you must not be abased to the other.
Loafe with me on the grass. . . . loose the stop from your throat.
Not words, not music or rhyme I want. . . . not custom or lecture, not even the best,
Only the lull I like, the hum of your valved voice.
I mind how we lay in June, such a transparent summer morning;
You settled your head athwart my hips and gently turned over upon me,

And parted my shirt from my bosom-bone, and plunged
your tongue to my barestript heart,
And reached till you felt my beard, and reached till
you held my feet.

Swiftly arose and spread around me the peace and joy
and knowledge that pass all the art and argument of the
earth;
And I know that the hand of God is the elderhand of
my own,
And I know that the spirit of God is the eldest brother
of my own,
And that all the men ever born are also my brothers . . .
and the women my sisters and lovers,
And that a kelson of the creation is love;
And limitless are leaves stiff or drooping in the
fields,
And brown ants in the little wells beneath them,
And mossy scabs of the wormfence, and heaped stones,
and elder and mullen and pokeweed.

Whitman's scene of lovemaking on the grass is
curiously elusive. Self and soul loaf tenderly, and yet
they hardly seem to touch each other. Instead of
touching, they listen: everything is in the voice, a
summer *bel canto* without words or rhyme; only a
"valved voice"—in effect, a new kind of poetry. At
last, the "tongue" brings self and soul together in an
act of phantasmic oral sex; an orgasm accomplished
by voice alone, surpassing "all the art and argument
of the earth." Whitman's lovemaking is also an act
of poetry, so intimate and vivid that whoever listens
becomes a loving partner and accomplice ("Stop this
day and night with me and you shall possess the
origin of all poems"). Whitman, here, is describing
his own poetry, this very poem. Self and soul embrace, as Whitman dreamed of embracing his reader.
The next poem in his book will begin:

Come closer to me,
Push close to me and take the best I possess,
Yield closer and closer and give me the best you possess.

This is unfinished business with me. . . . how is it with you?
I was chilled with the cold types and cylinder and wet
    paper between us.

I pass so poorly with paper and types. . . . I must pass with
    the contact of bodies and souls.

This unpredictable poem denies that it is a poem, yet it is always about the efficacy of poetry: as an erotic tool, as a voice, and an extension of the body:

My voice goes after what my eyes cannot reach,
With a twirl of my tongue I encompass worlds and volumes
    of worlds.

I have pointed out the curious resemblance between "Song of Myself" and the classical nineteenth-century novel. Both claim not to be "literature"; both want to be read naïvely, as windows on the truth; as mere daguerreotypes; history, not fantasy. On the whole, readers have probably done better with both than have critics. It is, after all, an austere wish to resist the novel's story-telling rapture in order to unearth its bag of tricks. "Song of Myself," too, I suspect, has been easier to read than understand. Analysis slides off the poem; yet the reader follows the shifting images and tone, the rising and falling cadence, the casual leap from theme to theme, as one follows the rhythms of a voice speaking its mind. The voice never lets one down. There is a flow, an exploratory reaching for the next thought and image, which is Whitman's profoundest verisimilitude. A mind must move like that; it must veer and surprise and amble forward, just like that. It must sidestep, change moods unpredictably, avoid statements in favor of suggestions, abstractions in favor of urgently physical images.

Critics have tried, with dubious success, to identify the five or seven or nine major divisions of the poem. They have enumerated the poem's central ideas, its statements, its developments. In short, they have tried to read it as other great poems have been read. Yet these critics have seemed, if not more wrong, somehow less useful than when reading, say, Keats's great odes, or Wordsworth's "Tintern Abbey," or Milton's "Lycidas." There is a danger in defying the author's instructions, and Whitman is unequivocal: this is no poem, he says; this is a reckless present tense; this is a voice becoming naked to you ("I will go to the bank by the wood and become undisguised and naked") and catching its own meanings as they fly; a voice discovering itself to you and to itself.

"Song of Myself" is an engine of self-making: that I believe is the clue we must follow to unravel its story. Whitman's "singer" is made and remade by his poem. He is a creature of language, grounded in his voice—as Whitman suggests through his conflation of themes. The poem is a body ("who touches this touches a man") but also a flirtatious commentary on itself as a poem. It is the flesh that is grass, but it is also a meditation on the capabilities of language. Flesh is grass, and grass is song: here Whitman's celebration of bodily feelings become doubled with artistic self-awareness, shaped by the poem's feeling for itself as a poem. Remember the double meanings that shimmer in Whitman's scene of lovemaking on the grass, which is at once erotic song and commentary on the new poetry Whitman invents in this very poem. No matter how fast the fit whirls him, the watcher still watches. The watcher is the dancing master and orchestrator of Whitman's themes. When watcher and dancer come together on the grass in an act of poetry performed by the "tongue," their partnership is sealed. Dancer and watcher, self and soul combine to answer the child's question which opens the next section of the poem: "What is the grass?" The

answer will be multitudinous and long—it will be the
poem itself; and the answerer will be caught up in the
whirlwind of his answer. He will take in his own words,
digest them, and become a new man:

> I find I incorporate gneiss and coal and long-threaded
> moss and fruits and grains and esculent roots,
> And am stucco'd with quadrupeds and birds all over.

This is the literal scenario of the poem; the process
by which Whitman's singer becomes a man of his
words. There are passages in Whitman's notebooks
where he plays with a grandiose fantasy of incorporation—as when we say we "digest" knowledge—and
that fantasy of incorporation becomes the underlying
figure for all learning and perception. Learning to be a
man, we take in what we see; we enrich our substance
with the perceived substance of what our senses, those
carnal hunters, bring to us as prey.

Aroused by his voice, Whitman's singer rises from
his bed of grass and journeys forth. What follows in the
poem is not so much catalogue as impressionistic
journey and gargantuan menu. It is the "open road" of
Whitman's senses, taking it all, as he says, "for me . . .
for me . . . for me." I called "Song of Myself" an epic, a
masterpiece of inclusion. Here is the epic work itself.
It is a labor of "merging"—Whitman's characteristic
figure—of becoming naked, in order to strip from
others their illusory separateness: "Undrape . . . I see
through the broadcloth and gingham whether or no."
Whitman's "open road" is also a tireless peristalsis: the
world enters the maw of the awakened self, who comments with a varied refrain:

> This is the grass.
> I fly the flight of the fluid and swallowing soul.
> All this I swallow and it tastes good.

Whitman's singer is not an ecstatic solitary; he is not a
solipsist, or an idealist. The world exists for him as food,

and he devours it with his song. Whitman's idea plays elusively throughout the text: the singer travels within his poem, which is a road going nowhere and everywhere; yet the poem is also a body feeding itself indiscriminately with all its sense. Before we insist, however, on Whitman's infantile magic thinking or on his naïve and primitive belief in the efficacy of language, we must remember the third strand in his play of meanings: the poem is, after all, a poem; the body and its digestive actions are figures of speech, they are maneuvers of the voice dramatizing its desires. The poem is a symbolic action, threaded with refrainlike commentaries on voice, body, and appetite as figures for the poetic act and the cognitive life of the mind. These are some of the double and triple takes of meaning that constitute Whitman's "indirections" in "Song of Myself."

Whitman's catalogues extend across half the poem, in a broad associative flow. They are the very workings of self-change. The digestive and devouring action of the poem passes through them. The open road is also an open mind, an open body, and an open mouth. The singer emerges from the journey, fleshed with his increased substance. "Who goes there! hankering, gross, mystical, nude? / How is it I extract strength from the beef I eat?" We know now what he's been eating—the very world— and we will learn shortly who he is. Meanwhile, we hear the boastful American voice that Whitman extracted from the booster journalism of his day, from the tall stories and the folklore—that American glamor of exaggeration that had made Mike Fink and Daniel Boone into frontier giants, and the Founding Fathers into saints. The shy solitary self, observing a spear of grass in the first lines of the poem, has "extracted strength" from his "beef," and now he will shout his name:

Walt Whitman, an American, one of the roughs, a kosmos,
Disorderly fleshy and sensual . . . eating drinking and
breeding,

No sentimentalist . . . no stander above men and women
or apart from them . . . no more modest than
immodest.

Unscrew the locks from the doors!
Unscrew the doors themselves from their jambs!

The anonymity is broken; the singer reveals himself as
an American, "one of the roughs." He has eaten and
drunk; he has lain naked on the grass and traveled along
an open road of appetizing sensations. He has also made
this poem, and now his name bursts from his lips. Like
Odysseus crowing his name to the blinded Cyclops,
Whitman's singer has made a name for himself. On line
499 of the first poem in his book, the name "Walt Whitman" enters literature. For more than a decade he had
been signing his short stories "Walter Whitman," and
his editorials, "WW" or "Paumanok," when they were
signed at all. His byline in James J. Brenton's 1849 anthology, *Voices from the Press*, had been "Walter Whitman." The receipts from his contracting work as late as
1854, are usually signed "Walter Whitman, Jr." To his
family and friends, on the other hand, he had been
"Walt" all along, "probably because his father was
Walter," George Whitman remembered. "It was a way
we had of separating them."

Now he would be "Walt" to everyone, as Emerson,
growing up, had decided to be "Waldo" instead of the
hated "Ralph," and Thoreau had decided to be "Henry
David" instead of the "David Henry" he had been born
with. While these are not new names, they are not quite
the old ones either. There has been a shuffling of identities; a choice subtly but definitely made to be this man.
Whitman chose to make his life and his work speak with
one voice and to name that voice "Walt Whitman." He
refused to separate his private and public identities, refused to climb the ladder of accepted ambitions. He has
not switched, for example, from the profession of jour-

nalism to the profession of literature. Unlike "Walter Whitman, Jr.," "Walt Whitman" did not claim to be a professional anything. He was simply himself: an irresistibly public man created by his poems, who lived in his words and was nourished by them:

I do not press my finger across my mouth,
I keep as delicate around the bowels as around the head
     and heart,
Copulation is no more rank to me than death is.

I believe in the flesh and the appetites,
Seeing hearing and feeling are miracles, and each part
     and tag of me is a miracle.

Divine am I inside and out, and I make holy whatever I
     touch or am touched from;
The scent of these arm-pits is aroma finer than prayer,
This head is more than churches or bibles or creeds.

If I worship any particular thing it shall be some of the
     spread of my body;
Translucent mould of me it shall be you,
Shaded ledges and rests, firm masculine coulter, it shall
     be you,
Whatever goes to the tilth of me it shall be you,
You my rich blood, your milky stream pale strippings of
     my life;
Breast that presses against other breasts it shall be you,
My brain it shall be your occult convolutions,
Root of washed sweet-flag, timorous pond-snipe, nest of
     guarded duplicate eggs, it shall be you,
Mixed tussled hay of head and beard and brawn it shall
     be you,
Trickling sap of maple, fibre of manly wheat, it shall
     be you;
Sun so generous it shall be you,
Vapors lighting and shading my face it shall be you,
Winds whose soft-tickling genitals rub against me it shall
     be you.

Broad muscular fields, branches of liveoak, loving lounger
in my winding paths, it shall be you,
Hands I have taken, face I have kissed, mortal I have ever
touched, it shall be you.

I dote on myself . . . there is that lot of me, and all so
luscious,
Each moment and whatever happens thrills me with joy.

These lines, climaxing a portion of the poem, contain
all Whitman's humor and sensuality and outrageous-
ness. He sings out about "worship" and "prayer"—the
language of churchgoing—but also about "armpits,"
"copulation," a charmingly timorous penis, the wind's
"soft-tickling genitals." Whitman's church is his body.
Aroused from head to toe, he describes himself as a
well-fed and bearded erection, so deliciously happy
that the trees, the fields, and the wind have become his
lovers.

But the song is not over. For there is a problemati-
cal side to Whitman's unbridled expansion. As he peels
away the boundaries of house, clothes, even place, as
social and moral distinctions fall away, he comes to
the very edge of language. He has been a voice, his
body has been the poem. Now body and poem blur
together:

My voice goes after what my eyes cannot reach.
With the twirl of my tongue I encompass worlds and
volumes of worlds.

Speech is the twin of my vision . . . it is unequal to measure
itself.
It provokes me forever,
It says sarcastically, Walt, you understand enough . . . why
don't you let it out then?

My final merit I refuse you . . . I refuse putting from me
the best I am.

Encompass worlds but never try to encompass me,
I crowd your noisiest talk by looking toward you.

Writing and talk do not prove me,
I carry the plenum of proof and every thing else in my
    face,
With the hush of my lips I confound the topmost skeptic.

There is overreaching here. This is not the mystic's
helpless admiration for an unsayable truth or Rousseau's romantic *je ne sais quoi*. Walt Whitman teeters
beyond himself. What does he need the poem for? He is
already the poem, and he is perfect. Whitman's question
is the ancient unanswerable one of the theologians.
Why did God, who is perfect and beyond need, create
anything at all? As the heroes of epic discovered, to be
"a little more than human" is to stand at the edge of a
strangely dissolving solitude. Is Walt Whitman in the
poem, or is he out of it? His silence is spoken: "the hush
of [his] lips" is, after all, a phrase. Yes, he is in the poem,
caught in it, carried by it. And now it becomes head-
long, more than he had bargained for.

His unfettered senses have been so aroused that
the experience of a sunrise almost destroys him. A
wild crescendo of sounds overwhelms him:

I am exposed . . . cut by bitter and poisoned hail,
Steeped amid honeyed morphine . . . my windpipe squeezed
    in fakes of death.

"Touch" floods him with fire, betrays and almost anni-
hilates him:

On all sides prurient provokers stiffening my limbs,
Straining the udder of my heart for its withheld drip.
Behaving licentious toward me, taking no denial,
Depriving me of my best as for a purpose,
Unbuttoning my clothes and holding me by the bare waist,
Deluding my confusion with the calm of the sunlight and
    pasture fields,

Immodestly sliding the fellow-senses away,
They bribed to swap off with touch, and go and graze at
    the edges of me.

I am given up by traitors;
I talk wildly . . . I have lost my wits . . . I and nobody else
    am the greatest traitor,
You villain touch! what are you doing? . . . my breath is
    tight in its throat;
Unclench your floodgates! you are too much for me.

The unshielded life is dangerous; physical ecstasy can be a kind of death. The poem will circle this danger several times. Several times, Whitman will push to the edge of his paradox: to be a self, with a name, and yet to be everything and everyone. And each time he will spiral into a wider orbit, discovering that "Walt Whitman's" journey is unendable, that his appetite can never be satiated, and the world never completely internalized. Having tried to end his poem in a swaggering celebration, he accepts at last that the poem can have no end.

Here begins the poem's second catalogue, grappling up into its language all religions, the geological past, the violence of history, walking with Jesus in Judea. Whitman's road opens ever wider:

Rise after rise bow the phantoms behind me,
Afar down I see the huge first Nothing, the vapor from
    the nostrils of death,
I know I was even there . . . I waited unseen and always,
And slept while God carried me through the lethargic mist,
And took my time . . . and took no hurt from the foetid
    carbon.

This day before dawn I ascended a hill and looked at the
    crowded heaven,
And I said to my spirit, When we become the enfolders of
    those orbs and the pleasure and knowledge of every
    thing in them, shall we be filled and satisfied then?
And my spirit said No, we level that lift to pass and continue
    beyond.

The Generation of Whitman

The sun that has begun rising on line 552—introduced casually, in the previous line, by an association with "morning glory"—continues to rise, clouded by panics and momentary fears, busy with "lovers," filled with an ever-more-solid acceptance of the unendable journey that is the poem. Finally, it is sunset. Whitman's singer sees himself as a wild hawk, sounding his non-language—his "barbaric yawp"—over the roofs of the world, while the daylight dims, and the almost-setting sun casts enormous shadows. The poem ends with dusk. But the grass will continue to grow; the singer will be waiting for you; the cycles of death and resurrection, like the cycle of day and night, will continue. The poem's end will not be a true ending, merely an articulation of endlessness:

I depart as air . . . I shake my white locks at the runaway
    sun,
I effuse my flesh in eddies and drift it in lacy jags.

I bequeath myself to the dirt to grow from the grass I
    love,
If you want me again look for me under your bootsoles.

You will hardly know who I am or what I mean,
But I shall be good health to you nevertheless,
And filter and fibre your blood.

Failing to fetch me at first keep encouraged,
Missing me one place search another,
I stop somewhere waiting for you.

7. Over-Soul as Orgone: The Case of Wilhelm Reich

STEVEN MARCUS

> Thoughtless people . . . do not distinguish between per-
> ception and notion. They fancy that I choose to see this
> or that thing. But perception is not whimsical, but fatal.
> If I see a trait, my children will see it after me, and in
> course of time all mankind,—although it may chance
> that no one has seen it before me. For my perception of it
> is as much a fact as the sun.—Emerson, "Self-Reliance"

The Romantic visionaries tended to confer on intuition
the status once occupied by divine revelation, and to
disencumber it from the accidents of an individual person's life history. To be sure, Wordsworth's "spots of
time" arrive only in the finite course of his personal
experience; but in *The Prelude* such moments serve to
explain his life, and not the other way around. To him
something like sacrilege would be entailed in the unin-
flected suggestion that his life alone might serve to
explain them fully. One unavoidable implication of
psychoanalytic theory, however, is that even a man's
perceptions occur on grounds prepared and foreshadowed by his experiences, actual and psychic. Wilhelm
Reich—the post-Freudian prophet of the orgasm, the
post-Romantic theorist of the reunification of man and
nature—began his career within the psychoanalytic
community, but ended it as a latter-day member of the
visionary company. The ideas of this physician-

cum-seer have had a large, though still largely unexplored, effect on certain tendencies in contemporary thought. Myron Sharaf's commendable biography, *Fury on Earth*, the work of a true believer who nonetheless struggles with the human terms of his own engagement with his mentor, offers a useful opportunity to reassess Reich's life and career, and to aid us in the effort to establish further connections between biography, prophecy, and culture.

Wilhelm Reich was born in 1897 in Galicia, then part of the Austro-Hungarian Empire. His father was a well-to-do Jewish cattle farmer, a man of dominating temperament, prone to violence and outbursts of jealous rage at his wife. When Reich was about twelve he discovered that his mother was having an affair with a young tutor who lived with the family. He observed this affair voyeuristically, with both horror and sexual excitement; finally, he managed somehow to inform his father of what was taking place. The father confronted the mother as the "whore" he had always accused her of being, and she then drank enough household cleanser to kill herself in the most painful way. The tutor was of course banished; the father never recovered from the event, and a few years later also did himself in, or tried to: he stood for hours in cold weather in a pond, "ostensibly fishing," but trying to contract pneumonia, which he did. He rapidly developed TB and died in 1914. One can only imagine what in the way of unbearable guilt, torment and anguish the young Reich went through. He, too, was never to recover from these horrible experiences and indeed in later life tended to repeat these primary crises in varied forms. His chief defense—as well as his partial repetition of the traumas—was the tendency to blame everyone else in quarrels, disagreements and fracases that were largely conflicts of Reich's own creation. There was also born in him at this time a "sense of a mis-

sion," a need to live "a heroic life," which, Sharaf
speculates, would bring him some surcease from the
unconscious guilt that he was always to feel and would
work to repare "the conditions that had produced the
early tragedies."

After a stint in the army during World War I, Reich
entered the University of Vienna. He had become a
social radical and was prepared to become a sexual
radical too. In March 1919, he wrote in his diary, "I
have become convinced that sexuality is the center
around which revolves the whole of social life as well
as the inner life of the individual." This is at once
much simpler than Freud but a good preparation for
the experience of Freud as well. That experience came
almost at once; Reich was immediately hooked, found
in Freud the surrogate for the parents (especially the
father) that he had lost, and entered upon a period of
discipleship. Freud took quickly to this bright and vig-
orous young man, and by the end of 1920, while he was
still in medical school, Reich was already a practicing
analyst. He also had two brief periods of analytic therapy at about this time, one with Isidor Sadger and one
with Paul Federn, both of whom eventually came to
detest Reich with exceptional intensity.

Some of Reich's early work retains an interest today both in itself and as part of the history of psychoanalytic theory and clinical practice. He was one of the
first psychoanalysts to become involved extensively in
the treatment of people who were suffering from what
was then called "impulsive character"—today the relevant pieces of terminology would be "character disorder" or "borderline personality." These patients were
not afflicted so much by specific neurotic symptoms as
by entire styles of life that were "chaotically disorganized." Reich's own early history had certainly prepared him to understand such people. He also learned
to direct attention to what he came to call "character
analysis"—namely the analysis of the entire array of

defenses that patients erect and that Reich characteristically termed "character armor." He was, in addition, among the first psychoanalysts to see that in such patients pieces of neurotic behavior are not treated as entities that are alien to the ego—as hysterical or obsessional symptoms are—but are instead regarded as an integral part of the self, as ego-syntonic. He tried to devise ways of dealing with these problems, and some of them were of considerable interest. For example, Reich was among the early analysts to begin to try to pay systematic attention to the nonverbal behavior of patients and to use such behavior as analytic material. He also directed very close attention to the latent negative transference in his patients and made every effort to elicit it and make it overt.

He made, as well, what he regarded as his first fundamental discovery—the phenomenon of "orgastic potency," which was for him the cornerstone to all his later work and his standard for human health. Reich was something of a Freudian fundamentalist; he believed that neuroses entailed literal, perhaps measurable, blockages of libidinal energies, and that the primary aim of psychotherapy ought to be to find ways and means of discharging these electro-physiological currents through the convulsive experience of the orgasm. To this end, Reich began to work directly with his patients' genital sensations; in due course this directness, always increasing, began to trouble his fellow analysts. There is no question that Reich is the key figure in the modern cult of the orgasm that has, so to speak, plagued Western middle-class culture for some decades now. And there is no question either that he rather simplemindedly equated sexual potency and responsiveness with psychic health in general. He was nothing if not utopian.

But these early achievements went along with the circumstance that from the beginning he kept getting into hot water with his colleagues. First, there was his personal behavior among them; with the exception of Freud, Reich could not resist the impulse to dominate, lead, compel and command everyone else in all situations. Second, Reich's own free—if not promiscuous—sexual life (he was always something of a womanizer), conducted openly, also added fuel to the fire that he was building. Then there was the manner in which he put forward his ideas among his analytic peers; Helena Deutsch, recalling the 1920s, writes with distaste about Reich's "aggressiveness" and "fanaticism" in advancing his ideas on sexuality. That is to say, he had no conception of how to behave collegially. Freud himself rather dryly recognized that there were problems brewing around Reich. In 1928, he wrote to Lou Andreas-Salomé that "we have here a Dr. Reich, a worthy but impetuous young man, passionately devoted to his hobby horse, who now salutes in the genital orgasm the antidote to every neurosis." Freud insisted on the irreducible importance of pregenital components of the sexual drive. And when, at an evening meeting held at Freud's house in 1928 or 1929, Reich held forth his views on orgastic potency, "Freud replied that 'complete orgasm' was not the answer. There were still pregenital drives that could not be satisfied even with orgasm. 'There is no single cause for the neuroses' was his verdict." Freud was right in his diagnosis of Reich's essentially reductionist and simplifying view of matters of exceptional complexity. But, when Reich at this meeting persisted in arguing for his theoretical view, Freud is reported to have replied sharply, "He who wants to have the floor again and again shows that he want to be right at any price," suggesting that he understood more about Reich than that his thesis alone was inadequate.

In addition to this, Reich had some years earlier fallen in love with, and then subsequently married, a female patient of his. Although Annie Reich was to be subsequently analysed by both Hermann Nunberg and

Anna Freud and become in her own turn a respected member of the analtyic community, there seems no doubt that Reich was at least in part impelled to this behavior precisely because it was tabooed. And it served to intensify the growing disapproval in which he was held by that community. This circumstance of deepening estrangement was not helped when, in about 1927, he sought a personal analysis from Freud and was refused. It was clearly becoming very difficult for Reich to remain one of the "good sons" that Freud needed to have around him, although it is also clear that part of him, during this period, tried to fulfill itself in that role. Things were not helped either by Reich's increasingly open social radicalism and his participation in the activities of the local Communist Party. Just as he sought rapid and radical character change in his own kind of psychotherapy, so also he believed that strong action on the political left would bring about analogous rapid, revolutionary liberation for the "oppressed masses" in society at large. He also, openly and publicly, took extremely advanced positions for the time on abortion, contraception and adolescent genital sexuality. It was at this time too that he came up with the crack-brained idea that there was nothing harmful in children watching their parents in sexual intercourse. In other words, Reich had made himself into a typical sexual-social modernist of the post World War I period—but his doing so pushed him further toward the periphery of the psychoanalytic movement, which deliberately maintained a generally low and conservative profile on such inflammatory matters of social behavior and morality.

It was from about this time—circa 1927—that colleagues would retrospectively identify perceptible changes in Reich's behavior: his fierce adherence to his theories and convictions was expressed with increasing belligerence, and a number of his associates believed that they could see "paranoid trends" emerging in his conduct. In 1930, with matters rapidly coming to a crisis in the German-speaking world, Reich moved from Vienna to Berlin. He joined the Communist Party there, tried to save the world through his personal campaign of sexual-political education and liberation of the working class, and continued to alienate almost everyone. By 1934, with Hitler now in power, Reich found himself in exile in Scandinavia: his love affair with the Communist Party was over; he had been expelled from the official psychoanalytic institutions and organizations; and his marriage had dissolved. He had broken with almost everyone and everything—including two young daughters. Reich believed that he was utterly right in what he had done: he had preserved "the integrity of his life and work," he would remark later on to Sharaf, and besides, it was everyone else's fault anyway.

In Scandinavia from 1934–36 (mostly in Norway) Reich pursued his own increasingly divergent way. He began to make experiments which were designed to discover the biological, physiological, and finally, electrical foundations of the libido. In 1939, he claimed to have discovered the "bions," vesicles which, he declared, "represented transitional stages between non-living and living substance." He was, in fact, looking for the secret of life itself. In this ambitious undertaking, he was surrounded and abetted by a specific group of people.

Most of the people who helped Reich were in therapy with him and, often, in a kind of "training analysis" to learn his techniques. With justification, Otto Fenichel has criticised Reich for abusing the transference situation—the patient's dependence upon and devotion to his therapist—by getting such people to help him through working or giving money or both. The fact that many were also students, eager for his stamp of approval, for referrals from him, heightened this situation.

Under these circumstances it is not altogether surprising that a number of his co-workers were also able to see the blue or blue-gray bions that Reich claimed became visible when he turned out the lights in his specially prepared laboratory.

A "kind of training analysis" is a kind way of putting it. Reich had passed from working analytically on the rigidities of "character armor" to working physically on the rigidities of "muscular armor." He no longer thought of himself as a psychoanalyst. Nudity, touching, the physical manipulation of the various segments of the musculature, in order to facilitate "the dissolution of characterological and muscular rigidities," the eliciting of strong emotions and energy "streamings," the emphasis upon respiration, the effort to breathe more freely by means of released "blocked feeling, through the expression of rage or sorrow," now came to be the central focus of Reich's therapy—a kind of psychiatric chiropraxis, which Reich himself now termed "character-analytic vegetotherapy." It is not difficult to make out the ancestral connections between these innovations and such latter-day developments as, to quote Sharaf, "primal scream therapy, Gestalt therapy, bio-energetics, and encounter groups." By the mid-1930s, then, Reich had become totally immersed in his own unique world, a world which, experientially, could be represented in condensed form by the "end phase" of therapy—a "world of intense sensation, of soft movements culminating in convulsions of the body (the orgasm reflex.)" He no longer had any friends, only students, helpers, and disciples. There were few limits that he placed on his own behavior: he did not hesitate to tyrannize over his patients and to take out his unending rage upon them; and in at least one "well-documented" episode, he did not scruple to have sexual relations with them either. And he continued with his momentous laboratory researches into the secrets of the universe.

By this time things were getting sticky for Reich in Norway—his activities were subject to public criticism in the daily press, and he was forced to look for a new place of exile. He was extricated from his difficulties by Theodore P. Wolfe, a young American psychiatrist, who had come to Norway to seek therapy and training from Reich, who became an unwavering disciple, and who, on his return to America, pulled strings in the State Department to obtain a visa so that Reich could immigrate. In August 1939, Reich arrived in New York and soon found a house in the unlikely region of Forest Hills—although, when you come to think of it, any place that he might settle down in would perforce become unlikely by virtue of his mere presence there. He needed patients, associates, money. To this end he secured a position to teach at the New School for Social Research. The course he offered was called "Biological Aspects of Character Formation," and he used it as a recruiting ground for patients and followers. His character continued to undergo change; in America, he became more distant and aloof from those who surrounded him; to his intellectual delusions he now added a touch of personal grandiosity. Thus he was prepared for the epiphany that appeared to him at Mooselookmeguntic Lake, near Rangeley, Maine, in the summer of 1940. There, looking out over the lake, at night and during the day, he observed flickerings and other phenomena of light and suddenly realized that he was seeing "an energy outside the body, outside matter itself." It was the fundamental energy of the cosmos that he had discovered, and he thereupon called it "orgone energy." Just as he had seen spontaneous movement in the "totally bodily convulsions of the orgasm" and in the "expansion and contraction of the bions," so now he saw it all around him in the "pulsation and movement of atmospheric orgone energy." This energy he believed to be the "same as the energy in the organism," in the body, and so it was the universal energy as well. It was visible everywhere and existed in everything; he had discovered the fundamental secret of Nature.

How had it come about that no one had ever seen this energy before? Sharaf offers this quite accurate, if not succinct, summary of Reich's ruminations on this question. (Reich himself was utterly incapable of succinctness.)

Unable to penetrate to the primordial, cosmic energy, man ... erected two systems of thought, mysticism and mechanism, which were essentially built around the concepts of "God" and "ether," respectively. God was behind all subjective, spiritual, qualitative phenomena; the ether behind all material, physical processes. Without intending to ... he had hit upon both the God and ether problem when he discovered the cosmic orgone energy. Orgone energy, like God and ether, was everywhere and permeated everything. It was behind both the physical processes in nature and the perceptual processes in the human organism. But whereas hitherto man had mechanically split up the cosmic energy into spiritual "God" and physical "ether" and then was unable to reach either, functional thinking discovered the cosmic orgone energy and was able to handle the concepts *practically.* And the same factor that throughout the centuries had prevented the discovery of orgone energy, of orgastic potency, of "what it is like to be a child"—man's armoring—now was at the basis of the tremendous fear and hatred of orgonomy.

With his delusionary system now in full bloom, Reich set about to observe the orgone energy closely, to gather, measure, and put it to use. He began, therefore, to build the orgone accumulator, in which the orgones would, naturally, accumulate and reach higher than normal intensities.

Early in 1941, Reich began to treat patients suffering from cancer with the orgone accumulator. He saw fifteen cases in all and claimed that the use of the accumulator caused cancerous tumors to disappear. He had now, he believed, discovered a widespread "biopathy" that might result in a cancer, but could make its appearance equally as "an angina pectoris, an asthma, a cardiovascular hypertension, an epilepsy, a catatonic or paranoid schizophrenia, an anxiety neurosis, a multiple sclerosis . . . chronic alcoholism," and so on into the pathogenic night. What he saw in all these afflictions was what he had been seeing all his life, "the pestilence of the sexual disturbances." "Cancer," he declared, "is living putrefaction of the tissues due to the pleasure starvation of the organism," as in their own ways are all the other ailments included in his encyclopedic "biopathy." The orgone accumulator was to serve—if not save—mankind by acting as a preventive measure or device against the development of such malign conditions.

In the meantime, Reich continued with his orgone therapy, and Sharaf has both the honesty and the courage (as well as the knowledge) to observe that Reich "never made clear publicly, though he sometimes did privately, that very few patients actually achieved orgastic potency." His degree of therapeutic success seems to have been even dimmer than that achieved by orthodox psychoanalysis, if such a thought is permissible. It is perhaps worthwhile, in this connection of unacknowledged failure, to note another involutional change in Reich's character that became visible at about this time (the mid-to-late 1940s). The former communist and social revolutionary had turned against the "masses", and in Listen, Little Man (1948), he wrote a jeremiad against the "average man," and in a tone, though not a style, that reminds one of D. H. Lawrence at his most shrill, accused the "little man" of not being able to give, of only being able to hold back and take, and of bringing the whole world to suffer from what he called "the emotional plague." He also had begun—again, like the later Lawrence—to identify himself with Jesus Christ.

In 1950, Reich pulled up stakes in Forest Hills and moved permanently to Rangeley, Maine, where he established his own little kingdom of 280 acres that he named Orgonon. During his early years in America, he had many patients but few colleagues, apart from the always devoted Wolfe. After World War II, however, Reich began to gather about him more colleagues from the medical and psychiatric worlds, as well as from elsewhere. Sharaf gives us a full run-down on all of them, and then wonders in a revealing statement why the work of all these people has come to almost nothing. "It says something," he writes, "about the lack of creativity or the blocks to independent productivity among the physicians who studied with Reich that only a few of them were able to write about and teach orgonomy after Reich's death." The only possibility that Sharaf leaves unnoticed is that this nullity may have something to do with the hopeless vacuity of the larger theory itself, if not of each of its specific components.

This period after World War II was also the time of Reich's widest vogue in the intellectual and cultural worlds. William Steig, best known for his cartoons for *The New Yorker*, was a patient and generous supporter. Paul Goodman and Saul Bellow had been in therapy with students of Reich. Isaac Rosenfeld and Norman Mailer were also touched rather strongly by what they found in Reich's writings, principally, of course, in *The Function of the Orgasm*. And here and there one ran into other people who were in Reichian therapy. If I may introduce a personal recollection, I remember from the early 1950s a conversation with a professional acquaintance of mine who, I thought, got particular pleasure in telling me detailed stories about his sex life. He was currently having an affair with a woman he had known long ago in high school and had recently met again. She wanted to be a musician and was working as a waitress to support herself. She was also in therapy with a Reichian. She lived in a small apartment in Washington Heights, and my acquaintance described it as being furnished with only three objects of significance: a bed, an orgone box, and a piano. Their relation apparently consisted in moving serially among these objects throughout the night. My interlocutor had sat in the orgone box but had no report on how or whether it affected him. It was all rather serious, slightly furtive and a bit absurd at the same time; it still seems to me an anecdote that preserves or illustrates something of the atmosphere of the decade following 1945. For all his notoriety in the literary culture, however, Reich was never able to build up much of a following or create an organization in any sense of the word. He was much too authoritarian, labile, demanding and emotionally uncontrolled to be the leader of a real group of colleagues and co-workers, to be *primus inter pares* among them.

Nevertheless, even as patients and followers came and went, Reich found plenty to keep himself busy with. The exploding of the atomic bombs and the subsequent development of nuclear science had set off a great wave of inner agitation in him. He was determined to find some way of enlisting orgone energy to counteract or neutralize atomic energy, nuclear radiation and the virulent fallout from the bombs. To this end he began to conduct experiments at Orgonon with radioactive material and orgone energy. The results, he reported, were catastrophic. When orgone energy came into contact with nuclear radiation, the former was altered by the latter and turned into DOR (Deadly Orgone) or Oranur. Mice died, the experimenters all got sick in one way or another, and the experiments had to be terminated. It was the discovery, Reich believed, of a planetary crisis—an entirely benign cosmic and organismic energy could be transformed into something lethal. It was most striking, he observed, in a remark whose meaning, I believe, he was only partly conscious of, "that a healthy person, when fighting evil, might himself change and develop the same characteristics he was fighting against."

Shortly thereafter, Reich became concerned with another new development. The atmosphere itself was changing. He saw "stillness" and "bleakness" fall over the once-sparkling Maine landscape. In particular, he noted the increased presence of "DOR-clouds," black and bleak, even in the midst of sunshine. It was all very much like John Ruskin, who in 1884 delivered his great lecture, "The Storm Cloud of the Nineteenth Century," a set of salient observations on changes in the atmospheric conditions of Britain and Europe brought about by industrialization, an analogous set of speculations upon how these outer changes were expressions of general inward spiritual deterioration, corruption and deadening in modern society, and a third series of remarks that are distinct intimations of the psychosis that was soon to overtake him. Reich's "DOR-clouds" also look forward to what was to become a wide public concern with atmospheric pollution and smog. But for Reich himself the clouds were made up of Deadly Orgone, and so he set about to do something about it. He invented a machine that he called a "cloud-buster," which, he claimed, could either concentrate or disperse atmospheric energy. The machine consisted of pipes and cables, and he asserted that he could either make rain with it or disperse the deadly clouds. So, in addition to everything else, Reich became a rain-maker, shaman, and witch doctor.

At the same time, this new phase of interest was marked, as usual, with "a burst of destructive rage in Reich's personal life." Reich still identified with his violent bully of a father; as Sharaf remarks, half-truthfully, half-wishfully, "Reich remained locked in repetitions of his past, even as he transcended them in his ever grander work." This alleged work was never brought to fruition because it was about to be stopped. And here, in the last years of his life, a very sad and rather disgraceful drama began to be played out. It seems to have actually begun when in May 1947, *The New Republic* ran an article that attacked Reich in general and insinuated that he was both a swindler and a megalomaniac. This article got quickly into the hands of the FDA, which began to focus its attention on what soon became known as the "Reich problem." By the early 1950s, the FDA, aided and abetted by the official organizations of both psychiatrists and psychoanalysts, was ready to move against Reich. It is a fairly painful story. Here was this aging and essentially harmless loony being treated by official establishment institutions as if he were some kind of public menace (in the early 1950s, orgone accumulators probably caused less harm and suffering than the measures that were then in use for treating cancer). As the FDA agents began to descend on Orgonon, Reich responded by turning up the gas under the pressure cooker of his own psychosis. The agents themselves he called, among other things, "Higs," an acronym for "Hoodlums in government." He developed an elaborate array of fantasies; among them were the conviction that President Eisenhower was a secret friend of his; that the U.S. Air Force was sending planes over Maine to protect Reich; that flying saucers, powered by orgone energy, and piloted by cosmic orgone engineers, were also about to make friendly contact with him and help his cause. (It was at about this time that Reich confided to Ilse Ollendorf Reich, who was then his wife, that he was the offspring of his mother and a man from outer space.)

The blow finally fell in February 1954, when, at the request of the FDA, the United States Attorney for the state of Maine filed a complaint for an injunction against Reich and all his work. Reich responded by refusing to appear in court. Instead, he sent the court a written document entitled "Response." That document contained such lulus as the following: "To appear in court as a *defendant* in matters of basic natural research would in itself appear, to say the least, extra-ordinary. It would require disclosure of evidence in support of the position of the discovery of the Life Energy. Such disclosure, however, would involve untold complications and *possibly national disaster.*" Undeterred by this incontestable lunacy, the court and the FDA pushed ahead and an injunction was issued: all orgone accumulators and all of Reich's in-stock soft-cover publications were ordered to be destroyed; his hard-cover books were ordered withheld from further distribution. Officials of the American Psychiatric Association and the American Psychoanalytic Association wrote letters of commendation to the FDA for its "effective action" against Reich. But the government was not done with him yet. Because he had failed to appear in court, Reich was now going to be tried for contempt. Reich decided to become his own lawyer and was tried in Federal Court in Portland for four days in May 1956. He was of course convicted and sentenced to two years imprisonment.

Quite evidently almost entirely gone by now, Reich was only confirmed by all these measures in his belief in a worldwide "Red-Fascist" conspiracy that was acting against him. He appealed his conviction, but to no avail. The Portland *Evening Express* for 11 March 1957 reported Reich's words in court as follows:

He pleaded against being imprisoned, saying that if the sentence were carried out, it inevitably would deprive the U.S. and the world at large of his equations on space and negative gravity.

These equations he said . . . are carried only in my head, known to no one on this planet. This knowledge will go down with me, maybe for millenia, should mankind survive the present planetary DOR emergency.

It would mean certain death in prison of a scientific pioneer at the hands of psychopathic persons who acted in the service of treason against mankind in a severe planetary emergency.

On 12 March Reich entered prison. It was a shameful business, as was the earlier destruction of all the orgone accumulators the FDA could find and the literal burning of tons of Reich's publications. On the morning of 3 November 1957 Reich was found dead in his prison cell. He had died of a heart attack during his sleep. Three parts crazy as he was, he had during these last bitter years behaved with greater dignity and decency than those who were opposed to him.

"To be great," Emerson also said in "Self-Reliance," "is to be misunderstood." It hardly follows, however, that being misunderstood is a demonstration of greatness. Sharaf wants his reader to know that in his view Reich was a "great man," someone who has "disturbed the sleep of the world more fundamentally even than Freud or Marx." In one sense, this remark recalls the project that Wordsworth announced, and to which Emerson among other visionaries subscribed as well: to "arouse the sensual from their sleep / Of Death." Despite the extended and displaced connotations that Reich's work attaches to Wordsworth's philosophic use of "sensual," Sharaf retains his faith in Reich's perceptions, and urges that the scientific community "pursue orgonomic hypotheses will all due speed." There is little likelihood of such pursuit being taken up, but in the meantime, popular culture continues intermittently to display a fascination with various reformulations of Reichian thought. The real task that Reich's life and legacy point toward is one that we seem to find still more vexing than did the Romantics: how and where are we to draw the line between intuition and hallucination, between prophecy and madness?

8. Talk Shows: On Reading Television

AARON FOGEL

I.

In the organization of American speech, Emerson is the exemplary personal lecturer, with the steadiest rhythms, so even that at times they seem to have been printed out in white ink. "Some of his periods quite majestic," someone says about Conversation Kenge in *Bleak House*; but Emerson's sentences don't try for majesty. F.O. Matthiessen's description of Emerson's belief that the public lecture was "the art preeminently fitted for democracies" suggests that, for all his Carlylean rejection of the idea of the "masses," Emerson's own rhythm in fact worked toward a democratic prose sublimity, an even scattering of powers that he also saw in the New England landscape. Matthiessen's remark should also remind us that Emerson didn't invent the social practice of the personal lecture, but moved into the already active speech-jobbing world at the Lyceums to supplement his income, and to get out of preaching. He worked inside a given speech context, like any professor. While scholars and historians have to scan previous Puritan rhetoric for the roots of his style, we might get a more incongruous but in fact equally useful perspective, a way of grasping the motives for his even prose rhythm, by considering the format of the television "talk show" as the same—or a later development of the same—predicament in which Emerson found himself when he wrote and spoke.

"Talk show," a blandly paradoxical, extraordinarily valuable phrase from television language, implies getting together for the purpose of watching spontaneous but controlled personal talk—a planned letting go with emphasis on the secret rhetorical control in the "letting"—put on for the general public by a celebrity. It is talk supposed to show something about the speaker's opinions and celebrated inner being, without focusing on the specifically political issues of the community. This sort of get-together grows out of an old American style itself derived from Protestant modes of priestless worship and spontaneous witness-bearing by those possessed. The sly but honest term "talk show" of the present is as touched with rhetorical genius about this American speech form as the term "jeremiad." One doesn't need to specialize in American literature to see in Twain, James, and Hawthorne, for example, or in Gerda Lerner's account of *The Grimke Sisters*, or in a dozen other places, that a kind of pseudo-intimate public speech-quackery was on the front burner in the nineteenth century. In a historically expanded sense, the phrase "talk show" might refer us back (and then forward) to such diverse manifestations as the Quaker meeting for worship; glossolalia; the style of poetry reading in which the poet affects joking intimacy; many classrooms now (where we work against and with the etiquette of the talk show because it is the dialogue regime many students have unconsciously learned); the Army-McCarthy hearings; and the Watergate tapes in their public exposure: metaphorically all "talk shows." Of course, anyone who participates in this variety of dialogue rites and solemn inquisitions might be grossly offended by this reductive naming of everything in our discourse. But the blandness and generality of the term are just what make it useful in thinking about what Henry James anxiously called "the question of our speech." One instance will illustrate how the image of the talk show could appear in a context especially conditioned by Emerson. In *The Bostonians,* chapter 8, James, always worried about the sounds girls make, puts Verena Tarrant on display as the young American girl speaking, trained by her mesmerist father to lecture precociously about social oppression and to rant seductively about women's rights; James writes down parts of her lecture to make the reader feel a kind of embarrassment for her as an abused child forced by phony parents to say more than she knows. Her speech—Tinkerbell as Jeremiah—is James's idea of Bostonian and post-Emersonian barbarity, a travesty of self-reliance. Personally, she can be rescued from this activity only because she in fact knows her speeches and ideas are "not me," knows that her public lectures are depersonalized. The plot of voice in the novel as something both personal and depersonalized is too complicated to go into here. To simplify: her lover Basil Ransom, in a story which reads like a caricature of Knightley's teaching of Emma, wins her over by stubborn insistence that her "thou" does not put on talk shows. Putting aside James's own highly productive obsession with the picture of young women speaking in public as, psychoanalytically, women making sexual noise, there is a core of specifically historical insight here also. James would have grudgingly welcomed the phrase "*talk show*" into his fat prose in *The American Scene,* enclosing it in some of the gas-mask quotations marks he used whenever he let what he thought of as slang, vulgarity, and neologism take over. But the phrase, in fact, doesn't need such marks: it has a dialogical force most fancier rhetorical terms don't. For starters, of course, James himself, in spite of fleeing from America and its talk shows, finally wrote books more and more as recorded speaking, dictation, until the late prose "bore witness" to his own speech processes and baroque Protestant consciousness as incessant verbal production. He himself, that is, came home with a vengeance to the talk show, to the Emersonian device of raising Protestant witness to a kind of prose so even that the reader has to disentangle any emphasis from the evenness. Even in James this is, finally, an image of strong democracy. It is important that in *The American Scene*, for example, after saying with characteristic honesty about class barriers that he can't guess how the commercial travelers ("drummers") speak, he finally calls them, at the end of a long journey, his "friends." He hints that there was finally conversation between him and them which was not a talk show, and could not be transcribed.

To read America, then, we need first to learn how to read talk shows, which are the controlling contemporary form of public discourse. The scene of Verena's public lecture suggests a slightly different (if not necessarily contrary) gist to American public rhetoric from that described by Sacvan Bercovitch as the "ritual of consensus" hidden in the denunciatory jeremiad. James read America as a place of talk shows, and I think Twain and Melville, whose perspectives were different, did also. To read American rhetoric we need a critical approach to talk-showing which is somewhat different from classical approaches to oratory and sophistry. Raymond Williams, in *Television: Technology and Cultural Form*, gives an excellent account of television as "flow" rather than shows, but seems dead wrong when he calls the talk show its most trivial form, and then ignores it. This is probably because he writes in England. For American television, the talk show is not trivial but definitive; many shows thought of as something else (e.g., *Sixty Minutes*, discussed below), in fact belong more to the genre of the talk show than to the claimed genre. The difficulty is how to stop the flow for analysis without sounding to our own ears pretentious and phony. You make a fool of yourself if you interpret.

All sorts of rules make us ashamed to take television, and specifically talk shows, as objects of interpretation, but we ought to ask why this is the case. The answer is that television itself has succeeded in becoming the main distributer and organizer of our notions of shame and shamelessness, these two (and not sex and violence) being in fact the organizing themes of television. To define then, as abstractly as possible: the talk show is now the key to American television and perhaps American collective speech in general; it occurs when the main purpose of dialogue is not narration (cf., Erving Goffman), instruction, drama, or debate, but the suggestion and witness of personality; it distributes names; and its main task is to organize models of shame and shamelessness.

With this beginning definition of American speech as talk shows about shame and shamelessness, I want to take several shows, and do what is implicitly forbidden—read them. To do this, I have to reverse the usual notion that there is no intentional author of texts that in fact have authors, and read some television shows, in fact authorless, as allegories. For example, I will treat "real" personal names like Mike Wallace or Milton Friedman as allegorical, with hidden, sometimes sarcastic meanings intended by an Author. To read a talk show, we have to call the roll, or read the names as signifying something besides personal identity. In addition, we have to look at the proportions of monologue to dialogue. This emphasis on the verbal and the onomastic will be based on the possibility that television is in fact more "bookish," and less cinematic, than is usually thought. Descriptions of the time consumed in private, absorbing television, resemble earlier criticisms of the effects of novels on the middle class. As it is used in the consumption of private time, television is much more like books than like movies. Further, as is being increasingly recognized, the assumptions of film criticism have often misled television criticism into overemphasis on the visual. It might be useful to go to the other false extreme, and to argue that television is in fact primarily used as a marketing device for distributing words and names, with the pictures acting only as reinforcements: that television is radio with pictures, rather than a tiny "cinema" in the home. Our clichés about the "power" of television (as in ideas about Big Brother and surveillance), are distorted and perhaps paranoid when they become purely visual; it might be useful to describe television not as an instrument of panoptic control, but, in accord with a verbal model, as organized and pacified market Rumor, a new economy of words and names, in which political and economic rumor (news and advertisements), which used to come from "nowhere" (i.e., from "the people," anonymously), has now for the first time been successfully centralized, pacified, and controlled by the government or its surrogates.

Within this new peaceful displacement of the power of rumor, the talk show is a little sacred rite, nightly performed: a "host" organizes spontaneous personal talk, the revelations of idiosyncratic likes and dislikes; shames and shameless avowals; the personal rumors and private fictions of the congenial "guests." The dialogue itself is therefore a model of advertising, that is, a distribution of personal preferences supposedly free. This benign dialogue format, casual "freedom of speech," of course conceals what are in fact strict, genteel, and unstated rules. We all know, for example, how powerfully television, with its verbal etiquette, acts to censor or punish ideation. Ideas are the obscene on television: they are the collective and the general. Recall, for example, how Barbara Walters, on a talk show (called an "interview") during the 1980 campaign, successfully scolded Carter, then President, for mentioning war and racism in his campaign against Reagan. She shamed him into silence on these questions, though he was of course weak enough to be shamed. He was sup-

posed to talk about "real" and "concrete" things, i.e.,
his "feelings" about being President.

To pierce this dialogue-world, in which hosts deter-
mine the shame-frame of the dialogue, is obviously almost impossible. The talk show has the hegemony over
our contemporary dialogue-values. Written language is
cornered into insisting either on its obscenity or its in-
tellectuality: unfairness, abstraction, ideas, analysis.
Traditional critical language seems either like abstraction or libel (labeling, calling attention unfairly to persons and names). Even so, television's distributive rhetoric of names and shames within the Protestant (inner,
personal) talk show must be dealt with onomastically
and morally. If television's job is to market names, then
criticism of television has to address the names themselves directly, whether of common English words like
"Tide," "Cheer," and "Time" (which have been grabbed
as corporate properties), or of individuals whose names
are "household words." Those words must be read not
as individual or personal, but as meanings. The etiquette (and even the law) which forbids us to attack
names, while bombarding us with images and names, is
a form of censorship.

An anecdote may help to illustrate the point about
television's (largely) successful displacement of rumor.
Several years ago, on New York City television news, a
rumor story—they're increasingly rare—ran as follows.
A bubble gum company was near bankruptcy because
children had heard there were spiders in that brand. The
newscasters, as usual, tried to lead the audience by tone
of voice: though funny, the tone implied, this goes too
far. People were being put out of work. As in the lacing
of Tylenol with fatal poison, and all the discussions that
followed about the broadcasting of the story, anti-advertising moments—defamations of product names—give
us insight into the main function of television as a posi-
tive name-distributer. The archetypal critic of advertising may be Ralph Nader, but he, in fact, supports the

logic of commodities (he holds that there are real rational differences between one product and another, and that they can be known and publicized). The real irrational nemesis of advertising is popular rumor, starting up arbitrarily from "nowhere" to arbitrarily defame a commodity or a person or a social group—and it represents an intense threat to the main activity of television as the praise of products. Here we have a complex of feelings about television's marketplace benevolence and its organization of free speech into talk shows about personal likes and dislikes. Both the spontaneous bad-mouthing of the bubble gum (carnivalesque and funny, by itself), and the Tylenol poisoning involve a sudden translation of the image of the market as a place of individual choices into a place of general will. It is clear that sudden defamations, e.g., those preceding lynchings and genocides, are not innately good, and that, in fact, television often acts as a force of anti-defamation, which is why it is perceived as "liberal" by many hate groups. At the same time, it is also clear that television achieves this by playing consistently on the myth that all feelings, tastes, likes, and experiences are "individual," and that whenever (with the exception of elections) any general will or collective energy begins to peep through this mask it is demonic. The incessant moral of television is that whatever is collective is evil or, at least, terrifying. A history of anti-advertising in the United States in this century—of sudden general defamations of products caused by rumors true and false—gives us a broad feeling for one source of a general negative energy that has been whited out by television. It is because of the weight of the current economy of names—on television, the world is constituted by "real people's names" and "real brand names"—that we can't help being startled when this onomastic marketplace order is disrupted by some anti-advertising, no matter how poisonous. Adam Mickiewicz wrote, "Most terrible are words that are suddenly everywhere, and no one knows where they were started," referring, ambivalently, to the word "socialism."

2

Milton Friedman's *Free to Choose: A Personal Statement* appeared on public television in the winter of 1980, about the same time as a book with the same title, and both became the subject of critical articles that took issue with his ideas on economic and political freedom. The format of the show was as follows: after thirty minutes of entertaining lecture and soliloquy by Friedman in shifting economic settings (often with montage from nation to nation, with Friedman standing and talking in each land, comparing economic conditions), there followed thirty minutes of bickering with critics, many of them liberal, inside a small theatre room or lecture hall. That is, each lecture was an illustrated journey across the planet, and the debate which followed was academic and indoors. The debate was often spliced jerkily, hopping among topics to cut off extended thought. This format, whatever the theme of the show, gave it a broad structural resemblance to *The Tonight Show*, which begins with Carson's warm, sarcastic, populist "monologue," and then moves on to gossip and bickering with guests in a rule-governed format meant to seem spontaneous or bacchanalian. A specific discussion of Friedman's persona as a talk show host, of the balance of dialogue and monologue, and of the visual and verbal composition of the program, is necessary to understand its success as television.

Until about 1980, the television "conservative," as an image, was most often a little grotesque. He flaunted his obesity, his antique smoking apparatus, his sneer, his upper class accent: the shameless "heavy." The iconograpy was simple: defiant difference. The cartoon called "William Buckley," with its coffee-advertiser's voice (deep-brewed tonalities) and serpentine tongue, and the cleverest public television clown, "Louis Rukeyser" of *Wall Street Week*, with its deliberately ridiculous facial expressions and molasses sarcasm of extended metaphor, are two milder examples of television genius, self-stereotypy, by skilled actors; while such "real" figures as Nixon and G. Gordon Liddy also appeared as conservative grotesques, baritones, heavies, signifying their indifference to "phony," slick liberal norms of bearing and voice. More could be said about these stock images of the Tory or conservative, which are as old as Walter Scott, Dickens, and Gilbert and Sullivan. But what is important here is that during the 1980–81 period, this iconography changed. The persona called "Milton Friedman" in the show under discussion was part of the change. He arrived as something of a surprise, light-hearted, Zen, a Hasidic rabbi of the earliest (the holiest) phase—"sting like a bee." Friedman is no grotesque, no visible snob; on the contrary, he's sprightly, a sprite, anti-grave, almost weightless in his bearing, full of sharp but forgiving ridicule. He resembles Puck, or Shakespeare's Autolycus in *The Winter's Tale*, or Moll Flanders, in his mobility, and is an embodiment of the romance of pure exchange. Not addicted to heavy sarcasm, his voice does not stick in the throat with irony (unlike Buckley, Rukeyser, or Cavett, i.e., unlike the television "intellectuals"), but flows on: realistic, light, mobile, healthy. The "liberals" now became the "heavies." Friedman won.

Friedman's persona made great romance television. As puckishness, natural insight, Friedman was, personally and theoretically, "on the air" during the half-hour lecture that preceded the debate: thirty seconds in Japan, a minute in Berlin, five in Calcutta, and then off to the next mortal habitation, in which he showed how foolish mortals make the mistake of not realizing that the free market is the answer. The vertical plane of television, its unearthly light in the air in midroom, and its power by something that is not montage to juxtapose all places and create the image of a planet without distances, solidities, gravity, barriers (television probably does "on the airness," or risky heights and dives and semi-controlled flights better than any other medium)—all this suited Friedman's puckish economy and his idea of freedom easily. The economy here was aesthetic, not political. Though there is, in fact, no "global village" created by technology, the set is convincing. Television has done very well with Shakespeare's romances, with their deliberate violations of geographical reality, their spirit of natural exchange and free fall that turns into flight, personalized in the merry thief whose wicked acts only needle poor earnest earthbound buffoons (liberals) unable to see the larger natural patterns and freedoms. On television this hopeful romance of inevitable freedom can't help but ring true. Emerson and Thoreau and Whitman of course recognize geographical places even at their most transcendental, but Friedman enacted with absolute innocence what Quentin Anderson calls the "imperial self," the ability to make "A Personal Statement" which somehow includes everyone from Calcutta to Alaska: his personal statement was the world.

Not only television technology, but also the dialogue format gave formal support to this propaganda of the air. The transition from monologue to bickering suited the main thesis exactly. If an opening sermon endears us to the host who plays "The Natural" and has put us into his redemptive key, any following dialogue necessarily arouses the feeling that the questioners are jackals, a species of interference. In the Friedman talk show, we moved from the neat, carefully planned, spontaneously free global soliloquy, in which the individual theorized the world as his own freedom, to a dialogue form that was only quarrelsome, fragmented, and hectic, with no chance for sustained

thought. Opponents were edited back to demonic out-
cries (like the three-sentence letters to the editor that
appear in *Newsweek* or on *Sixty Minutes* to serve as
angry blurbs). There is no better argument for the definition of freedom Friedman implies than this fractured
dialogue form, edited to resemble the stock exchange
floor, each harried broker shouting. Whatever partial
truth there may be in such a picture of the world's
polyphony of ideas, the formal implication is that
organized and collective human relations (dialogue) are
necessarily chaotic, while individuality (the soliloquy
or monologue) is coherent inclusiveness. This is not
simply lecture followed by discussion, but a formal
proof of the individualist thesis: individuality is concentration, sublimity, and freedom, while community
is only interference.

Arguments against interference in the natural flow
go snugly on television. While readers of written words
may, as Bakhtin suggests, experience dialogical interference as ecstatic "polyphony" (individual voices themselves are for Bakhtin composites), or as comedy, interference on television is "static." "Don't gimme no
static." Static—accidents of transmission which remind us that the air is not simple transparency but a
substance—is sometimes a pleasure, as in the *Rice
Krispies* trinity Snap, Crackle, and Pop. Mostly, however, static interference is dreaded. Friedman's inter-
locutors appeared as negative "static," Job's counse-
lors, an evil Snap, Crackle, and Pop. The possibility
that interference can be good, as in rescue, or that social life is in fact filled with interferences, good and
bad, is evaded by this rhetoric. Television that tries to
choreograph interference is usually perceived as "radical" even when its morality is very conservative: the
endless jostling and regrouping in the style of *Hill
Street Blues*, for example, is an urban dance that often
affirms the feeling that collectivity is a "jungle"; but it
is considered an "ultra-liberal" show.

There was, however, one audible but unintended interference in the successful presentation of Friedman's monologue, though it requires a kind of atypical listening: the jarring coincidence between the "personal" name of the speaker, Friedman, and the key word, freedom, which he offered as a one word solution to the world's miseries. Middle class personal names, ideally, are meaningless, and don't identify job or social status—only the pure person. A personal name with a clear meaning has this purely personal reference interfered with by objective impersonal forces in language itself. Meaningful names are part of comedy in the novel: the more clearly meaningful, the more funny. The idea that names have meanings is itself funny, even obscene and contagious to us, from *Tristram Shandy* onward, because it reminds us that our names are not finally ours. The name ceases to be free when it becomes a meaning. In Friedman's "Personal Statement," there is a jar in Tennessee, though he remains seemingly unaware of it. Emerson (who admits in his journal that he can't help laughing at odd names) described how each thinker tries to elevate some personal image or word to universality and is astonished when others have not cathected the same images or words in the same way. Those who do succeed in making their personal ideas seem universal are "representative." But Friedman's enormous pleasure in and certainty about his own definition of "freedom" is complex. Is he a "representative man"? To say the least, the word is already one of the great ideas; but Friedman's personal appropriation and representation of it has a bizarre flavor. It is as if he were ridiculously and unconsciously appointed—and as if he had not himself freely chosen his personal totem word— because he is unaware of its connection to his resolution of the Oedipus complex by identification of the paternal name as the universal idea. Comic, Shandean coincidences between one's own name and one's terms (think of Hume's *A Treatise of Human Nature*) do not always invalidate the ideas, and when conscious often cohere drolly with poetic skepticism. But in Friedman's show the effect is more discordant, and the suggestion of an unconscious coincidence between his terms and his narcissism voids the romance and freedom of the show, to make for a feeling of embarrassment and shame for Friedman's Personal Statement, as for Verena Tarrant.

Friedman's statement, then, appears as an infatuation with his own name, not with freedom itself. We might recall what Freud says in *Totem and Taboo* about the influence of our names on our obsessions and ideas, as well as on our dreams; but if this seems reductionist, we might remember also that Emerson himself asks us to look through any discourse for its biographical motives. We are playing by Friedman's own individualist rules when we ask how his personal name dwells in his concept. If there is an Author, he is being mocked: he is not free, but freed. He has his name and his thoughts, like the rest of us, as given. At least in the economy of names and ideas, an invisible hand does exist. Reading Friedman's personal name on the personal talk show, we have freed ourselves to read television unfairly, personally, onomastically, in a literary way, as Blake read the names Locke and Newton to mean imprisonment and negation. Television's power to generate shame can work against the host as well as for him.

Friedman's show, then, turns into a selfish limitation of the inexhaustible idea, freedom. In this instance, by reading a personal name, the signature that we are not, according to the rules, supposed to interpret, we suddenly understand better why Friedman's version of freedom was so hard for the other speakers to confront, and so typical of the dramatic powers of the talk show. The name-idea identity worked on the audience's rhetorical unconscious. It isn't that there is "no such thing" as freedom, nor that freedom is just a bourgeois illusion, nor that everyone makes his own name his idea, or other such occult nonsense or cant, but that in particular Friedman's unconscious definition of himself as freedom was what might be called a burlesque of the Emersonian process of "representation" of a great idea by the self in action. Friedman, in this performance, was a contemporary incarnation of the monological: his public word was unconsciously identical to his private name: hence he was a celebrity or successful allegory for a moment, a perfect figure for a talk show, a man mechanically identical with a personal idea in a medium notoriously dishonest about the power of words. This aesthetic economy is not really representation, either in the usual senses or in Emerson's sense; nor (it doesn't have to be said) is Friedman's own psychic economy the economy of the entire world.

3.

There are two polar images in the production of entertaining talk on television. The first is dialogue as inquisition: coercion to speak; roasting; the grill. The second, apparently contrary idea, is the fantasy of a public gathering in which all participants talk equally, with total ease and freedom. Johnny Carson works as close as possible to the image of free-and-easy dialogue, though joking sometimes about actual "plugging" and lack of spontaneity. Mike Wallace does a version of the inquisitor. The two of them are probably the most popular, and most institutional, talk-showers on American television now. But in some sense, however antithetical they look, they are the same figure. There is an odd identity between inquisition and entertainment in Puritan consciousness. Carson forces the shameless pseudo-confessional celebrity talk easily and playfully, in prefabricated chats the audience knows are forced, and Wallace, though apparently a journalist twisting real shame out of real people, is an entertainer. *Sixty Minutes*, however, does take its special character as the *tour de force* of American talk shows (it is the most watched show) from being the show that openly exhibits the extortion of shame-talk, the most important commodity on television. It exercises a sort of eminent domain over private lives and speech, with little comic undertow. (To express its own symmetrical and demonic relation to *The Tonight Show*, *Sixty Minutes* finishes up, instead of beginning, with a comic monologue. A dry guy named Rooney, television translation of the *New Yorker* cartoon, talks for about five minutes, as a middle-class man harrassed, but resigned, to the irrationality and inefficiency of the market. He is a sit-down comedian, often behind a desk with a display of knickknacks. This after-inquisition mint is provided to soothe any bad feelings aroused by the dialogical terror. Rooney returns us to the norm of the genial talk show from which *Sixty Minutes* is in fact a fantasmal departure.) As a sort of Sunday religious ritual, *Sixty Minutes* seems to fulfill a need for inquisitorial process glimpsed as the hidden ground of the benign daily talk show. The public need to have weekly scam overrides everything else. Sunday shame must be produced. "Real people" must be pursued. Doors must slam on the camera. How could this be anything but funny?

It's not. In many democratic tragic spectacles of coercion to speak before the people, the speech-forcer—like Oedipus, Lear, Joe McCarthy—extorts speech and plays inquisitor only to have the answers punish or destroy himself. The sublime and tragic pathos here comes from the democratic undoing of the insane paternal inquisitor: "justice." In the production of language by *Sixty Minutes*, however—as in the contemporary "nonfiction" novel, and other gimmicks whereby professional writers dig up vulnerable lower-class lives, keeping their "realistic" hands off those with real power—the reporter himself stands objectively above the events, not, potentially, an Oedipus. America is shown to be a great summa of little scams, but the talk-showers, with their own array of stammering Dickensian names—Harry Reasoner, Morley Safer, Dan Rather, and Mike Wallacer—are never clearly spotlighted as scammers themselves. No one asks Wallace what he earns, whom he can't roast, whom he can't quiz, and what mystery privileges him to interrogate without any apparent Oedipal (that is, democratic) risks to himself. Put more simply, there is no possibility that an interrogation by Mike Wallace will lead to his own incrimination, as it does for Oedipus. At the same time, the show *deliberately* arouses the audience's resentment of Wallace and the Oedipal fantasy that some day he will be caught in his own inquiry. It is an extraordinary exploitation of the public's Oedipal (in the dialogical sense) fantasy that the speech-forcer will be punished, the judge arraigned.

The real invulnerability of the inquisitors, however, is responsible for the show's lack of either humor or Oedipal depth, and therefore its terror. The feeling of terror aroused—though it isn't the worst of shows— is amplified by the sense that the hosts can't exercise real journalistic freedom. In its weekly portrait of evil and confidence games, it hounds corporations and persons equally. But because the screen describes individual faces much more explicitly than abstract organizations, there is disproportion: the individual caught by the talk show dragnet is humiliated; the corporation is only needled. People are massacred, institutions, teased. This disproportionate terror, however, is what makes *Sixty Minutes* accurate. It almost admits that it is a sponsored persecution of individuals, not an exercise of the freedom of the press to criticize institutions. (As an aside, it is almost too clear that the individual names of the inquirers—or at least the show's original cast—are allegorical, i.e., that, from a psychoanalytic perspective, these people became interviewers *because* of their names. If we saw "Harry Reasoner" in a text of Dickens as the name of an interviewer we would say it was grossly heavy-handed. A "Mike Wallace" is all too obviously someone who uses a microphone to get other peoples' ass against the wall. "Dan Rather" comes from the Hebrew *dan*, meaning *judge*, the name obviously meaning "I'd rather judge." The subtlest name, "Morley Safer," as Louis Zukofsky noted (see *"A"-18*), is freighted with allegorical meanings, *sefer* in Hebrew being a book of wisdom, but with the *a* grotesquely displacing the *e* (cf., Friedman/Freedom) to show the safe position of the inquisitor. "Morley" is obscure, and may be a corruption.)

Carson may be the only host on television strong enough, secular enough, to beat Wallace, and so his interview by Wallace on *Sixty Minutes* had a special clumsiness. Carson first maintained the comedic stance that all dialogues, including inquisitions, are "routines": he started off by confessing preemptively to the theft of candy at age twelve. Wallace, looking envious, seemed to resent Carson personally for getting away with an innocent and silly production of forced talk that earns more money. It was a little like Satan's hatred for Adam. He wouldn't let Carson joke. He earnestly demanded "moral seriousness." Why didn't *The Tonight Show* address serious social issues at bedtime? Carson allowed as how he was just an entertainer. And so on. At last, Wallace alleged Carson's alcoholism, and Carson seemed taken aback, but became serious and "human." This typical mawkish dialogue between the two best-known hosts on television had the value of showing the antithetical images of speech-production together: inquisition and burlesque.

In one sense, Carson won the match in spite of the final throw. His speech, funnier and more conscious, succeeded in making Wallace's look like a routine. As a comic genius, he knows more about inquisition than the inquisitor, and has long carnivalized question and answer. In the routine "Carnak the Magnificent," for example, he wears an oversized turban and receives at his desk a pile of sealed envelopes that contain questions. He places the envelope near his brow to untuit to the question inside, and announces an answer. He then tears the envelope at the side, blows into it a little gratuitously to open it, and reads the question. The reversed connection between question and answer is usually obscene and infantile. In this routine, which fits at least some of the rules Bakhtin describes for carnivalization of philosophical dialogue, the answer precedes and burlesques the question. The forms of authoritarian examination, catechism, interrogation, and testing get a sort of mild party-game comeuppance. The audience often becomes particularly manic during this routine.

Yet because of the Puritan confusion of inquisition and entertainment, Carson's mask seems sad, America's version of The Grand Inquisitor, pale Gilles. This much is clear: in spite of the laughter of Carson's comedy, he is as much undercut by the role of inquisitor as Wallace is by the role of unconscious comedian. They are the same, shame hosts, organizers of speaking models and shamelessness. Obviously the "battle" I have just described adds up to nothing, no difference. By comparison, if we look at classical organizations of dramatic speech, we will see lasting differences, whatever deconstructive criticism might suggest. Aeschylus's Clytemnestra and Cassandra, for example, though they might seem to be at first the same or similar because both speak obscurely in the field of generally dark, politic speech in the *Agamemnon*, turn out to be radically different: we are shown enough to see that prophecy is not the same as tyranny no matter what the resemblance in their double talk, and no matter that all "political" speech must be self-obscuring. With

Carson and Wallace, the difference, at first apparently
so clear, between an inquisition and a chat, dwindles
to nothing. Television is the production of forced talk
shows, and there must be incessant confession before
the public, in one form or another. Speech is the last,
not the first, commodity.

4.

In this context of speech-sameness, in which free entertainment and inquisition have become the same
things as produced commodities, we ought to look
back at the rhythmic samenesses in Emerson's writing
with a changed respect. He copied into his journal this
slogan from Schlegel: "In good prose . . . every word
should be underlined." Aware that his own gifts were
lyrical and not dramatic, he also complained of the
absence of dialogue in his period: "It is no easy matter
to write a dialogue. Cooper, Sterling, Dickens &
Hawthorne cannot." The charge seems startling (Dickens can't write dialogue?), but then just. Recognizing
an absence of dramatic dialogue in himself and his contemporaries, as talk-showers rather than dialoguers,
Emerson chooses to underline talk-showing until it becomes an emphatic prose in which each sentence
stands alone but linked. His form tries to tear itself off
from the demand by the culture that he provide talk as
show, by appearing to meet it, and then subverting it
with concentration and force. That is partly why his
compositional method was a continuous reordering
and reshaping of journal entries. In his lectures and
essays, it's as if someone came overprepared to an in-
formal gathering, so that in the steady pressure of the
style, he denies (even while seeming to practice and
preach), the ideal of easy spontaneity. The effect of this
prose style of underlined talk showing is to seem
neither artificially dramatic on the one hand, nor insip-
idly conversational on the other, but instead disturb-

ingly even, rebelliously calm. Compared to Santayana's sanctimoniously dependent phrasing or James' self-mesmerizing and self-criticizing syntax, Emerson's sublime of prose evenness has great lyric force which quietly detaches itself from other American rhetorics. His even, constant emphasis, equal weight given to everything, lack of subordination in syntax and sentence connections, was not just whitewash or naive optimism (though those charges are of course valid), but something more like trickery, an invitation to do away with democracy as weakness and replace it with democracy as force. This kind of rhythm leads directly to Faulkner's italicized historical voices, in which emphasis is constant and incessant, everything is stressed. This style, slightly thinned out by Whitman's metaphysical image of a "uniform hieroglyphic," the grass as writing, might be called democratic distribution: every particle is to be strong, not weak. Emphasis should fall evenly everywhere.

Most commercial talkers we now have are eirons—Carson, Wallace, Rukeyser, Cavett, Brinkley—winning their credentials and their right to interview by a prior display of thick cynicism and juvenile sarcasm in what might be called the "ornery ornate" voice. We know they're fit to interview because they scoff in mixed metaphors first. This "intellectual" style is, as a student of mine miswrote on an exam, "socrastic." Emerson seems to have suppressed his own scoffing and sarcasm for a kind of whiteness. It may be partly a racial tic, or too angelic, but it is also an attempt to overcome irony as the forced production of speech, in which the writer is either the confessional author, or the organizer of a dramatic inquisition. In his even emphatics, Emerson tries to project the ideal replacement of forced ironic talk-showing by a maturity arrived at without resort to the two antitheses, grand inquisitorial drama (possibly Catholic) on the one hand, and voluntary confession to everyone (possibly Protestant) on the other. Emerson

wanted a public speech which had outgrown this dialectic, in fact, a public speech whose sublime was not that
of compulsively generated guilt or shame.

Of course, we could say that he failed. We could
say, as all dramatic consciousness does, that no one gets
past, or ought to get past, the Oedipal form of public
inquiry: the forced exploration of the guilts and shames
of social selves. He goes very far, however, in trying to
purify this process of itself: to purify Puritanism of its
idea of process as guilt and shame, and its feeling that
the only valid dramatic speech reveals these feelings.
Sometimes our consciousness can't even recognize
speech that lacks these features as meaningful, and calls
it "nonsense." An American in the Emersonian line
easily dismissed for nonsensical egalitarianism of emphasis, Gertrude Stein, wrote a play about Woodrow
Wilson, the whitening idealist, which begins, "First
scene. Not a drama. Not a dream"—and another play or
libretto, *Four Saints in Three Acts,* whose heroine,
Sainte Therese, has a name which resembles "s'inter-
esser," to interest oneself, or self-reliance as sanctity.
We could say critically about her, as about Emerson,
that the time-sense, the "continuous present," is only a
secularization of the *Acta Sanctorum* which Emerson
described Carlyle as reading, exclusively, in old age, or
that it is "masturbatory." But Emerson and Stein both
register the comedy in the continuous present more
than the piety, and seem unthreatened by their own
"masturbatory" affect to the extent that it is that. They
were not the inventors of the fundamentalist free-self-
show as guilty masturbation in public, but its healers.
They recognized the duplicity of these rituals, and tried
to reuse the act of self-reliance for purposes less hysterical and more droll. Wallace Stevens, loading his conscious and comic diction with words that, like his own
names, repeat one vowel (e.g., sigil, eve, virtuoso), is
another comedian in this vein. As against the telling
criticisms of Emerson by Anderson or by Melville, the

Emerson I'm describing knew American speech from the inside, as a participant, and knew it as a scene of forced-dialogue-talk-shows energized by hysteria about sex and cash: guilty witness of what the private self has done, in its shameful scams. The lack of any dramatic form in Emerson is, of course, a limit. But Emerson has to kill the (to him) false dramas and orations generated by guilt and shame first. If no free confession really exists, if all dramatic confession ("no dialogue in Hawthorne") is not freeing, but only forced speech masquerading as moral revelation or visionary spontaneity, the calm and even distribution of light through his (secretly bitter) emphatic prose is an effort to "transcend" the Oedipal art of confessional societies, and to point out the delusion that the speech they generate is finally "free" and "true" because publicly confessed. Emerson tries to bypass confession, outer or inner, to suggest calmly that these processes may be only the mannerisms of forced dialogue, not of freedom. Whether he succeeded in this large ambition won't count; the prose rhythm succeeds in persuading us that another kind of poetics, neither inquisitorial nor confessional, might be possible.

9. *Quentin Anderson, Redux*

JACQUES BARZUN

"Those were the days!" The exclamation is always true; it is not the sign of an illusion created by a long perspective; for unless the time recalled was marked by disaster (in which case the warm feeling does not arise), there is in any past something wonderful that has since been lost—its uniqueness, to begin with. And then it is the very nature of history to create and destroy, so that all one can hope from the passage of time is that the new will make up in another fashion for what it kills. Memory has every right to bring back the dispossessed hour with its former glow.

"Those days" were the mid-1930s. The moment resembled that stage of convalescence when strength is felt to flow back like a slow sweet tide through the veins. Yet one did not want to stir excessively, because there is a rare comfort in being a coddled patient and because the illness may return. In the autumn of 1934 the Great Depression was not over, but the fear that it might be fatal was. Measures were in hand; action no longer seemed pointless; the contemplative mood could be indulged in about prospects other than the bleak.

The far world, to be sure, was still full of horrors and menaces: violence in France, madness in Germany and Italy, state crime in Russia, tight-rope walking over the abyss in Spain, and folly in England. But on the American scene the renewal of faith went with a quiet cultural revolution. The Paris Exiles' return had brought over modernism in full force, coupled with many agreeable European ways of living and feeling. The success of the WPA Theatre acclimated government aid to the arts. The claims of Marxism and of Neo-Thomism on young minds showed for the first time (or so it seemed) what the battle of ideas means in a civilized country. The paperback book (Pocket Book at twenty-five cents) was promising a great extension of the private bookshelf, and the gramophone disk, soon to be long playing, was providing for the first time in history the full repertory of music, independent of current fashions in program making. The Paris World's Fair showed the free countries of the West still original and superior in taste to the regimented powers dedicated to a conventional "People's culture" without reality.

Meanwhile, the Columbia scheme of general education was gaining converts everywhere. It revolutionized the University of Chicago under Hutchins and Adler; it even reached Harvard—in theory. By extension, outside the academy, little groups of business and professional men (soon to be know as Fat Cats) gathered at night to discuss the Great Books and then went about their social ways naming names unfamiliar to boardrooms, such as Hobbes or Diderot, and quoting subversive sentiments about morals, the state, or a market economy.

These thoughts and acts were so many expressions of a conscious intellectualizing of the United States by its own means, an unspoken denial of the "materialism" and "practicality" long imputed to a country which in fact had always been ready for another moral crusade or Great Awakening. Even the restoration of Drink by the repeal of Prohibition in 1934 looked like the Second Coming of Culture.

In the fall of that year in Columbia College, the course in great books known as The Colloquium had for its senior-section leaders two young instructors of disparate backgrounds and dispositions—Lionel Trilling and myself; he from the English Department, I from History. We had been undergraduates at the College, one year apart, but had never been friends, had not even appeared together in the same literary magazines. During that semester of our first encounter Lionel was struggling with Matthew Arnold for a dissertation that was to prove a masterwork and I was trying to readjust myself to a teaching schedule after sixteen months of research abroad, mostly in Germany. We had had no time to confer on ways of conducting the course or to begin forming a team by acquaintanceship over more trivial things.

But despite many differences of opinion we fell into an easy partnership and we were helped during the first few years by a remarkable group of students. A good many of them remain in the memory to this day for some outstanding trait. The most remarkable, without question, was Quentin Anderson. One could not help being immediately struck by his commanding stature and leonine head. What was the indwelling mind and spirit like? It is a relevant point that between teacher and taught the difference in age was less than half a dozen years; the personalities of students therefore made a deeper impress than they would later, when academic experience begins to repeat itself and undergraduates tend to become types.

Quentin could never have been a type. That calm yet anything but stolid countenance, that deep resounding voice, obviously betokened something formidable in its kind, not necessarily good—stubbornness, perhaps, or its intellectual counterpart, bigotry—except that the nobility of the brow and candor of the eye excluded anything low and mean. Such speculations naturally did not occur at once and in the blue. They arose when prompted by the subject's behavior during class discussion. The Colloquium answered to its name and purpose only if it was a running conversation, guided as unobtrusively as possible along a reasonably straight line. After the opening challenge of an astute question on the book of the evening, every member must participate without further proddings. Anderson was not completely silent, like the occasional student who feels both shy and superior and has to be jolted out of his ivory turret; but Anderson did not, would not, break in, argue, outvoice the others. He waited for the periodic pause and let fall a few words. Laconic, often aphoristic, they always sounded as if to the point but were not always easy to follow. They had to be met by the moderator's eternal "What do you mean, Mr. X., by —— ?" which would in turn yield from Mr. Anderson a statement even more cryptic.

The remarkable thing was that neither Trilling nor I thought for a moment that Quentin was bluffing. On little or no evidence, we *knew* that he had done the reading and—what is more—had thought about it. We were not being kind to the youth who, we were aware, was the son of the most thoughtful of playwrights, Maxwell Anderson. We did not feel kind, we felt exasperated. The cause of this oracular reticence was beyond us, but not the fact that it was thought-full too. We tried the direct question: "How would you compare the politics of Hobbes with those of Machiavelli?"

A long pause: "Well, of course, Machiavelli came first." Silence. Then, somehow, by tactics akin to those of the picadores at bullfights, we extracted the notion that Hobbes must have read *The Prince*, digested the experience of over a century of religious and civil wars and, combining it with a Protestant outlook and an empirical philosophy, took the next step in formulating political dualism. (I do not vouch for the literal accuracy of this example, but *se non è vero è ben' trovato*.)

Uphill work?—yes, in one sense, but excellent training for the young instructors and the other students. It was soon clear that Quentin's apparent taciturnity was also a dualism, a pairing of innate modesty with high intelligence. When his first response to a direct question was a barely voiced exhaling of breath, which in someone else would have meant condescension or even arrogance, the true cause was fear of stupidly offending by stating the obvious. Hence, no doubt, the habit of wrapping up what was clear and simple in brief phrases, all uptight—minimal art.

But for the instructors there was worse to come. The program called for the writing of several short essays three or four pages long. Each paper was read and painstakingly "edited" by each instructor, for we were determined to help our students learn the ways of good prose, most of these exceedingly bright boys having suffered neglect in high school and Freshman English. The first essays tended to be full of jargon, abstractions, and pretentious images that were also incoherent. Amid this display the point or thesis was lost. By the third or fourth essay prose usually regained its rights. But first and last, Quentin's papers remained baffling. Being free of the common faults they deserved high marks; but since we could not make out what they said, owing to excessive compression and jumps in thought, it would have been unfair to reward their stylistic purity.

We conferred with the writer and with each other behind his back—three cryptologists at work on what all knew contained a significant message. I remember one conversation in which I countered my own discouragement by saying: "You must admit he is sui generis," to which Lionel came back like a flash: "sui generis to a fault." A more productive idea—also Lionel's contribution—emerged from that exchange. It was the recommendation (which we urged thereafter on all our writing students) to keep steadily pedagogic; that is, write as if teaching; do not allude or comment—explain. It was indeed a counsel of despair—the world was already too full of teaching and telling and educating. But the imagined model of the pedagogue did help, and it freed Quentin by assuring him that he was not being fatuous in writing and speaking what seemed to him painfully obvious.

In other words, the change toward increasing lucidity was really toward explicitness; the lucid mind was there all the time. His close friendship with Charles Frankel, also in the group, was a sort of warrant for his instructors' trust in that lucidity. The voluble, uninhibited Frankel had a classmate's insight into his friend's meditations and would act as spokesman-interpreter when words seemed to Quentin superfluous or otiose. The willingness to use them more lavishly came just in time, for the final examination in the Colloquium was oral—an hour of questioning not just by one's own pair of instructors, but by two or three from the other sections as well. Mr. Anderson did nobly, this side garrulity.

Recollecting these incidents would be of slight value—possibly picturesque and no more—if they were not indicative of important characteristics in the mature Anderson's mind and work. Unmistakable in them is, first, the tone of authority. It is a pleasing authority, born of intellectual self-confidence, not conceit or complacency. The prose suggests that we are in good hands; we feel sure of moving forward to a definite result. That feeling is what led a reviewer to say of Quentin Anderson's first widely read book: "it is the work of a mind large enough to confront the hardest questions raised by the fate of a very great American writer," Henry James.

The reticence that goes with the authority in Anderson points to another quality, which is that of synoptic vision. All the parts and relations of a complex state or event seem to mirror themselves quickly and fully in his perceiving center, and to stay there so plainly that utterance seems at once unnecessary and difficult. Ordinary minds sometimes experience the same paralysis of words when surprised by a stranger's failure to catch on to what any fool could see. Anderson's fellow-feeling for the elder Henry James contains this emotion, which might be called the feeling of revelation. The whole brightly lit mental scene makes words, few or many, appear powerless to reproduce it—especially since the vision was reached without climbing successive steps. Hence no mediating ideas to be described for others' benefit. That is why William James remarked that his father did not sufficiently understand other men's intellectual difficulties. Henry, Sr., kept lecturing and writing in the tone of one offering the world manifest truisms, and the world had not a glimmer of what he saw.

The work of Quentin Anderson, let me hasten to add, has had a very different fate; it was favorably received from the outset and it has been deservedly influential, on readers and students alike. One reason is that the frame of mind I have tried to describe—the French might call it *l'esprit de constatation*—is complicated in Anderson by a contrary movement of thought and feeling: his conviction, namely, that individual experience is unique and important. I should like to think that the kind of teaching prevailing in his day in Columbia College and embodied in the Colloquium reinforced young Quentin's native bent toward this view. For that teaching was rooted in the historical sense, the sense that individuality is not illusory and that the ultimate arbiter of truth is experience.

These two beliefs keep the mind from espousing reductive systems of the kind that has been so popular for half a century in the study and criticism of literature—the "methodism," akin to science, which dissects the work of art to find what it really consists of, as if its surface aspects were misleading details obscuring the law of its being. Anderson was never seduced by the glamour of such analytic procedures; and although he takes into account, from one such analysis, the workings of the unconscious, it is never with the intention or effect of reducing a writer's life and significance to the common denominator of a clinical formula.

So far from performing this fashionable trick, Anderson's contribution to the understanding of American thought has been to delineate what he calls the Imperial Self, the overarching entity projected by Emerson, Whitman, and others, and in which the unique individual self is meant to disappear, fused with other selves—not a conglomerate, but a merger: "When me they fly, I am the wings"; in short, the Absolute of the nineteenth-century transcendental idealists. Their spirits were so fine and their minds so much at home in the abstract that the chronological crossing of German philosophy with Hinduism captured them without a struggle. It provided, besides, a welcome translation upwards from the commercial reality of that rough, developing country, the United States.

Anderson, in his superb introduction to Walt Whitman's analysis of *Leaves of Grass*, shows how the same dilation of the self to cosmic size superficially fits the temper of actual democracy, which the Transcendentalists acknowledged only in spirit. In Whitman, the egalitarianism is applied to perception and emotion as well as to the social status of persons. Differences, preferences no longer subsist. "All" is a leveling word, a word with which to worship the "divine average"; All (which embraces things, too), All is (or are) equally deserving of love—a totalitarian state of nonchoice Anderson repudiates and distinguishes from the truly democratic. The Imperial Self is of course the negation of history as a fact and as a form of thought. But read this virtuoso essay, which draws on a stunning breadth of knowledge and imagination and which matches for lucidity of thought and phrasing any critical prose written in our time.

The Whitman piece shows that when Quentin wants to he can make his meaning as transparent as plexiglas. But in private life and sometimes, it is said, in his teaching, he has always reserved the right to be sibylline when he wishes. He must be still afraid to tell you what he thinks you know, which you will therefore resent being told. But that does not in the least make him an unprofitable conversationalist. I remember a trip we took together to Rutgers as university representatives, to see (I think) a new president installed, or perhaps it was to witness a prizegiving—the cause is dim in the past, but not the pleasure of a journey accomplished mostly in companionable silence, but lit up by wonderful comments from Quentin on the shifting scenes: humorous, sympathetic, allusive, and profound. The lunch, I know, seemed to him foreshadowed in the sound of the word "Rutgers." As for the language of academic convocations, he said it called forth the highest Christian virtues: its meaning can only be found by the exercise of faith, hope, and charity.

Despite the sharpness of his vision and his wit, Quentin's attitude toward his fellow man is uncommonly free of prejudgments. He visibly prefers amity, agreement, reciprocity to argument and ascendancy. His large deliberate motions of limb and head betoken an ample patience. His mental reflexes are controlled, and what controls them is a high sense of honor. For him, the conflicts worthy of thought occur in the inner life, and once resolved they call for courage. An anecdote reported by a devoted student gives a glimpse of these traits in action.

It was in the 1970s, during one of the student protests that followed the main outbreaks of 1965–68. Anderson was teaching a seminar whose members had decided without prompting that the class should be held, despite the one-day strike just declared. At some point in the session, two hefty undergraduates, one of them carrying a guitar, walked into the room without knocking and demanded that the students file out and join the protest. Quentin questioned his group with a look and, since no one rose in answer to the intruders' summons, concluded that the class adhered to its original resolve. He therefore told the two and their guitar to please leave. They muttered something and did not budge; whereupon Quentin slowly got up, took one each by the elbow, and marched them out the door. As the guitar player crossed the threshold, he turned to Quentin and said, "Well! if you're going to use violence!"

Did Quentin know—or remember—his great predecessor in this little one-act play? In 1803 William Blake found an intruder—a soldier—in his garden at Felpham. "I insisted on his leaving . . .he refused. I therefore took him by the Elbows and pushed him before me till I had got him out." Unlike Blake, Quentin did not further "push forwards down the road about fifty yards" and so avoided the trouble that ensued for the poet. But it must be recorded that these two historic and honorable Knights of the Elbow had equal courage, for the mood of menace in the days of student activism showed up the academic community as peopled almost entirely by moral and physical cowards.

Now that the campus struggles are "the past," it is pleasant to return in thought to the time of his beginnings and recall others of his Columbia generation who have also made a name. I have mentioned Charles Frankel, philosopher of history and assistant secretary of state for cultural affairs. In the same years the College graduated Carl Schorske, cultural historian of Middle Europe; Reed Harris, journalist and government official in charge of U.S. Information abroad; James Wechsler, editor and columnist; Herbert Jacobson, wartime U.S. Radio director in Italy and later head of the U.N. Tariffs and Trade agency; William Davenport, biographer, author of travel books, and unofficial envoy to the world of French culture; Robert Giroux, scholar, editor, and publisher; Arthur Morales, scholar and minister for education in Puerto Rico; Herman Wouk, novelist; John Berryman, poet; Robert Marshak, physicist and president of the City College of New York; Charles Wagley, anthropologist and leading authority on Brazil—the list could be made longer by a better memory.

But this sampling is perhaps enough to substantiate the claim to special notice of the time to which Quentin Anderson belonged and which his achievements conspicuously adorn. Indeed, what the mid-thirties offered those young men and others of their stamp exemplifies what Anderson had in mind when in the Whitman essay he disputed the conventional idea of Whitman as the poet of democracy. Glorifying a state of consciousness and behavior in which no distinctions subsist strikes Anderson as the negation of freedom. Such an equality of emotional result "would clearly make it impossible to realize the variety of talent for which equality of opportunity might provide the conditions." No simpler, shorter, neater way could be found of marking the difference between the democratic ideal that deserves the wise man's allegiance and the homogenizing process which upsurps the name and which is only the final, anonymous phase of civilization.

10. The Shape of a Career: A Conversation with Quentin Anderson, January 1984

DIANA TRILLING

DT: Quentin, can we start by having you tell me when and where you were born?

QA: I was born in Minnewaukan, North Dakota, on 21 July 1912. At that time my father was the principal of a high school in Minnewaukan. He and my mother had met at the University of North Dakota. They moved east in 1919, to Rockland County, on the Jersey side of the Hudson. Subsequently, we moved to Manhattan.

DT: Where did you go to high school and college?

QA: The Lincoln School of Teachers College, and then I was a member of the Class of '37 at Columbia. Earlier I spent a year at Dartmouth. I graduated from high school in 1931 and attended Dartmouth in 1932–33; then there was in interval when I was out of college because the family was out of money and in those years I was doing things like cutting firewood for sale and making experimental booze with a chemist friend.

DT: As a way of earning a living?

QA: No, we made it for our own consumption.

DT: For a moment it sounded as if you'd been in the bootlegging business. Then you came back and entered the class of 1937 at Columbia?

QA: As a sophomore. It was '34–'35, '35–'36, '36–'37 that I was at Columbia as an undergraduate.

DT: Did you stay on for graduate work?

QA: No, I won a fellowship and went to Harvard for two years of graduate work.

DT: That takes us to 1939. Then what?

QA: Then I was employed by Columbia in the humblest assistant role.

DT: As an assistant in the English department?

QA: Yes.

DT: Do you want to take us forward from that quickly?

QA: I lingered a long while over a dissertation and finally assumed an assistant professorship in 1953.

DT: You took your advanced degrees at Columbia, or only your Ph.D.?

QA: I took an M.A. at Harvard.

DT: That would have been between '37 and '39. Let me ask you something here, Quentin, that hasn't to do with your academic career. Was your father successful as a playwright in the thirties? Wasn't *Saturday's Children* his first successful play?

QA: No, his first successful play was *What Price Glory*. In 1924.

DT: Yet there wasn't enough money for you to go to college?

QA: Well, the money would come in and go out like the tide and it happened that in the early thirties there was a period of low water. My father did not accumulate money. He received and dispensed money.

DT: But wasn't *What Price Glory* one of the spectacular successes of all time?

QA: Yes. He had been an editorial writer on the *New York World* at a salary of $150 a week and during the winter of 1924 he was suddenly receiving $1,500 a week, which for that time was quite a lot of money.

DT: And yet he was so hard up that you couldn't go to college?

QA: During that first winter after I had been forced to leave Dartmouth, I recall that we owed the grocer $2,000.

DT: Where was your father living at that time, and who were some of his associates in the theater?

QA: We had purchased a house in Rockland County in which he lived much of the time after 1922. We also had various apartments in New York and early in the thirties we purchased a house in what is now Harlem on 112th Street, just off Manhattan Avenue, and we went back and forth between the Rockland County house and that house thereafter.

DT: Did you have any experience in the thirties of the WPA or the Federal Theater Project? What about the radical movement of that time?

QA: My own adventures with radical politics actually came later, in a period—during the candidacy of Wallace in '48—when I might well have been accused of being totally innocent of what had gone on earlier. But I had had some experience in the theater in the thirties. I was an assistant stage manager on one of the plays my father produced in the thirties, *Both Your Houses*. I was thereafter a walk-on in *Mary of Scotland* with Helen Hayes. That would be, I think, '33. It was not until the next year that I went for the first time to Columbia College. But I did have in that first production some contact with the world of radical politics but it was a peripheral one. A number of members of the Group Theater figured in the cast of that first play where I was assistant stage manager—Phoebe Grant, Morris Carnovsky, Joe Bromberg, Collins—and I remember gathering a sense of their attitude toward the society out of the experience of that production.

DT: Were they fellow-travelers, is that what you're saying?

QA: Yes, I would say that.

DT: Were you at all sympathetic to their view? Did you find it exciting and think that they were out there in the real world?

QA: I thought it was wonderful. During the period that *Both Your Houses*, the first play I worked in, was on tour, Roosevelt closed the banks.

DT: That was early '33, wasn't it?

QA: I recall a moment of apprehension of attitudes toward the capitalist society. Watching, for example, one of the actors, a very well-known one, casually snatch up a pair of opera glasses from a sofa on which they were lying as he walked through a lobby into the hotel. He liked the look of them so he took them, and my conviction was that he did that because ownership was not of the first importance. It's a very small incident but it impressed me.

DT: Was your father involved in the radical politics of the time?

QA: No. My father's early attitudes, which I knew something about because I'd read his poetry and heard him talk, had very much to do with a sense that arbitrary power was of the nature of government and he was an anti-government man. There was a tinge of radicalism which one might even speak of as a sort of anarchism. But earlier he had made his mark protesting various kinds of injustice and censorship. For example, he had written a famous editorial called "The Blue Pencil" directed against those who employed him on San Francisco newspapers. His early reporting involved, say, the mining strikes in Virginia and so on, so that in our household there was that sense of the possibility of opposition to the character of the society. But my father's only involvement in politics that were deemed left-wing came much later when he entertained the Spanish Loyalist ambassador and that got him on some lists. Actually, the political or quasi-political episode that I best recall from my earlier life in Rockland County centers on the Sacco-Vanzetti case back in the twenties. For everybody who lived on South Mountain Road, the artist's colony where we lived, the execution was a sort of day of mourning, and indeed it led my father to write his first play about the Sacco-Vanzetti case—one in which he made the central figure a Wobbly. That was called *Gods of the Lightning* and it was actually written in collaboration with a member of the Communist party, Harold Hickerson. The second play was some time later, *Winterset,* in the thirties.

DT: In other words, what you're saying is that your father's life and that of his friends, and therefore yours as well, were rather peripheral to the radical activities of the thirties.

GA: Yes. John Howard Lawson had lived across the road from us during our first summer on South Mountain Road, in 1922, but that had no direct meaning for me. It was only much later that I learned that he had been an active member of the Party.

DT: So you really came quite pure to your Columbia years?

QA: In the political dimension, yes.

DT: Now, when you left Columbia in '37 and went to Harvard, were you already planning to have an academic career or were you just going to see what happened?

QA: I was just going to see what happened.

DT: Whom did you study with at Harvard?

QA: Chiefly F. O. Matthiessen and Perry Miller.

DT: Was it the experience of studying with those two men that led to your special interest in American literature?

QA: Yes it was, although there, too, there was a happenstance. The great Lovejoy was teaching a seminar and I got turned down for that one and I took a seminar with Howard Mumford Jones in American literature, a seminar in which Henry Nash Smith was also a student, and that, I think, was decisive.

DT: Wasn't that an awful lot of Americanists at Harvard at one time: Matthiessen, Perry Miller, Howard Mumford Jones? Were they all teaching at the same moment?

QA: Oh yes. And of course Matthiessen and Miller were extraordinary men.

DT: Wasn't Jones extraordinary, too?

QA: Jones was extraordinary in the sense that he commanded a great deal of knowledge. He once described himself in my presence as the best title page scholar in America. I think he was notable more for conveying information than a view of how to tackle literature.

DT: Yet you say that your course with him was decisive.

QA: Well, one had to take a seminar and to do a seminar meant doing serious work. After doing a 125-page monograph on James Fenimore Cooper's *The Spy*, I was involved. Under Matthiessen I wrote a paper on Emerson and William James, and this I think was a pretty decisive event with respect to my interests. But it shouldn't be forgotten that in Columbia College I had also been exposed to the Romantics and the Victorians and that I therefore regularly taught courses in Romantic and Victorian literature when I became a Columbia teacher.

DT: In those years at Columbia between '39 and '53, what did you teach?

QA: I taught my own course in American literature when I became senior enough to do so and carried it on at the same time as I taught in the sequence of courses which dealt with the history of English literature. In that sequence my period was, as I say, the Romantic and the Victorian period.

DT: When you came back to Columbia in '39, Quentin, who was in the English department? Was Fred Dupee already there?

QA: He probably arrived a year or two later, I'm not sure of this.

DT: And what about Richard Chase?

QA: Richard Chase was in the department in the sense that he was at that time a graduate student. He began to teach in 1940. He was an assistant in English and became an instructor in '43 to '45. And then there was an interval when he was not at Columbia. I can't at the moment tell you where he was.

DT: I believe it was Connecticut College.

QA: Connecticut College, right. And then he rejoined Columbia in 1949.

DT: I may be wrong about this, Quentin, but it's my impression that when I was at Radcliffe in the twenties, American literature didn't have any real standing. Was that just my way of looking at things or was it so?

QA: Although American histories of American literature began to appear around the turn of the century, it was an exceedingly marginal academic study. You really have to date a change from the moment when Parrington and Brooks were superseded by the appearance of my teacher F. O. Matthiessen's *American Renaissance.*

DT: What was the nature of the influence that Parrington and Brooks first had and then of the change that took place?

QA: In a sense, the Parrington volumes were very much concerned with the nature of the American political inheritance. They centered on that and on the Jeffersonian attitudes, as Parrington understood them and advocated them. The three volumes of Parrington are shaped by that concern—what he thought of as the high political destiny of the United States. That meant, of course, that the things that were happening in Cambridge, England, the things that came across the ocean as influences from I. A. Richards and others—T. S. Eliot and his criticism—had a rather late impact, if you like.

DT: What about *The Flowering of New England?*

QA: Well, if you mean the five-volume series, that appeared as a sort of failed competitor of the Matthiessen book once the Matthiessen book was on the ground. And indeed the later aspect of Brooks' career, the presumption which suffuses *The Flowering of New England* that since we were a nation of considerable importance we had a literature which would somehow match that importance, was hardly thought to be serious by those who were regarding literature with the kind of scrutiny that—beginning with I. A. Richards and thereafter—literature invited. After all, although one wouldn't quite call Matthiessen a New Critic, he was one of those who felt that the examination of the literary text was the fundamental task of the critic. He combined this concern with his own political concern for a democratic socialism or a Christian socialism, as he liked often to put it. Yet the structure of *American Renaissance* reflects these political convictions in a rather indirect way: that is, he found in the five classic writers whom he wrote about a preoccupation with the values of democracy and incipiently with the values of socialism which were very far from any rather loose selection of things that had a political implication for Parrington. Matthiessen examined these figures of the American renaissance—Thoreau, Whitman, Emerson, Melville—as at once writers and people who might further the large project of making America truly America as he conceived it. In other words, his book isn't really organized because so much of the time it seems to be implying that if we would but listen to these classic authors, we might achieve the kind of political awareness which is appropriate to a democratic socialism. But what now remains in the minds of students about that book seems chiefly to be those passages in which he carefully examines particular portions of the work of the classic American writers. They became classic, so to speak, in his hands and in the minds of a great many of his readers.

DT: Did you have the sense while you were studying at Harvard that there was another intellectual center, in New York, and that you were carrying on an enterprise which might not have been entirely consonant with the chief enterprise of the other center?

QA: I can't claim that. I seems to me that I was remarkably unaware of New York. I was also unaware of what was going on at Harvard by way of political activity. I wasn't aware of Matthiessen's involvement in the Teachers' Union and the other movements on the Left which were noticeable at Harvard in those years for those who were paying attention.

DT: I bring this up, Quentin, because the years when you were at Harvard roughly coincided with the budding years of *Partisan Review,* and *Partisan Review* was actually looking for its sources of energy not in the American past but across the ocean—the continental novel even more than English writing. I was wondering about the fact that while this was so much the emphasis in New York, you had so contrary an emphasis at Harvard.

QA: Well, graduate students very often have their eyes very narrowly focused, and I must think of myself as of that order. I wasn't concerned with politics in an active way.

DT: I'm not talking about politics as much as about what we might call political culture.

QA: Nor was I concerned with newness, so to speak. I wasn't reading contemporary writers with any particular devotion. I had my Dostoievsky period as I had earlier had my Thomas Wolfe period, but my sense of the things that were occupying *Partisan Review* in those years was really almost nil.

DT: Oh, I don't mean to make *Partisan Review* the sole source of intellectual energy in the country. But let me ask you this. What was your awareness of Henry James while you were a graduate student at Harvard? What was your awareness of all the Jameses?

QA: I had caught from Jacques Barzun early on a sense that William James was a figure of great importance and attractiveness. That happened when I was an undergraduate. I don't think that I had read any Henry James at the time that I was a graduate student at Harvard.

DT: They weren't reading him at Harvard at that time?

QA: I should think not.

DT: How do you date and where do you place the beginning of the revival of interest in his work?

QA: The centennial of his birth in '43 led to an issue of the *Kenyon Review* which dealt with James. Earlier, in '34, there had been something I was quite unconscious of at the time, an issue of *Hound and Horn* devoted to him. But it was really at about the time of the centennial that that interest grew lively.

DT: What was the date of Fred Dupee's collection of critical essays?

QA: As I recall, that was '45, so it was very timely. But there was an earlier stirring. It somehow coincided with the war.

DT: Wasn't the Ralph Barton Perry biography of William James earlier than the forties?

QA: I recall it perhaps just starting the case in connection with my interest in William James while I was at Harvard. And indeed one of the things I did at Harvard was to read in the Houghton Library William James's collection of Emerson volumes with its annotations, which I carefully transcribed. It was the subject of some of the work I did for Matthiessen.

DT: In other words, in some ways when you first came to Henry James you were coming to him as part of a larger American configuration. He wasn't this alienated person, this expatriate that the *Partisan Review* liked so much; he was an American figure.

QA: I came to him as a scholar. I happened to read his father and the first thing that struck me was that here was a subject for a dissertation which hadn't been exploited. As I read the father and as I read the son, it seemed to me that there was a far closer relationship in their sensitive world than had earlier been assumed by anyone.

DT: Then it was as early as that, while you were at Harvard, that you read Henry James, Sr.?

QA: No, I'm now talking about something that happened to me at Columbia.

DT: So it was some time, say, in the forties, that the subject first posed itself to you of dealing with the father Henry and the son Henry.

QA: In fact, I'd made an abortive attempt under the direction of Lionel Trilling. I knew that I wanted to do a dissertation and he was willing to have me do one under him and I first tackled Henry Adams and found that subject resistant. I think it was earlier on that I had undertaken to work out an Emerson topic under Professor Rusk but having found Rusk not a congenial director for a dissertation, I asked Lionel Trilling whether he would direct me and I shifted my subject from Adams to James. Then I read James for the first time.

DT: Let's go back to the population of the Columbia English department at that time that you were teaching and doing your dissertation. Who were some of the people? As I recall, Charles Everett was there, was he not?

QA: Yes.

DT: And Lionel and . . .

QA: We had Harry Dick, who had written about biography. But the figures who were most in the public eye were Mark Van Doren and Joseph Wood Krutch.

DT: Not Raymond Weaver?

QA: Weaver was certainly known as the man who had written the first modern book on Melville.

DT: Wasn't that very important to you?

QA: It was important only historically, because I felt that Melville had been noted and seized on by Weaver. But the book itself already had successors that I regarded with more interest.

DT: And then among the younger men at the beginning of the forties there were Fred Dupee and Richard Chase. And of course Andrew Chiappe.

QA: Chiappe was certainly important. He was indeed one of the younger men but he was certainly visibly a growing power.

DT: As a cultural historian, how did you feel about the difference between the approach to the teaching of literature at Harvard and the approach at Columbia in those years?

QA: Having been a Columbia undergraduate, I was accustomed to the relatively small classes and the relatively intimate sort of instruction that Columbia afforded. Since Harvard threw its graduates and its undergraduates together in many courses, the character of the Harvard courses was far more a matter of a teacher at a lectern in a room with 150 people. I did, of course, have the advantage of the tutorial attention of eminences like Matthiessen and Miller. But for the most part, the instruction, as I say, was in very large classes and had nothing of the sort that I'd experienced at Columbia as an undergraduate. I had been an undergraduate in the colloquium on important books which was taught jointly by Jacques Barzun and Lionel Trilling. That had been the most exciting of my classroom experiences and remains so. Columbia, after all, had given me a sense of a way of pursuing literature.

DT: Can you describe what that sense was?

QA: One didn't dream for a moment of seeking to detach literature from its cultural matrix, even to the extent that it seemed detached at Harvard.

DT: "Even" to the extent that it seemed detached at Harvard? Didn't it seem very detached at Harvard?

QA: I thought so.

DT: I certainly thought so in an earlier period. Did you in any way relate that to something going on in New York or did you think of it as peculiarly Columbia?

QA: I don't know how much I'm reading back but it does seem to me that one could have the sense that by comparison Harvard was provincial. This dawned on me fairly early. After all, in New York I knew that my teachers were writing and publishing in current journals that I found interesting. I knew that they were choosing books for their courses, as Barzun and Trilling chose them, which broke the customary academic molds and made the curriculum seem much more a matter of current and even agonizing current concern. One wouldn't have dreamed of a course at Harvard in which one read *The Origin of Species* or Trotsky's *History of the Russian Revolution.*

DT: Had you read Trotsky's *History of the Russian Revolution* in colloquium?

QA: Yes.

DT: Did it come before or after Freud's *Civilization and Its Discontents?*

QA: I'm not sure that that book figured on the list. But as soon as I returned to Columbia, it surely was one of the things that would have occupied me.

DT: Was that your first reading of Freud? Speaking of your dissertation topic, you haven't yet specified that any knowledge of Freud had led you to your interest in the relation of the Jameses, father and son.

QA: Surely it was not unimportant. It was something I was very much aware of—the character of the relation of fathers and sons as Freud might have suggested it to me. But I thought I had something straightforward to propose, to wit, that James's own sense of himself and of humanity had in large measure been framed by the way in which his father regarded the world.

DT' That's a matter of a sort of intellectual history of that family, isn't it, and hasn't very much to do with any of the assumptions of psychoanalysis. That was what I was wondering, whether you had any knowledge of psychoanalysis when you came to the writing of your James book.

QA: Indeed I did. I was in analysis from, say, '42 until '47. For me, that meant a rather religious avoidance of reading Freud. I felt that that would confuse my own attempt to redirect my own energies. So I was certainly involved in some sense in Freud but it was therapeutic rather than anything else.

DT: I'm struck by how casually, in 1984, you can say that you were in analysis forty years ago. Did you talk about it that readily then? I know that if you had spoken about it with Lionel at that time he would have told you not to discuss it at all around the University. He always advised anyone he knew who was in analytical treatment not to discuss it at the University because it would harm his career. Not analysis, not any therapy was accepted then the way it is now.

QA: Well, Lionel of course would have been wholly conscious of attitudes among those who were at that time my elders. I had no hesitation among my friends in talking my head off about what I conceived to be emotional reality as I was discovering it and uncovering it in analysis. I mean my contemporaries, I don't mean my elders. Indeed, I must have been rather a nuisance and even possibly to some people a danger because I was so persuaded that I had a sense of the emotional life which was denied to the unwashed who hadn't any links with analysis.

DT: The other day, somewhere or other, I came across the strange statement that in the forties the New York radical intellectuals, having become disenchanted with communism, had turned from Marxism to Freudianism. That struck me as being one of those contrived historical formulations; it isn't at all my recollection of how it was.

QA: It's very misleading to say that. The turn, if we may speak of a turn—let's say, at *Partisan Review*— was from the administration of a great authority about political affairs and political reality to an authority about art. Literary figures such as Proust, Rilke and Joyce started to loom, it has always seemed to me, with an authority in some way almost comparable to that which people had earlier felt about the dictates of the Party. But that meant that the administrators, if they were commissars (although the term is a wrong one) of literary and cultural authority, had assumed a new kind of authority. This I was rather persuaded of.

DT: I want to talk with you about Richard Chase. Did you and he become very good friends in those early years of the forties.?

QA: I can't speak of our being very good friends. I don't know whether Richard had very good friends. He was most friendly, most charming, most ready to talk about intellectual matters. He moved very largely in a circle which was not my own—Dwight Macdonald, William Phillips, Mary McCarthy, the *Partisan Review* group of which I was not a part.

DT: How interesting that you say that because he doesn't figure at all in my recollections of the *Partisan Review* group! When I think of *Partisan Review* parties or evenings with editors and their friends, I don't recall Richard Chase being there at all.

QA: Well, you and I may be saying the same thing, embraced by the same ignorance. If Richard, a contributor to the magazine, was as removed from them as he was in a sense from me, he was alone indeed. I made the wrong assumption: I thought of him as part of that social group. Before we began this discussion, I had a fresh look at his best-known book. He had earlier, in '49, published his dissertation, *The Quest for Myth*, and he published his Melville book in the same year. His best-known book, *The American Novel and Its Tradition*, quite vividly suggests a sort of personal presence that Richard had. He had a tone of easy authority and he was wholly persuaded that to talk about literature was to talk about the quality of a culture; that literature exhibited the quality of a culture and that it was indissoluble from the culture in which it appeared. And when he turned to write about Americans, and indeed elaborated a thesis about the American novel which became very well known and held the field for a number of years, he had a sort of Yankee tone. But he spoke with a great assurance that used to stagger me.

DT: What was the thesis of his book about the American novel?

QA: *The American Novel and Its Tradition* took as its point of departure a notion of which Lionel Trilling had made use, that the American novel existed in a dialectical relation to the culture, that its heroes, its principal figures, tended to be people who had set themselves in opposition and but whose opposition revealed things about the character of the culture. It was Chase who first nailed down the thesis that the American novel had a relation to romance that the English novel had not had and was indeed different because the country was so new.

DT: Is that what he traced the romance to, the fact that we were a newer culture?

QA: He traced it, I think, to what he calls in one passage 'the romance of the self.' And what he meant by that, obviously enough, I suppose, was that in a country which was not yet defined by institutional manners and occupations or by the weight of its own past, the self had freer play. Therefore, an attempt at definition of the self inevitably led one to romance rather than realism because the substance of realism was, so to speak, not present in the form of institutions, manners and so on.

DT: I remember that this was felt to be very much in opposition to the way that Lionel had been writing about the novel. How would you define the opposition?

QA: I would say that when Lionel wrote about the novel he was most occupied with novels which emerged from dense cultures such as the nineteenth-century cultures in which, for instance, there was the attempt to translate money into class. Richard was in effect saying that that sort of density, which was appropriate to either a George Eliot or a Trollope, was simply not available to the American writer and that—to put it as Richard and indeed I, in those days, often did, and of course as Henry James had put in in his *Hawthorne* book—the American novelists had, so to speak, to contrive a scene on which the characters were to appear. For the English or Continental novelist, the scene existed and was simply one that the writer was able to employ and deploy.

DT: What would you do with Howells?

QA: Howells was an interesting subject for discussion among Richard Chase, Lionel Trilling and myself because the notion that someone had tried to find the grain of existing American life and to represent it was indeed attractive. But the question whether Howells had what James called the 'grasping imagination' was always to the fore. And indeed we arrived at a position, the three of us, about one Howells novel which made us appear rather eccentric. We said *The Vacation of the*

Kelwyns, the last one, really does it. And indeed both Lionel Trilling and Richard Chase wrote about that book as an instance in which Howells had at once managed to catch the awareness of an American cultural situation and to reveal it in the centennial year, 1876, with a depth of awareness that other novelists had not contrived. It was published in 1920 but he wrote it as early as 1910. It wasn't that Chase didn't believe that realism was a word worth using. As against, say, Dick Poirier's later book, *A World Elsewhere,* which is devoted in large part to American novelists, Chase felt that it was worthwhile to articulate the actualities of a social scene and that an imaginative work in part derived its strength from the capacity to do so.

DT: What was there in his differences with Trilling that somehow led Chase to feel, as I remember he did, that he was a far more radical character than Trilling, more in rebellion against tradition and against the given of middle-class society? How do you get to that from what you have been describing as his view of American literature?

QA: He had a strong impulse to see society as in some way corrigible and needing correction. But it did not lead him to large formulations about the right to go about being a socialist. In fact, the distance you felt when you talked to Richard with his sweet smile was a distance he preserved in relation to the resolution of all the large social issues. Yet he wanted to be thought of as someone who was blowing his horn for the right cause even if that cause was not defined by a program. It's very hard to describe.

DT: Perhaps I'm pushing this too far but isn't it a constant situation among American intellectuals that they are looking to be radical, looking to be in opposition to that which is established and given? Wasn't

Richard Chase really trying to find in his view of the American self something that testified to his own youthful rebelliousness?

QA: That's interesting but I'm not sure that I would accept it. The most vivid episode in his career for me is the moment when he got very enthusiastic about Arnold Toynbee and the notion he seized from Toynbee was a notion of withdrawal and return; indeed, when it came to writing his Melville book, he literally enacted it. He withdrew to the Cape, wrote the book and, so to speak, laid it before us as a species of political document. I call it political because what it argued was that Melville was incipiently a critic of all the bad aspects of the politics of the time—the time when the book was published—that Richard wanted to denounce. And so it was a polemical and somewhat tendentious book. But it was a book in which, for example, he made great play with the figure of Melville's Bulkington in *Moby-Dick* and Bulkington was the developed democratic hero, the one who Melville simply consigned to one chapter and then had silently drowned. If that hero had appeared he might have remade the culture as well as the economy of the sailing ship on which Melville planted him. And I think there was something suggestive about Richard's own sense of the world, in that he was looking for the image of the hero that he said Melville had suppressed. His actual politics, however, remained for me a bit unformulated. They reminded one of Irving Howe's desperate attempt of late to be a certified radical.

DT: Let me try to say more sharply what I'm getting at here. Let's make a jump forward to the student uprisings at Columbia in '68. I remember that one of the top secretaries in the University said to me at the height of the uprising, with a kind of wild look in her eye—she had been a perfectly orderly person up to that moment—"Everybody's asserting rights, I'm going to assert my rights, too. If this is a moment of revolution and everybody's asserting rights, I have rights, too." I asked her what rights she had in mind and of course she hadn't even thought of any rights she was going to assert. It was a moment for asserting rights, a moment of radical definition, and therefore she must make her radical self-definition, too. Well, this is a bit of what I'm talking about in relation to Richard Chase, that in dealing with the American self he was trying to find some way that would help him define himself as a radical individual. Is that a fair statement? And I want to generalize from it; I don't want to stay with Richard. You see, Quentin, I think you and he parted company at that moment. You speak sympathetically of his views but how did you get from there to the "imperial self?" That's the point I really have in the back of my head. It seems to me that when you went to the imperial self, you had found something different and much truer to say: that the self is not a radical agent but an imposing agent, an aspect of power, of the wish for power. I think it's an important difference I'm trying to make here.

QA: I've read—re-read, in fact—a review by Richard of Leslie Fiedler's *Love and Death in the American Novel* and I was startled by its harshly polemical tone at moments and its assertiveness as to how things had really gone. Now, it's easy to attack *Love and Death in the American Novel*. It, so to speak, unpacks itself. It has a very good opening about the meaning of the novel as a sort of cultural form and how people have avoided and responded to it. But later on it is full of misreadings of American literature. And Richard tags these. But in doing so, he assumes a very lordly position which is almost above the battle, as if *he knew*. I used to be puzzled about the measure of his assurance because there were so many things that were unclear to me and so many things that seemed to be clear to him. I frankly don't know how to relate his sense of authority to his sense of—what?—political expectation. But clearly he meant, as you noted, to place himself to the Left without being in any way programmatic. But I can't at the moment carry this further. I don't see further on it.

DT: Maybe you can't carry it further because *he* didn't carry it further. I think your analogy with Irving Howe is a sound one. It was a *stance* that Richard required. He had to think of himself as in rebellion.

QA: Yet consider how very conventinal was the pattern of his life.

DT: Oh yes indeed. Well, I really am much more interested at this point in wherever it was that you agreed with him and where it was thay you moved away from him. I'm using Richard as a figure in your landscape.

QA: Let me recall one tiny episode in my encounters with him on a question of literature. I once said to Richard, "You know, when I read Whitman's 'Crossing Brooklyn Ferry' I get scared." I was saying this because I felt that in that poem, as I told him, all the appearances of the world were sopped up and aggregated within the self: the world disappeared. Richard chuckled at me and said he didn't understand at all why I thought that was happening. I must confess that I myself felt that he was not subjecting himself to the poem, that he had found it convenient to write about Whitman as he did in relation to Whitman's own authority as a sort of judge of American affairs. And I didn't think that in that poem one could speak of Whitman as a judge of American affairs. One of the shrewd things he did was to point to moments when it seemed to him plausible that Whitman was being comic, but many of those moments seemed to me not to be comic at all but deadly serious. Now what to make of that episode, one isn't quite sure. But what I made of it was that he thought he had Whitman tagged, that he was surer of the function of the self as he envisioned it in America than I was. He thought of Whitman as more firmly planted in a going society than I did. However, that doesn't seem to carry us much further with your question, does it?

DT: I'm afraid that my question goes perilously close to something almost too personal—personal to Richard, I mean—to deal with, so let's go back to your book *The American Henry James.* You know, I was looking at it the other day in preparation for this interview and I saw that in the acknowledgments you mentioned Francis Fergusson. I was struck by that because, as you know, Francis Fergusson's *Idea of a Theater* was one of the first books put out in Anchor Books and one of the best-sellers of our first quality paperback publishing in this country. I haven't seen many references to Fergusson in recent years. What did he do for you, intellectually?

QA: He did something very important for me. Before my book appeared, he read the long essay that I had published in *Kenyon Review* in '43 called "Henry James and the New Jerusalem," and he read it with the kind of sympathy and interest which was accorded it by only two other critics, V. S. Pritchett and Lionel Trilling. F. R. Leavis also responded to it but in a different way that I might describe in a moment. Fergusson found what I was suggesting in that essay both interesting and worth differing with on some points.

DT: Perhaps you should summarize that essay.

QA: It's a long and complex affair, but I suggested that many of James's ruling motifs and emblems had a direct connection with his father's sense of human psychic economy and indeed with how things went for humanity in the succession of its churches. His father was very insistent on the succession of churches, as Swedenborg had been, but he rather reduced it so that the first church was the Jewish church, the second the Christian, and the third was that of the realized new Jerusalem which extant Swedenborgians didn't really understand but he, the elder Henry James, did. And in this succession there was also a reenactment of the growth of individuals so that as in Marxism you had an account of the history of the West which was recapitulated in the growth of individual persons. One began as a greedy grasper and, necessarily, one seized on the world as matter to fill one's cup or, as later in Henry, Jr., one's bowl, and went on until a moment of crisis arrived when you perceived the nature of your own activity—which indeed had been that of engorgement, of filling the self. And therafter you came to realize that the world was not there to be seized but was there to illustrate the perfections of your own fully realized nature. So that the world, as the elder Henry James saw it, was a scene of a vast providential experiment but what the God had done was to bury himself (and one is tempted to say "herself" here because it often turned out to be herself) in humanity; and so presently you recognized that you were inhabited by the God and finally realized that the God would not come to full embodiment except in humanity at large. And not until everybody's realization that greed had to be discarded and that the great enterprise of humanity was to create beautiful forms and to create beautiful things and to exhibit the beauty of its nature by its garmental forms, its artistic forms, and so on—not until that third stage was realized by everyone would the condition of divine natural humanity be realized.

Well now, to connect this with Henry James in 1943, as I did, was practically an act of impiety because James was known as the 'author's author' and he was known also as a species of realist, as an investigator of the relations between Europe and America. To propose that in writing what he had written he was actually giving the world an account of how humanity was fated to develop and what its ultimate realized state ought to be like was just about as far from anybody's presumptions as one could possibly have gone.

DT: And what was the response of Francis Fergusson?

QA: Fergusson found this account (and here I must suggest that the account best fitted the last three completed novels of James and that my essay, as did my later book, emphasized these last three completed novels) quite plausible.

DT: Did he write to you?

QA: He didn't write, he published. That's the point, he published an essay in, I believe, *Sewanee,* in which he recorded his sense of the matter.

DT: Quentin, we'll come back to your life as a scholar in American literature and American culture. But for a moment I want to move aside a bit and find out what was going on in your life apart from your teaching and writing. Were you living in New York or Rockland County? Let's take it from about the mid-forties—you weren't in the war, were you?

QA: No, I had a bum leg. I lived in Rockland County for a time in what I conceived to be a political atmosphere. The Fourth Estate was very prominent in my community. People on the *Times,* people on *Life.* I got involved in the National Association for the Advancement of Colored People—it had a branch in Nyack. I clearly was inclined to liberal politics. When the American Labor Party, which in New York was already well known to be under the thumb of the Communist Party, appeared on my scene I embraced it with what I now regard as incredible ignorance and indeed consented at one point to become a candidate for county treasurer. The people with whom I was associated at the time were, many of them, quite passionately Left. The newspaper *PM* was greatly exercised about the

school segregation fight in the neighboring village of
Hillburn and when I realized that people in the Labor
Party I was working with were far more interested in
having a cause that would make newspaper headlines
than they were in solving the segregation problem in
Hillburn, I took an ad in the county paper and denounced the whole enterprise and effectively got out of
the American Labor Party and made a great many local
enemies. One of the amusing episodes there was that I
had gotten quite a number of votes in Stony Point and
no one could work out why it was that I was so influential in that one place; but I knew it was because I
belonged to a fishing club in Stony Point and the members loyally supported my candidacy. I came out of that
campaign for county treasurer with the clear sense that
I no longer wished to be pushed around, and it later
occurred to me that my involvement with these people
who were presumably carrying out the orders of the
Party had become repugnant to me, not so much because I had changed my political views as because I
had a couple of vivid instances of the fact that I was
expected to act under orders. I simply did not want to
be under orders.

DT: What year are we talking about, Quentin?

QA: I would have to go back to records and search. But
it was close to '48. The atmosphere was that of pre-
Wallace and the Wallace campaign.

DT: But you talked about your having been very close
to Lionel in that period. Didn't you learn anything
about how Communists operated from having known
him? Hadn't you picked this up from conversations
with him?

QA: No. I don't think that actually our conversations
touched on politics at that period.

DT: That's quite important.

QA: I might have learned from an earlier experience when I was a member of Actors' Equity and saw the attempts of the Communists to take over Actors' Equity.

DT: That had to have been the early forties, or even earlier.

QA: That would have been the thirties. But I didn't learn, and indeed I appear to have been a slow learner on the question of people's actual political orientations.

DT: The actual political orientations were often hard to discover. But weren't you prepared for the general atmosphere of Communist manipulation?

QA: I was not.

DT: So then we come to the Wallace campaign. There was active support for it on the Columbia campus.

QA: By that time, I was off the boat. In fact, I never did get involved in politics on the Columbia campus. My only memory there is of standing at a window with Charles Frankel at an earlier period, the period of the Oxford Oath, and having him remark as has always seemed to me very acutely: "They're holding a meeting against war and peace." That is, against the human condition in general.

DT: That's very good. Who were the people around you at that time? By now you were a rather senior member of the faculty.

QA: I was a senior member of the young faculty and I was much interested in their views on intellectual matters and on books but apparently never very much interested in their views on politics, which I don't think were in many cases very strongly developed. In fact, I would in general say of my junior colleagues, and I was a junior myself, the last thing they were talking about actively was politics.

DT: Well, what about the war?

QA: I guess my most vivid memory is of a very early moment of the war, sitting for the first time in the Faculty Club. The war was the topic of discussion but as a young aspirant I was most impressed by the fact that I was sitting with colleagues in the Faculty Club during my very first semester of teaching.

DT: There's some kind of lesson in that, Quentin, but I'm not quite sure I want to say what it is.

QA: It might be a comment on the single-mindness of the graduate student.

DT: Going forward to 1957, when your James book was published, did you see any relationship between the way that book was received and whatever it was that was happening in the fifties in the general literary culture?

QA: I saw an agonizingly close relation between the publication of that book and the kind of reception it received. On the one hand, in *Partisan Review*, Irving Howe denounced it and called it a bad book. On the other, from a quite different academic perspective, R. W. B. Lewis took it to task in, I believe, the *Yale Review*. Indeed, the only really favorable responses I had from people whose names are well known were those from my sponsor, Lionel Trilling, and as I've earlier mentioned, Francis Fergusson, and the very pleasant, very favorable review by V. S. Pritchett in England. There was another person who responded to that book and that was F. R. Leavis. Leavis, however, seemed to regard it as part of his armory directed against the late James. Since, for him, the middle James was far more important in the novels he rejoiced in—*The Princess Casamassima*, *Portrait of a Lady*, *The Bostonians*, and so on—when someone came along and suggested that the late James was deeply influenced by a symbolism which carried him away from what Leavis regarded as the prime task of the novel, that person was someone who was indirectly backing him. He even gave me a voice in *Scrutiny* to expound my sense of the late James.

DT: And did you?

QA: Yes, I published two pieces in *Scrutiny.*

DT: Which were those?

QA: I think one of them was called "Henry James and His Critics"; I don't recall the title of the second.

DT: Tell me, did you have a sense of there being any problem about the appropriateness of relating biographical information to literary criticism?

QA: Well, at that time, James was often called the 'artist's artist,' and his performance in the novel was thought of as something that should be considered quite apart from any cultural matrix or even his own family. To mix into the culture and assert that he had been peculiarly American, almost Emersonian, in his attitudes towards humanity was regarded as a kind of impiety in a number of quarters. I offended those who felt that symbolism in James was of primary concern and I offended those who felt that James should not be associated with the society. Also, in not altogether defensible terms, I'd associated quite particular assertions and positions of Henry's father with quite particular moments in the structure and in the emblems employed in the novels, and this troubled certain people.

DT: And you seemed to assume that it was natural to see a father's influence in the work of his son: wasn't that in itself inconoclastic?

QA: I suppose that it was. It was not only inconoclastic but it might be easily made to appear an imposition.

DT: Why?

QA: If you didn't have any sympathy with the possibility that a father might influence his son. So for a time the book led an underground life; I discovered later that there were those who had accepted it in part. The English were more inclined to say that I had actually made a point which was worth discussing than were the Americans. But a number of Americans—Roy Harvey Pearce, for example—took it quite seriously without being able wholly to define the relation of its merits to its defects. On the whole, though, I'd suffered a setback in my career. The book had made a splash but it hadn't established itself—I think of the arc of my career from '57 to, say, '65 as having been cut, stopped. It was in '65 that I got a remarkable letter from Lionel Trilling in which he reproached me for not making use of my energies and asserted that they were of some use. For me, this marked a kind of a turning point; I went to work.

DT: Did that letter just arrive out of a clear sky?

QA: It came in response to a gloomy letter of my own. But it was a very heartening occasion for me and I think it helped to loosen energies that had been frozen for some time. I launched out on the book which, years later, became *The Imperial Self*—in fact, one of the chapters of *The Imperial Self* is a version of my early attempt at that point to cope with Hawthorne. Actually, the evolution of *The Imperial Self* was a slow one in anybody's terms—anyone who thinks of himself as a practicing writer and critic. I had been teaching a course called English 19 on American writers through the years, and developing attitudes and convictions. Between, say, '65 and late '69, or early '70, when *The Imperial Self* was actually finished, I was gathering together ideas that I had long entertained. And as the manuscript neared completion, about the time of Woodstock, I recall saying that the culture was catching up with me and everybody would find that I was a commonplace by the time I got the book into print. *The Imperial Self* had an odd kind of entrance into the world from the point of view of its author because, for one thing, it was published in '71. Since '68 to '70 marked the high-water mark of that period of student rebellion, the book came to be associated with the rebellions as if it had been my response to them.

DT: Really? Who made that association?

QA: A number of reviewers spoke of it in those terms. It left me gasping because I certainly don't write so fast.

DT: But what was the connection? I don't understand this.

QA: I was speaking in behalf of society and that meant, in the eyes of these reviewers, that I was speaking in behalf of the existing institutions. The fact that I started out with the premise that the very being of any kind of society was what had been questioned by those I had called the 'imperial selves' seemed to have escaped the attention of those readers. I was talking about the way in which people related themselves to each other but the reviews did not reflect that. They seemed to regard the book as an assertion about the extraordinary merits of America as it existed at the moment. But what writer is ever satisfied with his reviews?

DT: The book has a permanent place in American Studies and in our understanding of our past. Surely it's a major contribution. Whether the reviews were favorable or whether they were understanding or not, they yet added up to that.

QA: The phrase for a moment passed into current usage . . .

DT: You think just for the moment?

QA: I believe that. I think that Christopher Lasch's *Narcissism* succeeded it.

DT: No, I don't think that displaced it at all.

QA: At any rate, there it was and I was in some ways satisfied with it because I had given an account of these people with whom I had struggled for so long as a teacher. Subsequently I came to feel that in saying, as I did in the book, that the mode of self-elevation which had long existed in this country and which declared that one didn't need the support of society or family or community in order to define oneself was all very well, but that one might attempt to explain the origin, or at least the necessary condition, in the culture itself that might lead people to feel this. And the matter of the book I'm currently working on is precisely that: what is the character of a society in which one seeks to assert that one can define one's own identity through one's own efforts alone?

DT: You spoke just now, Quentin, of the student uprisings as having come in the middle of the period or near the end of the period in which you were working on *The Imperial Self* and that leads me to ask one more question. Do you feel that anything was accomplished by that rebellion?

QA: I think my answer would have to be at least double. To say that the uprising was, so to speak, a species of aberration or accident is probably wrong. Some sort of tide of feeling was clearly washing over the students at that time. But that that tide of feeling had results that we can in some way be happy about, I can't quite say at all. I feel, and perhaps this is derived from my own position as someone occupying a responsible office at the time, that the vulnerability of the staff to the sort of assertion that was being made is what sticks with me as the most distressing and troubling aspect of the whole affair. I accuse myself of having failed to see precisely what my responsibility was in the given situation.

DT: But how can you define that except in terms of an authority that's forbidden by the very terms of our liberal culture? The father who says, "I'll have none of this because there's another pattern of behavior that I insist upon" is now an authority figure only in a very pejorative sense. If there were another such occasion, would you be prepared, even with the wisdom of '68 behind you, to say, "I want none of this?" I'm not sure it would be possible.

QA: Something very elemental, and perhaps even touching, happened. To tell a professor that there is nothing he can do to persuade his students of something is to tell him someting that he finds very hard to absorb. We tried to talk, we tried to reason, we tried to accept enough of what was being offered us as a position to reestablish our sense of ourselves and of our students. We went over the mark. And yet in retrospect we pulled ourselves together and performed very much as we had before. Nonetheless, there were wounds. And some of the wounds survive.

11. The *Imperial Self* and the Study of American Literature in the 1970s

PETER SHAW

The impact of the 1960s was felt as surely in the study of American literature as it was everywhere else in the culture. Until about 1970, the dominant treatments of American literature concentrated on the symbolic and the existential. After 1970, the emphasis shifted decidedly to the social and political. In view of this important change of approach, Quentin Anderson's *The Imperial Self*, published in 1971, takes on a new significance. Anderson's book set out to challenge the older criticism. Yet in view of what was to follow, it now stands as a monument of the tradition it criticized. As such, the book permits us to view with greater clarity the differences between the two periods that it separated.

The Imperial Self stood at the end of a distinguished line of works descending from D. H. Lawrence's *Studies in Classic American Literature* (1923). Lawrence virtually invented American literature as we now know it by redefining its major tradition. He singled out and made central a small number of largely neglected American works in which he found a hidden, subversive message. By the 1950s, it had become typical for scholars to generalize about the entire literature—and culture—through one or another extension of Lawrence's subversiveness formula. Like him, each of the later commentators found something hidden and dark at the heart of the literature. What that something might be was brilliantly explored in such works as *Symbolism and American Literature* (1953) by Charles Feidelson, *The Power of Blackness* (1958) by Harry Levin, *The American Novel and Its Tradition* (1957) by Richard Chase, and *Love and Death in the American Novel* (1960) by Leslie Fiedler.

There was also a sunnier view of American literature. It tended to find its expression in studies of the American Transcendentalists and the American West. James Fenimore Cooper, Emerson, Thoreau, Walt Whitman, and Mark Twain were favored over the authors usually discussed by the darker critics: namely, Hawthorne, Poe, Melville, and Henry James. The sunnier view descended from Lewis Mumford's *The Golden Day* (1926), which had offered something of an alternative to D. H. Lawrence in its time. Both *The American Adam* (1955) by R. W. B. Lewis and *Virgin Land* (1950) by Henry Nash Smith, celebrated the American spirit in a Mumfordian way when they praised the setting aside of conventions in favor of starting out with first things. (Celebratory in different ways from Mumford in his time were V. L. Parrington, Van Wyck Brooks, and F. O. Matthiessen, who is discussed immediately below.)

Anderson faulted the dark, symbolic approach to American literature for being too much in thrall to the New Criticism. The symbolic critics' elevation of literary form and worship of the artistic imagination, Anderson felt, distracted them from grasping the cultural message that they had set out to uncover. More important, these critics failed to deal with the literature's tendency to elevate the solipsistic self over the values of civilization. F. O. Matthiessen's *American Renaissance* (1941) was the one major critical attempt to escape the trap inherent in the worship of form. But Matthiessen's emphasis on social context as a corrective unfortunately proved to be "feeble," partial, and in any case went largely ignored.[1]

Where the symbolic critics ignored the cultural implications of American literature, the celebratory critics became "emotional collaborators" with the solipsistic tendencies of Emerson, Thoreau, and Whitman. Emerson, it was true, frequently paid homage to history and tradition, but Anderson insisted that at bottom his message that "we could all start afresh" was "deeply subversive of society itself."[2] In contrast to both symbolic and celebratory critics, Anderson aimed in *The Imperial Self* to identify the cultural and social implications of the Emersonian message in American literature, and to hold it up to an adult, socially responsible critique.

The need for such a critique was lent urgency by cultural developments in the 1960s. Above all, the counterculture of that period had been fed and to a great extent legitimized by the literary-critical triumph of the irresponsible self. Taking Norman O. Brown's *Life Against Death* as the representative work of the 60s, Anderson singled out its rejections of the family and business civilization (society) in favor of that "fantasy of an adolescent sensibility": the polymorphously perverse sexual experience. Here was a clear case of late Emersonianism. Brown was basing himself on Whitman's celebration of the body, along with "the gigantesque claims of the infantile self" that Whitman shared with Emerson.[3]

Anderson strongly implied that parallel celebrations of the Whitmanian self by literary critics also had a hand in preparing the way for a programmatically self-indulgent youth culture. As the 1960s progressed, moreover, that culture was lent a certain historical legitimacy by the prevailing interpretation of American literature—namely, that it stood for the rejection of tradition, authority, and social boundaries. Surprisingly, though, the critics who found and applauded these tendencies did not consciously intend the encouragement of countercultural attitudes. Furthermore, they never clearly recognized the nature of the message that they were explicating. For example, F. O. Matthiessen softened Whitman's subversive impact by transforming him into an author of chiefly formal accomplishment. The critics, Anderson might have put it, were *unconscious* collaborators. In contrast, the more direct progenitors of the sixties ethos—Henry Miller, Norman O. Brown, Allen Ginsberg—well understood and applauded such tendencies as Whitman's "assault on the grown-up self."[4]

In the course of the 1970s, the critics of American literature might almost seem to have been responding to *The Imperial Self*'s plea to substitute social relevance for concern with the self. The dominant tendency of the period in both literary and cultural criticism, after all, was to replace the individual with society as the center of concern. Furthermore, literature came to be studied in terms both of history—usually the history of capitalism—and of social groups: women, Blacks, Indians, ethnic minorities. And yet, the critics who allied themselves with particularist movements in the 1970s did nothing to reconcile the individual to society and its ways. Instead, they typically conceived each of the groups that concerned them as being in its own adversary relationship to the whole of society. And the individual members of those groups, needless to say, continued to have personal adversary relationships with the same society. In other words, the critics had but elevated the drama of the isolated, imperial self to the group level.

In a 1972 review, Anderson found in *Democratic Humanism and American Literature* by Harold Kaplan a representatively inadequate attempt to unite art and life. Anderson criticized the professorial tendency to view American literature as "the most useful, or the only useful, engine of social change."[5] Paradoxically, though, Anderson pointed out, for contemporary literary critics, social change turns out to be predicated on *personal* relationships. And these relationships, insofar as they are conceived of in a manner derived from the nineteenth-century Transcendentalists, are decidedly not calculated to sustain society. Thus, Anderson concluded that despite its emphasis on society and social change, *Democratic Humanism and American Literature* had not really advanced toward socially responsible criticism.

Anderson perceived a greater failure in *Puritanism in America* by Larzer Ziff, which he reviewed in 1973. Here, yet another apparent shift to social concerns was based on Karl Marx. Ziff began by analyzing the culture of Puritanism as a reflection of material conditions. But in tracing the supposed influences of Puritanism on nineteenth-century culture, he jettisoned his Marxist-derived approach and shifted "into a curious cloudcuckooland" of analysis.[6] Ziff began to treat society, that is to say, quite as ideally and abstractly as the New Critics.

Anderson found still another failure to balance individual with social reality within the deconstructionist literary critical movement of the 1970s. That movement, too, intended a departure from the New Criticism. But in addition, it challenged an older convention in literary criticism whereby the evaluation of a critic's work is determined by the judgment of his peers. This collective opinion is the discipline's equivalent for the traditional wisdom of society. Thus deconstruction, with its "monstrous claims to personal power," acted out within critical theory the familiar struggle between the individual and society.[7]

For Anderson, then, American criticism in the 1970s remained subject to its old shortcomings. Though critics reflected the high social awareness of the period, they continued to derive their attitudes from the visionary individual and his fantastical ideas.

On the other hand, these ideas now grew political—in keeping with the politicization of culture that had begun in the 1960s. Thus, in addition to pointing out the Marxist technique in Larzer Ziff's *Puritanism in America*, Anderson might well have gone on to emphasize the degree to which Ziff's hostility to nineteenth-century American society derived from that society's *capitalist* identity.

Anderson did point out deconstructionist criticism's source in French radical, anti-capitalist politics. But he regarded American deconstruction as having developed independently of this source. More recently, though, other analysts have argued that American deconstruction, dominated by what Gerald Graff terms "textual leftism," is as much wedded to political radicalism as its French original.[8]

Outside of the deconstructionist movement, the politicized critics of the 1970s fervently wished to denounce American racism, sexism, technocracy, and Imperialism. In addition, some felt compelled to reject capitalist civilization itself. No consensus developed on exactly how harshly America should be judged. But there was growing agreement that classic American literature offered ideal models of resistance. In Anderson's terms such critical projections onto the past always misconceive the nature of American literature, which was to both grow out of and be independent of social reality. Criticism most decidedly needed to observe the workings of that reality, but also to remember that it was not reflected directly.

To make his point, Anderson asked on the final page of *The Imperial Self:* "why did industrialism have no imaginative consequences proportionate to the profound changes it worked?" The disaffected critics who followed him have obviously assumed that industrialism did have its direct imaginative consequences. Thus in *The Incorporation of America* (1983), Alan Trachtenberg offers a reading of nineteenth-century American literature based almost exclusively on such a connection. The process of business incorporation, he argues, pervaded nineteenth-century culture at every level, providing a central imaginative theme. Literary rejections of society in that period were really political protests against the dangers of incorporation.

Among literary critics, those who differed with views such as Trachtenberg's have responded not by defending capitalism or society but by arguing the related issue of authority. In fact, not only in literary criticism but in other disciplines as well, the central political debate of the period has been over personal, familial, and social authority. As it happened, *The Imperial Self* anticipated this debate by making the problems of fatherhood and authority its central concerns. Anderson set forth his critique of the tyranny of the self in American literature in a chapter called "The Failure of the Fathers." Here, he located Emerson's most influential assault on society in his attack on the authority of "the divine father"—god.

In passing, Anderson speculated on the cultural nexus of Emerson's attack in a manner that further anticipated the 1970s—this time touching on the later decade's fascination with the group psychology of the father-son relationship. Anderson found it significant, in the first place, that the young Emerson, along with several of his contemporaries who went on to become influential writers, all lost their fathers. Anderson further observed that in the nineteenth-century "the authority of the father was not very firmly based in the culture." He therefore speculated that the Emersonian process of usurping or "incorporating the powers of the father" also took place in the culture at large—hence the enthusiastic response given to Emerson's program.[9]

In the course of the 1970s, this kind of psychohistorical analysis was vastly elaborated. One senses in historical and sociological books of the decade, for example, a special sensitivity to the consequences of lost paternal authority. This sensitivity, one may say, was a product of a loss of authority in the 1960s. Eventually, the theme of authority became explicit in such books as *The Culture of Narcissism* (1979) by Christopher Lasch and *Twilight of Authority* (1975) by Robert Nisbet.

Perhaps the most striking application of the weak-ened-father concept appeared in studies of the American Revolution. First came two essays whose insights reverberated down the decade. "The American Revolution: The Ideology and Psychology of National Liberation" (1972) by Edwin G. Burrows and Michael Wallace set forth the language of protest in the Revolution as an expression of dissatisfaction by the colonists at their dependent, childlike status in the British Empire. "Familial Politics: Thomas Paine and the Killing of the King, 1776" (1973) by Winthrop D. Jordan showed how rising colonial resentment of England was suddenly given its collective expression in Paine's *Common Sense* (1775). In this tract, the true author of the colonists' distress was for the first time named: it was the king, conceived of as a father. Paine, by excoriating this father and raising up the image of patricide against him, satisfied a national need to express the point of view of the son.

Subsequent to these two essays of the early 1970s, a series of books built on evidence presented in James Henretta's *The Evolution of American Society 1700–1815* (1973), showing an actual loss of authority among the fathers of the pre-Revolutionary older generation. These books explored the psychological consequences of the culturally evolved father-son relationship as it affected the Revolution. Each analysis tended to emphasize a particular discipline: *Sons of the Fathers* (1976) by Catherine Albanese, was sociological; *A Cultural History of the American Revolution* (1976) by Kenneth Silverman, and *Prodigals and Pilgrims* (1982) by Jay Fliegelman, were literary; *A Divided People*

(1977) by Kenneth Lynn, was biographical; *The Protestant Temperament* (1978) by Philip Greven, was cultural; *American Patriots and the Rituals of Revolution* (1981) by Peter Shaw, was anthropological; and *Revolution and Regeneration* (1983) by Peter Hoffer, was psychohistorical. Together with other books and essays on the Revolution, these works represented an outpouring of analytic energy and ingenuity all directed to the issues of the father and authority raised by Anderson.

In the field of psychoanalysis itself, where the subject of fathers and sons had provided a central focus since the beginning, there has been a detectable shift in recent years toward the father. In a number of professional papers, for example, the traditional discussion of the Oedipus complex has shifted to what is now referred to as the "Laius complex." The term refers to the experience of Oedipus' father, who in Greek legend was threatened with death at the hands of his son. In psychoanalytic readings of the legend, Laius' partial responsibility for his own and his son's tragedy is now emphasized. But if assigning part of the blame to Laius amounts to yet another assault on the father, at least it is an assault accompanied by active sympathy with his experience. This sympathy has led to—or perhaps been influenced by—psychological studies of middle-aged experience, and especially of the maturation process. All in all, the psychoanalytic pendulum, too, has swung away from the son.[10]

It would hardly be logical to look for a comparable change in the study of American literature, so decided is its bias against both the father and adulthood. Yet, it needs to be pointed out that American literature follows a universal pattern in taking up the point of view of the rebelling son.[11] The differences from other literatures consist in a greater emphasis on the youthful hero, and in the likelihood that he will be younger— often only a child.

Given the preponderance of young protagonists

in American literature, Quentin Anderson was not tempted to deal with the failure of the fathers by searching out exemplary literary fathers. Instead, he held up as an ideal the mature conception of society and human relations to be found in the works of Nathaniel Hawthorne. Here was a fictional universe in which fathers and authority were accorded their rightful places. This was not to say that Hawthorne upheld whatever might be done in the name of tradition. Rather, he pictured fathers and authority as ineluctable givens of life. Thus Hester Prynne, *The Scarlet Letter*'s unmistakable victim of injustice, goes awry when she becomes a feminist futilely bent on transforming the nature of human relations. For Anderson, "the emptiness of her categorization of Society as enemy of Woman, explains how injustice gives rise to distortion."[12]

In order to defend his presentation of Hawthorne as an alternative to Emerson and Whitman, Anderson had to deal with the argument that Hawthorne was *unconsciously* sympathetic to Hester and his other antinomian characters. Frederic Crews' *The Sins of the Fathers* (1966) had presented Hawthorne as, in Anderson's summary, "humped over his ever-intensifying Oedipal difficulties, attacking fathers." It could not be said in reply that Hawthorne has fictionally resolved his Oedipal conundrums in favor of the fathers. But Hawthorne could at least be described as speaking for "manhood" and "parenthood," and it was on these pillars that Anderson rested his critical case.[13]

That case, taken together with the literary-critical developments of the 1970s just surveyed, prompts the following reflections. The study of "American literature" is only technically concerned with the written word as it has been produced on these shores from the time of settlement until the present. Effectively, American literature means the work of a few authors and books of a single extraordinary period, the 1850s—along with selected works by earlier and later nineteenth-century writers (Poe and Fenimore Cooper; Mark Twain and Henry James). The Lawrentian singling out of a small group of substantially alienated and unrepresentative authors is based on the theorem that these particular authors succeeded in penetrating deeper into the heart of the American experience and therefore came closer to creating a "classic" literature than any others in the course of the American centuries.

This heavily tendentious view of the matter contrasts sharply with the ways in which other literatures are studied. English literature, for example, is not thought of as being defined by some particular tendency within it. F. R. Leavis's *The Great Tradition*, which studies the novel alone, comes closest to the partisanship of the American approach. But Leavis's work is surely the exception that proves the rule. With American criticism, in contrast, the Lawrentian approach's built-in affinity with iconoclastic private vision has most certainly prevailed. It is true that Anderson's demurrer from sympathy with the rebel outlook has come to be recognized as a position.[14] But this position is hardly a popular one: *The Imperial Self* stands unrefuted yet alone. Such an outcome confirms Anderson's characterization of American literature as possessed of a fatal attraction for its critics. In the 1970s, as it developed, it was not so much the individual heretic—the imperial self—who continued to lure these critics, so much as the literature's intrinsically subversive thrust itself.

For those who wish to stand back in Anderson's fashion and view the literature at a critical distance, this exercise of its power in the 1970s presents a sobering spectacle. For here is a demonstration that in the ongoing struggle over who shall possess the heart of American literature in each critical generation, those who are complicit with the adversary spirit have an evident advantage. On the other hand, *The Imperial*

Self has permanently altered the terms of discourse by raising to consciousness what had previously existed as unconscious complicity. Thus, whatever the outcome of the debate over American literature, Quentin Anderson will have had a hand in the result.

Notes
Bibliography of Quentin Anderson
Notes on Contributors

Notes

1. Emerson as Itinerant

1. Williston Walker, *The Creeds and Platforms of Congregationalism* (1893; rpt. Boston: Pilgrim Press, 1960), 210–11, 145; Donald M. Scott, *From Office to Profession: The New England Ministry, 1750–1850* (Philadelphia: University of Pennsylvania Press, 1978), 1–17; William T. Youngs, *God's Messengers: Religious Leadership in Colonial New England* (Baltimore: Johns Hopkins University Press, 1976), 17–39.

2. David D. Hall, *The Faithful Shepherd: A History of the New England Ministry in the Seventeenth Century* (Chapel Hill: University of North Carolina Press, 1972), 29–34, 102–5, 78–80; Nathaniel Mather, *A Discussion of the Lawfulness of a Pastor's Acting as an Officer in Other Churches* (London: Nath. Hillier, 1689), 8, 11–12, 29–30. On the question of whether in special circumstances ministers might perform certain offices outside their own congregations, see Cotton Mather, *Magnalia Christi Americana* (Hartford: Silas Andrus, 1853), 2, 237–39.

3. Edwin S. Gaustad, *The Great Awakening in New England* (New York: Harper, 1957), 25–41; Alan E. Heimert, *Religion and the American Mind: From the Great Awakening to the Revolution* (Cambridge, Mass: Harvard University Press, 1966), 118–23; Jonathan Edwards, *The Works of Jonathan Edwards: Volume IV, The Great Awakening*, ed. C. C. Goen (New Haven: Yale University Press, 1972), 378.

4. Ola Elizabeth Winslow, *Jonathan Edwards, 1703–1758: A Biography* (New York: Macmillan, 1940), 287.

5. Edwards, *The Great Awakening*, 69, 549–50; Stuart C. Henry, *George Whitefield: Wayfaring Witness* (New York: Abingdon Press, 1958), 18–19; 61–2; Ralph Waldo Emerson, *Journals and Miscellaneous Notebooks*, ed. William H. Gilman et al., (Cambridge, Mass.: Harvard University Press, 1960–1982), 2, 334 (hereafter referred to as *JMN*).

6. Perry Miller and Alan E. Heimert, eds., *The Great Awakening: Documents Illustrating the Crisis and Its Consequences* (Indianapolis: Bobbs-Merrill, 1967), 186.

7. Edwards, *The Great Awakening,* 565–66; Charles Grandison Finney, "What a Revival of Religion Is" (1834), in *The American Evangelicals, 1800–1900: An Anthology,* ed. William G. McLoughlin (New York: Harper, 1968), 87.

8. Charles Chauncy, *Seasonable Thoughts on the State of Religion in New-England* (Boston: Rogers & Fowle, 1743), 47.

9. William Emerson, *An Historical Sketch of the First Church in Boston, from Its Formation to the Present Period* (Boston: Hunroe & Francis, 1812), 189–90, 184, 192. Joseph Stevens Buckminster's funeral eulogy, printed with the history, refers to William Emerson's attitude toward the past ministers of the church. "He looked back with veneration almost unbounded on some of his predecessors here; and while he breathed much of their spirit, he successfully emulated their merits" 226–27. See also Joel Porte, *Representative Man: Ralph Waldo Emerson in His Time* (New York: Oxford University Press, 1979), 99–104.

10. William Emerson, *Historical Sketch,* 226.

11. Charles C. Forman, "Elected Now By Time," *A Stream of Light: A Sesquicentennial History of American Unitarianism,* ed. Conrad Wright (Boston: Unitarian Universalist Association, 1975), 27–29.

12. *JMN,* 2: 239.

13. Ralph Waldo Emerson, *Letters and Social Aims* (1904; rpt. New York: AMS Press, 1968), 127–28.

14. *JMN,* 2: 369.

15. Ralph Waldo Emerson, *Miscellanies* (1878; rpt. Boston: Houghton Mifflin, 1906), 24.

16. Ralph Waldo Emerson, *Young Emerson Speaks,* ed. Arthur C. McGiffert (1938; rpt. Port Washington, N.Y.: Kennikat Press, 1968), 32.

17. Gay Wilson Allen, *Waldo Emerson: A Biography* (New York: Viking, 1981), 187–90.

18. *JMN,* 4: 27.

19. In his journal entries of this period he notes, almost in self-criticism, "It seems not worth while for them who charge other with exalting forms above the moon to fear forms themselves with extravagant dislike" (*JMN,* 4: 30).

20. *JMN,* 4: 31.

21. *JMN,* 4: 52, 58, 87, 278–79.

22. Ralph Waldo Emerson, "The Divinity School Address" in *Nature, Addresses, and Lectures,* ed. Robert E. Spiller (Cambridge, Mass.: Harvard University Press, 1971), 85 (further references to the Address are given in the text).

23. William Ellery Channing, *The Works of William E. Channing* (1882; rpt. New York: Burt Franklin, 1970), 272–73.
24. *JMN*, 4: 384.
26. *JMN*, 4: 383.
27. Wordsworth, *The Prelude*, lines 10–12; Coleridge, *The Rime of the Ancient Mariner*, lines 605–9.
28. *The Letters of Ralph Waldo Emerson*, ed. Ralph L. Rusk (New York: Columbia University Press, 1939), 2: 167.
29. Norton identifies the earlier form explicitly: "But at the present day there is little of that avowed and zealous infidelity, the infidelity of highly popular authors, acknowledged enemies of our faith, which characterized the latter half of the last century. Their writings, often disfigured by gross immoralities, are now falling into disrepute" (Andrews Norton, *A Discourse on the Latest Form of Infidelity* (1839; rpt. Port Washington, N.Y.: Kennikat Press, 1971), 8–9.
30. Wesley T. Mott, "Emerson and Antinomianism: The Legacy of the Sermons," *American Literature*, 50 (1978), 369–97; Sacvan Bercovitch, *The Puritan Origins of the American Self* (New Haven: Yale University Press, 1975), 174–76.

3. Seeing and Saying: The Dialectic of Emerson's Eloquence

1. *The Journals and Miscellaneous Notebooks of Ralph Waldo Emerson*, 14 vols., ed. William H. Gilman et al. (Cambridge, Mass.: Harvard University Press, 1960–1982), 5: 376. Additional references to this inestimable source will be cited in my text, as *JMN*, followed by volume and page numbers. For the sake of simplicity, I have silently incorporated all the punctuation marks which the editors supply in brackets, and, with one exception, have left out all the phrases cancelled by Emerson which they print in broken brackets.
2. *The Letters of Ralph Waldo Emerson*, 6 vols., ed. Ralph Rusk (New York: Columbia University Press, 1939), 2: 46.
3. Kenneth Burke, "I, Eye, Ay—Emerson's Early Essay on 'Nature,' " *Sewanee Review*, 74 (Autumn 1966): 891.
4. M. H. Abrams, *Natural Supernaturalism* (New York: Norton, 1971), 309.
5. Cf. *JMN*, 5, 373 – an entry from September 1837, in which Emerson is obviously reflecting on the success of "The American Scholar": "It occurred the other day in hearing some clapping of hands after a speech, that the orator's value might be measured by every additional round after the first three claps."
6. "If I am the Devil's child I will live from the Devil. I can

have no law sacred but that of my nature" (*JMN*, 5: 49). This aphorism, for example, was entered into the journal in June 1835 but was withheld from the public for almost six years, not being used until "Self-Reliance" (1841).

7. Compare *JMN*, 5: 203, with the conclusion of "Literature" (rpt. in *The Early Lectures of Ralph Waldo Emerson*, 3 vols., ed. Stephen Whicher et al., [Cambridge, Mass.: Harvard University Press, 1959–1972], 2: 68). This journal entry is a draft for the lecture, and only one part of it was not used: "When I spoke or speak of the democratic element I do not mean that ill thing vain & loud which writes lying newspapers, spouts at caucuses, & sells its lies for gold . . . There is nothing of the true democratic element in what is called Democracy; it must fall, being wholly commercial. I beg I may not be understood to praise anything which the soul in you does not honor, however grateful may be names to your ear & your pocket." When we see what this passage becomes in the lecture, where Emerson still speaks of "the democratic element," we note that apparently he would rather be misunderstood than confront his culture so clearly—and note too the oblique return of the suppressed in his private attempt to absolve himself for the passage he did not dare to read aloud: "All questions touching the human race, the daily press now discusses. I stand here to describe, not to praise. I will not say there is no dark side to the picture or that what is gained in universality is not lost in enthusiasm."

8. My favorite example of the way Emerson could exploit the authority Jesus had with his audience is at the end of "Holiness": if "the aspirant . . . would know what the great God speaketh [namely; that the Highest dwells with him; that the sources of nature are in his own soul], he must 'go into his closet and shut the door,' as Jesus spake" (*Early Lectures*, 2: 355). In this passage, however, Jesus was commanding men to pray to God, not to commune with their own souls—and to pray according to the formula he went on to give them: the Lord's Prayer (Matt. 6). An analogous strategy can also be mentioned here: Emerson's stylistic addiction to the verb forms (spake, speaketh, etc.), the phrases and the rhythms of the King James Version. Despite his journal indictments of those Unitarian preachers who gave "scripture phraseology" instead of the living speech of men (cf. *JMN*, 5: 471), Emerson regularly fell back on an evocation of the Bible in his style—not, I believe, because the habits of a minister die hard, but rather because sounding like the Bible his audience still professed to revere could soothe any reservations about his own message that may have been growing in their thoughts.

9. *Early Lectures*, 3, 95, 97.

10. *The Imperial Self* (New York: Knopf, 1971), 22–23.
11. "Religion" (1840), *Early Lectures*, 3: 276–77.
12. There is a journal entry, headed "Vocabularies," that suggests the same trope: "Our journey, the journey of the Soul, is through different regions of thought, and to each its own vocabulary. As soon as we hear a new vocabulary from our own, at once we exaggerate the alarming differences,—account the man suspicious, a thief, a pagan, & set no bounds to our disgust or hatred, and, late in life, perhaps too late, we find that he was loving & hating, doing & thinking the same *things* as we, under his own vocabulary" (*JMN*, 7: 117).
13. "Eloquence," in *The Complete Works of Ralph Waldo Emerson*, 12 vols. (Boston: Houghton Mifflin, 1903), 7: 66.
14. Ibid., 65.
15. "Society" (1837), *Early Lectures*, 2: 109.
16. Indeed, from the journals it is clear that the doctrine of self-reliance was actually articulated under the pressure of this conflict between seeing and saying: self-reliance for Emerson was primarily not a metaphysical issue, but a rhetorical one—which is to say that it involved less the soul's relationship to spirit than the public speaker's relationship to his society (cf. *JMN*, 5 92–93, etc., especially all the entries in *JMN*, 7, in which he works up many of the most familiar passages from "Self-Reliance" itself in the specific context of the reaction to "The Divinity School Address").
17. "The Divinity School Address" was Emerson's most Oedipal attempt to assert himself. Joel Porte is right to see it as a kind of existential effort to arrive at an identity of his own, and right to point out how important the presence of the father-figures from the faculty of the Divinity School was to the attempt. But Porte, who seems to know nothing about what Unitarians had been saying for over a generation by the time Emerson spoke, and to have them confused with the Calvinists, is surely wrong to see the Address as an unqualified attempt to shock the auditors. Even this performance is full of regressive misgivings; Emerson's Oedipal impulses, which here were given the fullest expression they ever got, had to compete with his much stronger narcissistic needs. (Cf. Porte, *Representative Man* [New York: Oxford University Press, 1979], 89–160.)
18. "Eloquence," 63.

4. English and American Traits
1. References are to the edition edited by Howard Mumford Jones (Cambridge, Mass.: Belknap-Harvard University Press, 1966). The introduction and notes are useful. For the sake of brevity,

when my essay makes clear from what chapter of *English Traits* a quotation comes; no page reference is given, since the chapters are relatively brief, and references easily accessible.

References to Emerson's *Journal* are to *The Journals and Miscellaneous Notebooks*, ed. William H. Gilman *et al.* (Cambridge, Mass.: Harvard University Press, 1960–1982, hereafter cited as *JMN*.

In the correspondence, references are to *The Letters of Ralph Waldo Emerson*, ed. Ralph L. Rusk (New York: Columbia University Press, 1939), hereafter cited as "Rusk, *Letters*," and to *The Correspondence of Emerson and Carlyle*, ed. Joseph Slater (New York: Columbia University Press, 1964), cited here as "Slater, *Letters*."

The most extended treatment of *English Traits* is by Philip L. Nicoloff, *Emerson on Race and History: An Examination of English Traits* (New York: Columbia University Press, 1961). Among other discussions is a provocative brief account by Joel Porte in "The Problem of Emerson" in *Uses of Literature*, ed. Monroe Engel, *Harvard English Studies*, no. 4 (Cambridge, Mass.: Harvard University Press, 1973.)

I read Joel Porte's essay after drafting my own. I take as confirmation of Emerson's effectiveness in this work that we both find the first and last sections of the book structurally appropriate to Emerson's purposes, and chap. 16, "Stonehenge," crucial to the work's aims. Porte argues that *English Traits* represents a negative judgment of England as artificial and constrained, in contrast to the great promise of America. My sense of the book, while not in all ways contradictory, moves much in the other direction. As evidence, Porte provides apt quotations from the work, but the problem—as always in Emerson—is that equally apt quotations can be gathered to argue the other way. One traces an Emersonian argument rather as one watches the progress of a sailing vessel: harbor is often gained by an alternating series of movements oblique to the aim.

2. One can, of course, find Emerson saying admiring things about England's continuing vitality. While there in 1847–48, he noted that "In America we fancy that we live in a new & forming country but that England was finished long ago. But we find London & England in full growth, the British Museum not yet arranged, the boards only taken down the other day from the monument & fountains of Trafalgar Square." (*JMN*, 10: 244.) See H.M. Jones' note in his "Introduction," xxi; he objects that "Nicoloff thinks that Emerson was demonstrating the coming decadence of Great Britain. Is this not to read history backward?" The point is rather that Emerson sees England as being at the height of its

power; he knows that industrialization will bring many changes internally, and that English power will wane.

3. Chap. 17: 191–93.
4. All quotations in this paragraph are from chap. 18.
5. *JMN*, 10: 79–80.
6. *JMN*, 10: 303.
7. *JMN*, 11: 284.
8. 4 June 1847. Rusk, *Letters*, 3: 400.
9. Chap. 18: 199.
10. Chap. 3: 21.
11. *JMN*, 10: 397.
12. *JMN*, 11: 346.
13. *JMN*, 11: 385.
14. Slater, *Letters*, 486.
15. Rusk, *Letters*, 442.
16. *JMN*, 10: 311.
17. *JMN*, 10: 553.
18. *JMN*, 10: 345.

5. Emerson, Poe, and the Ruins of Convention

When I have quoted from well-known works by the authors considered here, I have not provided specific citations to any particular edition; these texts are readily available in many places, and the passages to which I refer are not difficult to locate.

1. The assertion by Baudelaire may be found in his *Correspondance*, 4: 277 [*Oeuvres complètes de Charles Baudelaire*, ed. Jacques Crépet (Paris, 1923–1953), 19 vols.]; quoted in English translation by Patrick F. Quinn in *The French Face of Edgar Poe* (Carbondale and Edwardsville: Southern Illinois University Press, 1971 [1957]), 135–36. Nietzsche's remarks about Emerson are cited in Walter Kaufmann's "Translator's Introduction" to *The Gay Science* (New York: Random House, 1974), 12.

2. James's observation is contained in an essay on "Charles Baudelaire" [1876], in Morris Shapira, ed., Henry James, *Selected Literary Criticism* (New York: Horizon Press, 1964), 28.

3. Review of Emerson's *Nature*, originally published in *The Christian Examiner*, January 1837 and November 1837, in Milton R. Konvitz, ed., *The Recognition of Ralph Waldo Emerson* (Ann Arbor: University of Michigan Press, 1972), 3.

4. *Ibid.*

5. Robert Ginsberg, "The Aesthetics of Ruins," *Bucknell Review*, 18, no. 3 (Winter, 1970), 92.

6. Preface to *The Altar of the Dead and Other Tales* (New York: Charles Scribner's Sons, 1909), xix–xx. This preface is in-

cluded with all the others written for the New York Edition in Henry James, *The Art of the Novel*, ed. with an introduction by R. P. Blackmur (New York: Charles Scribner's Sons, 1937); the specific passage to which I refer may also be found in James E. Miller, Jr., ed., *Theory of Fiction: Henry James* (Lincoln: University of Nebraska Press, 1972), 113.

7. *Ibid.*, xix.

8. "Introduction" to *Edgar Allen Poe: Selected Prose and Poetry* (New York: Rinehart, 1950), in Eric W. Carlson, ed., *The Recognition of Edgar Allen Poe* (Ann Arbor: University of Michigan Press, 1966), 222.

9. E. P. Peabody, "Emerson as Preacher," in F. B. Sanborn, ed., *The Genius and Character of Emerson* (Boston, 1885; rpt. Port Washington, N.Y. and London: Kennikat Press, 1971), 162–63, 163–64.

10. The sentence is taken from Emerson's lecture on "Shakespeare; or, The Poet," included in *Representative Men* (1850); it is singled out for special praise in "Some Recollections of Ralph Waldo Emerson" by Edwin Percy Whipple, who regards it as "the best prose sentence ever written on this side of the Atlantic." Whipple's essay, first published in the September 1882 issue of *Harper's Magazine*, is reprinted in Carl Bode, ed., *Ralph Waldo Emerson: A Profile* (New York: Hill and Wang, 1969).

11. *Studies in Human Time*, trans. Elliott Coleman (Baltimore: The Johns Hopkins Press, 1956), 332.

12. Letter of 1 February, 1835, the relevant portion of which is included in Stephen Whicher, ed., *Selections from Ralph Waldo Emerson* (Boston: Houghton Mifflin Co., 1957), 19.

13. Rodin's reflections appear in his book *On Art and Artists* (the English version of the work originally entitled *L'Art*), trans. Romilly Fedden, intro. by Alfred Werner (New York: Philosophical Library, 1957), 228–29; cited by Albert Elsen in his *Rodin* (New York: Museum of Modern Art, 1963), 180–81.

14. *Search for the Real and Other Essays*, ed. Sara T. Weeks and Bartlett H. Hayes, Jr., rev. ed. (Cambridge, Mass., and London: Massachusetts Institute of Technology Press, 1967 [1948]), 49.

11. The Imperial Self and the Study of American Literature in the
1970s

1. Quentin Anderson, *The Imperial Self: An Essay in American Literary and Cultural History* (New York: Knopf, 1971) 200; 35.

2. *Ibid.*, xi, 17, 88.

3. *Ibid.*, 98, 100.

4. *Ibid.*, 96.
5. Anderson, *Commentary* (October 1972), 84.
6. Anderson, *N. Y. Times Book Review* 16 December 1973, 4.
7. Anderson, *Partisan Review* 2 (1980), 265.
8. See Gerald Graff, "Textual Leftism," *Partisan Review* 4 (1982), 558–76.
9. Anderson, *Imperial Self*, 16, 55.
10. See Erik H. Erikson, "Themes of Adulthood in the Freud-Jung Correspondence," In *Themes of Work and Love in Adulthood,* ed. Neil J. Smelser and Erik H. Erikson (Cambridge, Mass.: Harvard University Press, 1980); John Mander Ross, "Laius and the 'Laius Complex" *The Psychoanalytic Study of the Child* 37 (New Haven: Yale University Press, 1982); Peter Blos, 'Son and Father,' plenary lecture, American Psychoanalytic Association mid-winter meeting, December 1982.
11. Harold R. Isaacs, 'Bringing Up the Father Question,' in *Generations*, ed. Stephen R. Graubard (New York: Norton, 1979); Kenneth Lynn, 'Adulthood in American Literature,' *Daedalus* 105 (Fall, 1976).
12. Anderson, *Imperial Self*, 80.
13. Ibid., 69.
14. See Carolyn Porter, *Seeing and Being: The Plight of the Participant Observer in Emerson, James, Adams, and Faulkner* (Middletown, Conn.: Wesleyan University Press, 1981), 5.

A Bibliography of Quentin Anderson

TIMOTHY TRASK

Quentin Anderson came to literary criticism in the 1940s from a career on the stage. Some of his early publications (see 2 and 4) reflect this transition. His use of the words "role," "acting," "drama," and "character," for example, indicates the lasting impression this earlier career has left on him. These words are not arbitrary vestiges but indications of the conscious acceptance of society in his role as a critic. The play is incorporated in Anderson's thinking as a representation of the human drama we call history. His critical responses during the last four decades indicate that he has from the beginning assumed the full burden of his chosen role—a burden of making judgments from the consciously acknowledged limitations that such a role entails.

Anderson's stance does not derive wholly from his theater period. There are probably many sources for it: his father was the playwright Maxwell Anderson; he grew up in New York City; and he studied at Columbia College with (among others) Jacques Barzun and Lionel Trilling, and at Harvard with Perry Miller and F. O. Matthiessen. All of these teachers would have helped Anderson to ground his work in the human realm, especially Trilling, who placed himself in a tradition of cultural history deriving from Burckhardt. As early as 1937, in his valedictory address (1), Anderson wrote: "We exist in our perceptions and responses; these are the matter of intelligent action, of artistic organization. The ends we desire are forever implicated in our social relationships." This is the statement of a man already committed to a point of view which is developed in subsequent publications. While critical fancy was turning to explication, Anderson was concerning himself with implication, with the involvement of individuals in their culture.

Anderson's first major critical piece, "Henry James and the New Jerusalem," (3) challenged the ascendant perspective on the work of Henry James. To a public schooled by Eliot's assertion that James's mind was so fine that it could not be violated by an idea, Anderson's thesis, that James's manner and style derived from early immersion in his father's religious, philosophical, and psychological ideas, seemed like heresy. This was a generation which did not believe in belief, and Anderson was challenging its notions of the purity of James's art. In this first essay, the basis Anderson gives for his assertions is a "truth written large in the theology of the elder James— every individual implicates a society and every society implicates a personality type." Explications based on the assumption that a work of art stands by itself or is not a response to a cultural dilemma won't help us to understand a James who 'built upon this truth' of the mutual implications of societies and persons.

The response Anderson did get (most notably from F. R. Leavis, who invited him to continue his work in the pages of *Scrutiny*) led him to write "Henry James, His Symbolism and His Critics" (6). This essay, the second of two in a series, clarifies Anderson's position on James and leads us into Anderson's later works of cultural history. It amplifies the basis for the authority of Anderson's critique of James, and it leads toward an assessment of what he would later call the Emersonian urge in American culture. It was his answer for those who had responded to his first article on James, and it signalled the entry of Quentin Anderson into a public dialogue, which means that it established Anderson with a critical identity. This is due not so much to the new ideas in the essay as to the quality of the clarifications. He had entered a public forum with his first essay on James, but in this one he showed himself able to respond to others.

This is not the place to recapitulate Anderson's argument on James, but it may be helpful to look at his full statement of James's "implicated" role in culture:

Unless we perceive a continuity between the artist's moral sanctions and the rooted popular myth of his time we cannot really judge him at all. If James had not felt in himself the very impulses which he saw crystallized in American manners he could not have understood American manners. Had he not felt himself a sinner he could not have condemned self-righteousness. The courage to do this is rare. It is surprising to us that James had a belief because we seek to hide our beliefs from ourselves. Lionel Trilling has pointed out that Mark Twain's strength as a moralist comes from his sense of participation in the evils he denounced. James's critics love to think of him as alienated or uncommitted because they dare not acknowledge themselves committed. The abstractions *artist* and *society* hide us from ourselves.

James overcame the impulse to hide from himself. He was wholly conscious that he both loved and hated himself—and he knew what in himself he loved and what he hated. That love and that hate were to be found in his culture as well. Its institutions and its manners expressed both. These emotions determined people's relationships to one another as they determined James's relationship to himself.

Bibliography of Quentin Anderson

The complexity of the discourse between James and his culture helps explain why he is not adequately met by exclusively Marxian or Freudian analyses. Any treatment of our writers which does not treat their works as "perceptions [of] and responses" to their culture will fail.

These two essays were to become the germ for *The American Henry James* (11 & 18), a book which is still causing critical reaction. And the larger concern of these works on James—the implications of individuals and their culture—is the theme which informs the historical appraisals Anderson would later make of Emerson, Thoreau, Whitman, and those who followed them. Emerson is cast as an enabling predecessor to James in some of Anderson's early work, but it is his *The Imperial Self* (42) which most fully puts our great nineteenth century writers into a historical context. With the exception of Hawthorne (whom Anderson had early called "a far greater moralist" than James [3]), the writers he deals with are *imperial* selves, "imperial" because they sought to conquer history by dissolving it in consciousness. Anderson suggests that at their most powerful, Emerson and Whitman, along with James, Thoreau, and, to a lesser extent, Melville, were able to surmount the difficulties posed by the stubborn materials of life (what Fitzgerald's Gatsby would later call the merely "personal"). The thesis is dynamic in that it shows that a tendency begun in the early works of Emerson receives impetus in Whitman's "Crossing Brooklyn Ferry" and culminates in Henry James's *The Golden Bowl*. The problem in this for us, who inherit the "emotional and intellectual consequences" of their struggles to become "fully conscious" Americans (see 57), is that we are not aided in our own *different* moral struggles by their work. Instead, they offer an all-too-tempting avenue of escape (which is not what they were up to at all; they were contending with different circumstances). Only an historical perspective like Anderson's can show us this.

By the early 1970s, when *The Imperial Self* appeared, it had long been clear that Anderson's own work emulated in its moral awareness the work of Hawthorne and Trilling, both of whom made it a characteristic of their work to acknowledge the presence of societies as historical facts involving (and limiting) the individuals within them. This moral awareness is present in Anderson's reviews as well as in the essays and books. He has responded to many of the recent critical and biographical treatments of American writers. His basis for judging the merit of these works is the same as his basis for judging our imaginative writers: he examines the ways in which they are implicated in their culture. His assessments are helpful because they do not immerse themselves in the terminology of the books at hand but rather put the books and their writers into a historical frame. Read through in sequence, they give evidence of a lifetime of thought. The reviews dovetail into the essays and the latter in turn complement the books. The best are responses to a culture which seems to have lost track of itself by a mind which has not.

It should be worth restating that the mind writing these responses came to us from a background in theater. He tells us that we are playing a role, that the role we play is the thing we are to be judged by, and that this role is, in fact, our character. He began by telling his fellow graduates that "the ends we desire are forever implicated in our social relationships." And he has since shown us how this must be the basis of our response to literature just as literature, if it is worthy of our notice, is based on the involvement of a writer with his culture. If he has been the first to notice the imperial urges of our cultural figures, that tendency of selves toward hypertrophy, that is because, like Henry James before him, he has not hidden from himself. We cannot ask more of a person than that he implicate himself in his work, but we should recognize that it takes courage, the courage required for gaining self-knowledge, to be able to do so.

Anderson is now working on a book on American views of personal identity. He has already given us his own view of the origins of personal identity in many different ways, but the most startling, perhaps, is this one (from 45): "My relation to other people is what made me, if I had none I wouldn't be a person at all. The babe leaps up on his mother's arm in response to her and the world she proffers; there isn't any escape from the conditioned character of our lives." This is a long way from the infinitude promised by Emerson, Whitman, and James. It has the ring of hard-won victory. We should be grateful to have this sort of critic about. He reminds us who we are.

I am indebted to Quentin Anderson's family for giving me most of the information contained in this bibliography.

Bibliography

1937
1. "Valedictory: An Undergraduate Appraises Education." *Columbia University Quarterly* 29, no. 3 (September 1937): 144–47.

1946
2. "Notes on the Theatre." *The Kenyon Review* 8, no. 3 (Summer 1946): 477–83.

Bibliography of Quentin Anderson

3. "Henry James and the New Jerusalem." *The Kenyon Review* 8, no. 4 (Autumn 1946): 515–66.

1947

4. "Theatre Letter." *The Kenyon Review* 9, no. 3 (Summer 1947): 481–86.
5. "The Two Henry Jameses." *Scrutiny* 14, no. 4 (September 1947): 242–51.
6. "Henry James, His Symbolism and His Critics." *Scrutiny* 15, no. 1 (December 1947): 12–19.

1949

7. Review of *The James Family*, by F. O. Matthiessen, and *The Notebooks of Henry James*, ed. F. O. Matthiessen and Kenneth B. Murdock. *Modern Language Notes* 64 (February 1949): 116–19.
8. "Second Trip to Byzantium." Review of *Melville's "Billy Budd,"* ed. Baron Freeman. *The Kenyon Review* 11, no. 3 (Summer 1949): 516–20.

1950

9. Introduction to *Selected Short Stories*, by Henry James. Rev. ed. New York: Rinehart & Co., Inc., 1950; New York: Holt, Rinehart & Winston, 1961.

1953

10. Review of *The Philosophy of Henry James, Sr.*, by Frederic Harold Young. *American Literature* 24 (January 1953): 556–57.
11. "The American Henry James." Ph.D. diss., sponsored by Lionel Trilling, Columbia University, 1953.

1955

12. "Emerson Changed His Mind." Review of *Freedom and Fate*, by Stephen E. Whicher. *The Kenyon Review* 17, no. 4 (Autumn 1955): 642–45.

1956

13. "George Eliot's *Adam Bede*." Broadcast on CBS Radio Network, 18 March 1956 (discussion with Quentin Anderson, Gordon S. Haight, and Alfred Kazin); pub. in *The Invitation to Learning Reader: The Victorian Era: Discussions of Great Books and Significant Ideas as Broadcast Weekly on the CBS Radio Network* 6, no. 1 (no. 21).

14. Review of *Young Henry James,* by Robert Charles LeClair. *Modern Language Notes* 71 (June 1956): 457–60.
15. "The Context of Criticism." Review of *The American Adam,* by R. W. B. Lewis. *The Sewanee Review* 64, no. 4 (Autumn 1956): 651–57.
16. "Treasures of Literature." *The New Wonder World Encyclopedia* 8 (*Parents' Magazine,* 1956).

1957

17. "Saints or Single Hounds?" Review of *New England Saints,* by Austin Warren. *The Kenyon Review* 19, no. 2 (Spring 1957): 300–02.
18. *The American Henry James.* New Brunswick, N.J.: Rutgers University Press, 1957; London: John Calder, 1958.

1958

19. "George Eliot in *Middlemarch*." In *From Dickens to Hardy,* ed. Boris Ford, 274–93. Baltimore: Penguin Books, 1958/ rpt. in *Discussions of George Eliot,* ed. Richard Stang, 85–94. Boston: D. C. Heath & Co., 1960; rpt. in *A Century of George Eliot Criticism,* ed. Gordon S. Haight, 313–24. Boston: Houghton Mifflin Co., 1965; rpt. in *George Eliot: A Collection of Critical Essays,* ed. George R. Creeger; 141–60. Englewood Cliffs, NJ: Prentice-Hall, Inc., 1970.

1960

20. "All Discontents and No Civilization." Review of *Love and Death in The American Novel,* by Leslie A. Fiedler. *Columbia Daily Spectator* 1, no. 6 (27 April 1960):1ff.
21. Introduction to *Twice-Told Tales and Other Short Stories,* by Nathaniel Hawthorne. New York: Washington Square Press, Inc., 1960.

1962

22. "Henry James." *The Reader's Encyclopedia of American Literature,* by Max J. Herzberg and staff. New York: Thomas Y. Crowell, Co., 1962: 527–34.
23. "American Literature." *Collier's Encyclopedia,* 2, ed. William D. Halsey, *et al.* London: The Crowell-Collier Publishing Co., 1962: 43–74.
24. Introduction to *Wuthering Heights,* by Emily Brontë. New York: Collier Books, 1962.
25. Introduction and annotated bibliography for *The Deerslayer,* by James Fenimore Cooper. New York: Collier Books, 1962.

26. Introduction to *Middlemarch: A Study of Provincial Life,* by George Eliot. New York: Collier Books, 1962.
27. Introduction to *Moby-Dick, or The White Whale,* by Herman Melville. New York: Collier Books, 1962.
28. Co-editor with Joseph A. Mazzeo. *The Proper Study: Essays on Western Classics.* New York: St. Martin's Press, 1962.

1963
29. Introduction to *Lord Jim,* by Joseph Conrad. New York: Washington Square Press, Inc., 1963; New York: Pocket Books, Inc., 1963.
30. Introduction to *Portrait of a Lady,* by Henry James. New York: Washington Square Press, Inc., 1963.

1965
31. "The Critic and Imperial Consciousness." Review of *An Autobiography,* by Van Wyck Brooks. *The New Republic* 152, no. 16 (17 April 1965): 15–17.
32. "Willa Cather: Her Masquerade." Review of *Willa Cather's Collected Short Fiction, 1892–1912,* ed. Mildred R. Bennett. *The New Republic* 153, no. 22 (27 November 1965): 28–31.
33. "Wilson's Canadian Junket." Review of *O Canada,* by Edmund Wilson. *The New Republic* 152, no. 22 (29 May 1965): 26–28.
34. Foreword as General Editor, *American Literature Series,* to *The Ferment of Realism: American Literature, 1884–1919,* by Warner Berthoff. New York: The Free Press, 1965.
35. Review of *The Expense of Vision: Essays on the Craft of Henry James,* by Laurence Bedwell Holland. *English Language Notes* 3, no. 1 (September 1965): 76–83.

1966
36. "Nabokov in Time." Review of *Despair,* by Vladimir Nabokov. *The New Republic* 154, no. 23 (4 June 1966): 23–28; rpt. in *The Critic as Artist: Essays on Books, 1920–1970, with Some Preliminary Ruminations by H. L. Mencken,* ed. Gilbert A. Harrison, 16–26. New York: Liveright, 1972.

1967
37. "Frost's Way: Making the Most of It." Review of *Robert Frost: The Early Years, 1874–1915,* by Lawrance Thompson. *The Nation* 204, no. 6 (6 February 1967): 182–84.
38. Co-editor of *Adventures in English Literature.* New York: Harcourt, Brace and World, Inc., 1967.

1971

39. Review of *The Early Tales of Henry James,* by James Kraft, *The Fictional Children of Henry James,* by Muriel G. Shine, and *Henry James: Dramatist,* by Rudolph R. Kossman. *American Literature* 43, no. 2 (May 1971): 294–96.

40. "Thoreau on July 4." Review of *The Writings of Henry D. Thoreau: Walden,* ed. J. Lyndon Shanley, *The Annotated Walden: Walden, or Life in the Woods,* ed. Philip Van Doren Stern, *Thoreau's World: Miniatures from His Journal,* ed. Charles R. Anderson, and *The Best of Thoreau's Journals,* ed. Carl Bode, 1, 16–18. *The New York Times Book Review,* 4 July 1971.

41. Foreword as General Editor, American Literature Series, to *The Middle Distance: A Comparative History of American Imaginative Literature, 1919–1932,* by John McCormick. New York: The Free Press, 1971.

42. *The Imperial Self: An Essay in American Literary and Cultural History.* New York: Alfred A. Knopf, 1971; also pub. New York: Vintage Books, 1972.

1972

43. "Devouring the Hemingway Corpus." Review of *The Nick Adams Stories,* ed. Philip Young. *The New Leader Spring Book Issue* 55, no. 10 (15 May 1972): 13–15.

44. "Leon Edel's 'Henry James.' " Review of *Henry James the Master: 1901–1916,* by Leon Edel. *The Virginia Quarterly Review* 48, no. 4 (Autumn 1972): 621–30.

45. "National Character." Review of *Ten Versions of America,* by Gerald B. Nelson, *Democratic Humanism and American Literature,* by Harold Kaplan, and *The Novel of Manners in America,* by James W. Tuttleton. *Commentary* 54, no. 4 (October 1972): 84–88.

1973

46. "Arms (the Civil War) and the Man (the American Writer)." Review of *The Unwritten War: American Writers and the Civil War,* by Daniel Aaron, 4, 26. *The New York Times Book Review,* 11 November 1973.

47. "Did Marx Come Over on the Mayflower?" Review of *Puritanism in America: New Culture in a New World,* by Larzer Ziff, 4. *The New York Times Book Review,* 16 December 1973.

1974

48. "Whitman's New Man." Introductory essay to *Walt Whitman: Walt Whitman's Autograph Revision of the Analysis of Leaves of Grass (for Dr. R. M. Bucke's Walt Whitman)*, ed. Stephen Railton, 11–52. New York: New York University Press, 1974.

1975

49. "The Emergence of Henry James." Review of *Henry James: Letters, Volume I: 1843–1845*, ed. Leon Edel, 498–500. *TLS*, 9 May 1975.

50. "It Was Not Easy to Be or Become Edith Wharton." Review of *Edith Wharton: A Biography*, by R. W. B. Lewis, 1–2. *The New York Times Book Review*, 31 August 1975.

1976

51. "Classical Landscapes." Review of *The Classic*, by Frank Kermode, 371. *TLS*, 2 April 1976.

52. "Practical and Visionary Americans." *The American Scholar*, 45, no. 3 (Summer 1976): 405–18.

1977

53. "The Liberal Imagination." Review of *The Liberal Imagination: Essays on Literature and Society*, by Lionel Trilling, 30–32. *The New Republic*, 23 April 1977.

54. Co-editor of *Art, Politics, and Will: Essays in Honor of Lionel Trilling*. New York: Basic Books, Inc., 1977.

55. "On the Middle of the Journey." *Art, Politics, and Will: Essays in Honor of Lionel Trilling*, ed. Quentin Anderson, Stephen Donadio, and Steven Marcus, 254–64. New York: Basic Books, Inc., 1977.

1978

56. Review of *The Hole in the Fabric: Science, Contemporary Literature and Henry James*, by Strother B. Purdy. *American Literature*, 50, no. 1 (March 1978): 124–26.

57. "Legend with Buttons." Review of *The Journals and Miscellaneous Notebooks of Ralph Waldo Emerson, Volume 13, 1852–1855*, ed. Ralph H. Orth and Alfred R. Ferguson, 12, 42. *The New York Times Book Review*, 19 March 1978.

58. "New Critic Back Down South." Review of *William Faulkner: Toward Yoknapatawpha and Beyond*, by Cleanth Brooks, 7, 31–32. *The New York Times Book Review*, 21 May 1978.

Bibliography of Quentin Anderson

59. "Property and Vision in 19th–Century America." *The Virginia Quarterly Review*, 54, no. 3 (Summer 1978): 385–410.

1979
60. "American Classics, American Readers." Review of *Democracy and the Novel: Popular Resistance to Classic American Writers*, by Henry Nash Smith, 9, 22–23. *The New York Times Book Review*, 11 February 1979.
61. Review of *Educated Lives: The Rise of Autobiography in America*, by Thomas Cooley. *English Language Notes*, 16, no. 3 (March 1979): 266–68.
62. "John Dewey's American Democrat." *Daedalus*, 108, no. 3 (Summer 1979): 145–59.

1980
63. "Notes on the Responsibility of the Critic." *Partisan Review*, 47, no. 2 (1980): 264–68.
64. "Sweet Democratic Despot." Review of *Walt Whitman: A Life*, by Justin Kaplan. *The New Republic*, 183, no. 21 (22 November 1980): 27–31.

1981
65. Foreword to *Camus' Imperial Vision*, by Anthony Rizzuto, ix–x. Carbondale: Southern Illinois University Press, 1981.

1982
66. Review of *Nature and Culture: American Landscape and Painting, 1825–1875*. Intellectual History Group, *Newsletter*, (Spring 1982): 29–33.
67. Review of *After the Revolution: Profiles of Early American Culture*, by Joseph J. Ellis. *Early American Literature*, 17, no. 1 (Spring 1982): 87–89.

1983
68. "Henry James's Cultural Office." *Prospects: The Annual of American Cultural Studies*, 8 (1983): 197–210. (Original version delivered to the Henry James Society at the MLA Convention, Houston, 1980).
69. 'Making It Alone.' Review of *The Writings of Henry D. Thoreau, Journal, Volume 1, 1837–1844*, ed. Elizabeth Hall Witherell, William L. Howarth, Robert Sattelmeyer, and Thomas Blanding. *Review*, 5 (1983): 17–30.

247

70. "When the Singer Found His Song." Review of *Walt Whitman: The Making of the Poet,* by Paul Zweig, 1, 43–44. *The New York Times Book Review,* 6 May 1984.

Notes on Contributors

JACQUES BARZUN is University Professor Emeritus at Columbia University and the author of many works in cultural history and criticism, ranging widely in subject from aspects of romanticism to issues in contemporary education. His most recent book is a study of the thought and sensibility of William James.

STEPHEN DONADIO is Professor and Chairman of the Department of American Literature and Civilization at Middlebury College, and Director of the Program in Literary Studies there. Among other works, he has published a study of Nietzsche and Henry James, and he is currently engaged in completing a cultural history of the United States in the period between 1941 and 1961.

DENIS DONOGHUE taught for many years at University College, Dublin, and currently holds an appointment as the Henry James Professor of Letters at New York University. He has published studies of Yeats and Swift, and is the author of numerous works concerned with modern English and American poetry and with developments in contemporary literary criticism and theory.

AARON FOGEL is a poet and a teacher of English at Boston University. His first critical book, *Coercion to Speak: Conrad's Poetics of Dialogue*, will be published in 1985.

CARL HOVDE teaches at Columbia, where he was dean of Columbia College from 1968 to 1972. He has edited, with others, the Princeton edition of Thoreau's *Week on the Concord and Merrimack Rivers*.

STEVEN MARCUS who has served for many years as Associate Editor of *Partisan Review*, is Delacorte Professor of the Humanities at Columbia University. His writings have engaged a wide variety of cultural subjects, including the implications of Victorian pornography, Engels and the working class, the novels of Charles Dickens, and the development of psychoanalytic theory.

STEPHEN RAILTON was a student of Quentin Anderson and collaborated with him on an edition of Whitman's additions to R. M. Bucke's biography of Whitman. His first book, *Fenimore Cooper: A Study of His Life and Imagination*, was developed from a dissertation written under Anderson's direction. He teaches at the University of Virginia and is presently working on a study of the American Renaissance.

ORMOND SEAVEY teaches at the George Washington University, where he is currently the coordinator of the humanities program. He has written about Cotton Mather, Benjamin Franklin, and D. H. Lawrence.

PETER SHAW is retired from the faculty at SUNY, Stony Brook. In addition to two books, *The Character of John Adams* and *American Patriots and the Rituals of Revolution*, he has written numerous essays on contemporary culture. He is presently the book review editor of *Early American Literature*.

TIMOTHY TRASK, also a student of Quentin Anderson, teaches at Massasoit Community College in Brockton, Massachusetts, and is working on a study of Thoreau.

DIANA TRILLING is a cultural critic whose numerous published works have explored decisive shifts in contemporary sensibility. Her concerns have ranged from the complex achievement of D. H. Lawrence to the political attitudes and involvements of American and European intellectuals since the 1930s, and at the present time she is engaged in work on a personal memoir of this period.

PAUL ZWEIG, who died before this book reached completion, was the author of numerous works of literary and cultural history—most recently, an extended account of Whitman's development as a poet—as well as several volumes of poetry. He served as Chairman of the Department of Comparative Literature at Queens College, and also taught in the program in writing in the Columbia University School of the Arts.